D1243742

OPEN HEARTS, CLOSED DOORS

Open Hearts, Closed Doors

*Immigration Reform and the Waning
of Mainline Protestantism*

Nicholas T. Pruitt

NEW YORK UNIVERSITY PRESS
New York

NEW YORK UNIVERSITY PRESS
New York
www.nyupress.org

References to Internet websites (URLs) were accurate at the time of writing. Neither the author nor New York University Press is responsible for URLs that may have expired or changed since the manuscript was prepared.

Library of Congress Cataloging-in-Publication Data
Names: Pruitt, Nicholas T., author.
Title: Open hearts, closed doors : immigration reform and the waning of mainline protestantism / Nicholas T. Pruitt.
Description: New York : New York University Press, [2021] |
Includes bibliographical references and index.
Identifiers: LCCN 2020039541 (print) | LCCN 2020039542 (ebook) |
ISBN 9781479803545 (hardback) | ISBN 9781479803576 (ebook) |
ISBN 9781479803569 (ebook other)
Subjects: LCSH: Protestant churches—History—20th century. | Emigration and immigration—Religious aspects—Protestant churches—History—20th century.
Classification: LCC BX4817 .P78 2021 (print) | LCC BX4817 (ebook) |
DDC 261.8/3809045—dc23
LC record available at https://lccn.loc.gov/2020039541
LC ebook record available at https://lccn.loc.gov/2020039542

New York University Press books are printed on acid-free paper, and their binding materials are chosen for strength and durability. We strive to use environmentally responsible suppliers and materials to the greatest extent possible in publishing our books.

Manufactured in the United States of America

10 9 8 7 6 5 4 3 2 1

Also available as an ebook

To Barry Hankins

Mentor, Wordsmith, and Friend

CONTENTS

LIST OF ABBREVIATIONS

ABC—American Baptist Convention

ABHMS—American Baptist Home Mission Society

ABHS—American Baptist Historical Society, Atlanta, Georgia

AEC—Archives of the Episcopal Church, Austin, Texas

AMA—American Missionary Association

BGCT—Baptist General Convention of Texas

CCC—Congregational Christian Churches

CCUS—Congregational Churches of the United States

CHMS—Congregational Home Missionary Society

CLA—Congregational Library and Archives, Boston, Massachusetts

CWHM—Council of Women for Home Missions

CWS—Church World Service

FCC—Federal Council of the Churches of Christ in America

HMC—Home Missions Council

MEC—Methodist Episcopal Church

MECS—Methodist Episcopal Church, South

NBC—Northern Baptist Convention

NCC—National Council of the Churches of Christ in the USA

PCUSA—Presbyterian Church in the United States of America

PEC—Protestant Episcopal Church

PHS—Presbyterian Historical Society, Philadelphia, Pennsylvania

SBC—Southern Baptist Convention

SBHLA—Southern Baptist Historical Library and Archives, Nashville, Tennessee

UMAHC—United Methodist Archives and History Center–General Commission on Archives and History, Madison, New Jersey

UMC—United Methodist Church

UPCUSA—United Presbyterian Church in the United States of America

WABHMS—Woman's American Baptist Home Mission Society

Introduction

But the world has suddenly become very small. Space has wondrously shrunk, and we are face to face in a closely intertwined and increasingly interdependent life. Isolation is no longer possible. A new era is upon us. The question for us all is whether this is to be a glorious era of brotherhood and good-will, an era of interchange of our best spiritual treasures and material achievements, or an era of enmity, aggression and strife.
—Sidney L. Gulick, *Adventuring in Brotherhood among Orientals in America*

At the outset of the twentieth century, white Protestants still held a tight grasp on the cultural and social resources of the United States. Public school classrooms began each day with largely Protestant prayer, local stores closed on Sundays, national political leaders touted the centrality of Christian ideals to American identity, and an expanding overseas empire aimed to extend the reach of Christian civilization. For many Americans, such religious aspirations blended seamlessly with American cultural norms of personal enterprise, a shared English language, and democratic principles. This bold Protestant orientation simply would not last.

As the twenty-first century unfolds, Protestants still hold a disproportionate amount of power, but schools no longer expect prayer of their students and it is more common to witness a mosque or Hindu temple along the highway. Even long-standing Protestant denominations have surrendered much of their power to more recent evangelical groups and coalitions. When the 116th US Congress convened in 2019, while Protestants still claimed a majority of the body, 163 Catholic, 34 Jewish, ten Mormon, five Orthodox Christian, three Hindu, three Muslim, and two Buddhist members of Congress reflected a more apparent diversity.[1]

Scholars and pundits alike acknowledge the role more recent immigration has had in redefining America's cultural and social identity. Robert P. Jones's *The End of White Christian America* published in 2016 examines such trends and draws attention to shifting demographics, both racial and religious, that are occurring in the United States.[2] Twelve years earlier political theorist Samuel P. Huntington went so far as to lament these same developments in his book *Who Are We?*[3] No matter how one interprets these changes, the social and cultural landscape of the United States by the early twenty-first century is much more diverse than it was a century earlier.

This coming momentous change, however, was not evident to the Protestant figures and politicians who gathered in 1961 at a consultation to discuss immigration policy. Religious leaders representing most mainline Protestant denominations met with key policymakers in Washington, DC for two days to discuss immigration reform. Attendees believed the nation's immigration policy during the last four decades had enforced forms of racial discrimination that favored some nationalities over others. These liberal Protestants joined a chorus of voices at the time calling for the dismantling of the national origins system, thus allowing for more diverse groups of people to enter the country. Despite the pushback they would receive from their more conservative constituents, those in attendance were convinced that the nation could maintain a Christian identity while still tolerating the cultural diversity that accompanied immigration. Many in attendance also believed that the Cold War demanded liberal reform in order to distance the United States from the godless totalitarianism practiced in the Soviet Union. The themes of Protestant relief and Cold War concerns all converged in an endorsement the delegates received while at the 1961 conference. "Consultations such as this focus attention upon an issue that is important to both our international standing and our national self-respect," declared President John F. Kennedy in a statement sent to the gathering. "You who assume the daily burden of guiding the oppressed and the orphaned people of the world to productive and satisfying lives under the banner of freedom deserve our thanks."[4]

Four years later, the Immigration and Nationality Act overturned in large part a restrictive immigration system put in place 40 years earlier that discriminated on the basis of race and national origins. This watershed moment helped to unsettle the white Protestant hegemony which had held sway for most of the nation's history. What was once a nation whose leaders were steeped in Anglo-Protestant culture slowly came to accept forms of multiculturalism and provide opportunities for other ethnic, racial, and religious groups to participate in American political and social institutions, though much work remains. This book delineates the ways in which mainline Protestants in the United States from 1924 to 1965 facilitated and helped to define such pluralism as they responded to immigrants and refugees through home missions and political lobbying. During these four decades, Protestants contributed to the national debate over immigration policy; yet their positions would have unintended consequences. Largely overlooked, mainline Protestant leaders joined the drive for midcentury immigration reform, and in the process paved the way for a more plural nation. Mainline Protestant denominations tried to balance a limited form of pluralism and respect for cultural diversity with the conviction that America should be a Protestant nation centered on biblical tenets and church attendance; in short, they came to a pluralistic bargain. In so doing, they contributed to their own decline as cultural gatekeepers and aided in immigration reform that allowed for a cultural revolution as non-Western immigration changed the cultural and religious landscape of the nation.

Mainline Protestants, a collective label applied to numerically predominant, largely white denominations driven by ecumenism, entered the twentieth century maintaining a cultural prominence inherited from their nineteenth-century predecessors. During the early to mid-twentieth century, they retained their cultural clout and worked to preserve an American Protestant consensus despite rising pluralism.[5] Nativist and assimilationist impulses remained patent among American Protestants, but these dispositions were tempered by home missions, midcentury sensibilities, and internationalist views. Mainline leaders aimed to confront long-standing racial prejudice among their members and incorporate diverse immigrant groups into their churches.

Current events, such as World War II and the Cold War, also inspired more liberal Protestants to criticize immigration restriction during this time, and even to sponsor refugee resettlement. Melding their cosmopolitan ideals with postwar sensibilities, Protestant luminaries during these 40 years, including Sidney Gulick, Walter Van Kirk, G. Bromley Oxnam,

Thelma Stevens, and Francis B. Sayre, Jr., worked to overturn Asian exclusion and, by the 1950s, to challenge discriminatory quotas that had been applied to eastern and southern Europeans since 1924. Such efforts often put liberal, ecumenical figures at odds with more conservative Christians, Protestant fundamentalists, and anti-communist crusaders. Yet these Protestant dignitaries did not necessarily call for *increased* immigration, but for a more equal system. Through frequent communication with political representatives and testimony before congressional committee hearings, they advocated a more liberal immigration policy and encouraged postwar refugee resettlement, largely through the work of Church World Service, an ecumenical, mainline organization that led the way in coordinating Protestant refugee relief efforts following World War II. Mainline Protestant leaders rode the wave of progressive momentum fostered by the New Deal, the civil rights movement, and the Great Society programs of President Lyndon B. Johnson and reflected the political liberalism and internationalist spirit of their time, despite the reservations of more conservative church members. By 1965, mainline Protestant groups were helping lead the charge for immigration reform; their hopes came to fruition later that year when President Johnson signed the Hart-Celler Act, which overturned the quota system premised on national origins.

As they witnessed increasing diversity in the nation, mainline Protestants worked to shed the vestiges of virulent nativism from the prior century. They largely sought to confront their nativist demons by promoting cosmopolitanism and eventually a moderate form of cultural pluralism, rather than embracing religious pluralism. They hoped to challenge systemic racism and ever-present xenophobia while maintaining their hold on American society intact. But in their embrace of diversity, mainline Protestants helped to foster, quite inadvertently, both cultural *and* religious pluralism. By the end of the twentieth century, mainline Protestants simply could not support cultural diversity and still effectively maintain a religiously uniform nation. The pluralistic bargain thus helped bring to an end more than three centuries of white Protestant hegemony in American society.

The Immigration Act of 1924 had placed heavy restrictions, in the form of quotas, on southern and eastern European groups in an effort to curtail the rising number of "new" immigrants who began coming to America during the late nineteenth century, a demographic that was largely Catholic and Jewish, as opposed to the "old" immigrants who arrived from northern Europe earlier during the nineteenth century with a largely Protestant faith. Though their overall numbers declined, people from overseas still entered the United States under the new law, and others made it into America undocumented. The 1924 legislation did not apply the quota system to immigration from the Western Hemisphere, except for European colonial possessions, and during the 1940s, '50s, and '60s, the United States opened its borders to short-term contract laborers from Mexico known as braceros; Europeans displaced by the upheaval of World War II; previously excluded Asian immigrants; and refugees fleeing political turmoil during the Cold War. America's growing role in international relations only compounded the issues raised by people of various nationalities migrating to the United States. In addition, millions of immigrants who had already come to the United States since the late nineteenth century continued to settle into their new American surroundings. These immigrants from prior years continued to speak foreign languages and practice foreign cultures while putting down roots in American neighborhoods. And though in limited numbers, additional people arrived from other lands.[6]

Caught in the midst of these changes were Anglo-Protestants who had long worked to define the contours of American culture. When historians assess the ways Protestants regarded immigrants, they usually focus on efforts to assimilate them during the late nineteenth and early twentieth centuries and Protestant support for restriction leading up to 1924. According to the standard timeline, concerned Christians hoped to integrate the "foreigner" into American society through evangelization and assimilation, only to find by the 1920s that this approach was not working. As this line of interpretation goes, white Protestants then turned to immigration restriction, thus reflecting the nativist inclinations of American society at large that were codified in the legislation Congress passed during the 1920s. But this narrative abruptly ends in 1924, failing to account for subsequent Protestant attention to immigrants.[7] This book sheds light on the largely unknown story of mainline Protestants during the following years who advocated for cultural diversity and a more just immigration policy, while still grasping a narrowly defined Protestant and American vision for the nation.

Pluralism can be an amorphous term, a catchall for diversity in America.[8] The term is often used to describe the variety of religions practiced within the United States. But pluralism can also be applied in a more general sense as a label for cultural diversity. Historian David Hollinger identifies two key manifestations of such thinking during the early to mid-twentieth century: cosmopolitanism and cultural pluralism. Drawing from the work of early twentieth-century writer Randolph Bourne, Hollinger describes cosmopolitanism as an acceptance of cultural diversity while holding firmly to a common national identity. Within such a framework, the nation's multifaceted culture is celebrated, but not at the expense of national cohesion. The second school of thought that Hollinger identifies is that of cultural pluralism, which lauds the nation's diverse ethnic cultures and challenges assimilationist expectations. The origin of this idea is often attributed to Horace M. Kallen, a Jewish philosopher from Germany who immigrated to the United States during the late nineteenth century.[9] Beginning with his 1915 piece titled "Democracy Versus the Melting-Pot" published in *The Nation*, Kallen advocated the idea that immigrant diversity and American democracy were congruent. Then in 1924, the same year that Congress established the restrictive quota system, Kallen argued in *Culture and Democracy in the United States*, "Cultural Pluralism is possible only in a democratic society whose institutions encourage individuality in groups, in persons, in temperaments, whose program liberates these individualities and guides them into a fellowship of freedom and cooperation. The alternative before Americans is Kultur Klux Klan or Cultural Pluralism."[10]

Many of the Protestants discussed in this book reflected a more cosmopolitan outlook toward cultural diversity, while some liberal Protestant leaders began turning to cultural pluralism by the 1960s. As for religious pluralism, however, most mainline Protestants were still adamant that Protestantism best served the national interest, though some were amenable to including Jews and Catholics in the conversation.[11] This multilayered approach to pluralism helps to explain in part why mainline Protestants generally supported a more diverse America. They certainly understood the cultural pluralism they were fostering in America and justified this agenda on the basis of human equality and Christian love. Protestant leaders, however, did not have the foresight to recognize that in supporting cosmopolitanism and cultural pluralism, they were also setting the stage for a more robust religious pluralism that would undermine their own social standing.

This book confirms the fissures historian K. Healan Gaston has identified within midcentury America concerning the role of religion in society. As Gaston notes, many mainline Protestants embraced a "Judeo-Christian exceptionalism" as a way to spur religious tolerance while combating the rise of secularism and a stark separation of church and state. In the process, they downplayed ethnocultural differences in order to highlight the Judeo-Christian basis of America's immigrant heritage.[12] The pluralistic bargain amounted to an attempt by Protestant churches to incorporate progressive mores of toleration while bracing themselves against modern cultural forces that threatened to decenter Protestant Christianity within American society.[13]

Mainline Protestants and American Culture

Beginning in the colonial era, Protestants in America had positioned themselves as gatekeepers of culture. Ever since the Puritans formed the Massachusetts Bay Colony as a "city upon a hill," Protestantism and American identity had been woven inextricably together in the minds of many white Americans. This aspiration to link religious and national identity proved elusive during the colonial period as the religious practices of dissident Protestant sects, Catholics, and Native Americans challenged Puritan claims, and ever since then the task has remained just beyond the grasp of Protestants desiring a Christian nation that conforms to their beliefs. But this reality has not stopped white Christians in the United States from attempting to maintain social, cultural, and religious boundaries that define who is and is not American. Yet as the twentieth century unfolded, a host of developments began chipping away at their position of national prominence, none more so than the immigration of people practicing different cultures and religions.

As self-identified cultural gatekeepers, the white mainline Protestant reception of immigrants underlines multiple historical facets. While this book's primary focus is Protestant interpretations of pluralism and their outcomes, within its scope several themes intersect, including denominational institutions and home missions, politics and nativism, race, and gender. All of these topics are valid historical subjects in their own right, but considered together, they help to further illuminate Protestant attempts to grapple with immigration and pluralism during the twentieth century. Running throughout these themes is the internal tension between envisioning a shared religious identity within the nation and assenting to cultural diversity, a version of what historian John Higham referred to as "pluralistic integration."[14]

In approaching the topic of religion and immigration through the lens of denominational sources, this book works to historicize institutional Protestantism in the United States.[15] Examining twentieth-century Protestant denominations, however, presents several challenges for the historian. First, when addressing the Protestant establishment during the twentieth century, one must define "mainline Protestantism." Historians often interpret mainline Protestantism as denominations that cooperated ecumenically through the Federal Council of the Churches of Christ in America (FCC), renamed the National Council of the Churches of Christ in the USA (NCC) in 1950. These consisted of the denominations that came to be known as the "Seven Sisters": the Methodist Church, Presbyterian Church in the United States of America, Protestant Episcopal Church, Northern Baptist Convention, Congregational Christian Churches, Disciples of Christ, and United Lutheran Church in America. In 1921, the FCC, a veritable clearinghouse for mainline Protestantism, claimed to represent more than 20 million members of affiliate denominations, and by 1958, mainline Protestantism accounted for half of the nation's population.[16] But mainline status included more than just institutional membership in an ecumenical body; historically, it also reflected cultural influence, expansive membership, and a theological disposition that frowned upon divisive doctrinal differences. American mainliners represented a broad contingent of the white Protestant center, with fundamentalists on the right and modernists on the left. By the mid-twentieth century, mainline Protestant denominations affiliated with the NCC still dominated the American Protestant scene and, consequently, believed that they were responsible for steering the course of American culture.[17]

These white Protestant groups marshaled much of the cultural and social, and oftentimes political, resources of the nation. Black Protestant denominations, such as the National Baptist Convention and African Methodist Episcopal Church, were early members of the FCC and thus were also part of the Protestant mainline. But much like their immigrant counterparts, they were often marginalized or outright segregated by white leadership within Protestant groups. And in the nation at large, the significant number of black Protestant churchgoers was woefully disproportionate to the limited political and social power they actually possessed. While black mainline Protestant views on immigration require historical study, this book focuses specifically on white mainliners who still held a tight, though tenuous, grip on mainstream American culture.

With regard to institutional Christianity in the United States, this book also adds nuance to the concept of mainline Protestantism by highlighting the continuity of practice and sentiment among leading denominations by midcentury, including those not necessarily a part of the mainline consensus. I include in this book's analysis the Southern Baptist Convention (SBC) to provide a more complete sweep of twentieth-century Protestantism. While Southern Baptist churches did not participate in ecumenical endeavors and were not "mainline," their sheer numbers make the SBC one of the leading white Protestant groups in America during the twentieth century. The SBC included more than 3.5 million church members by 1926, outnumbering most mainline denominations, and by the late twentieth century, Southern Baptists comprised the largest Protestant denomination in America.[18] They represented a sizable white Protestant demographic that maintained considerable cultural influence. They were certainly not "mainline" in their theological and ecumenical orientation, but their responses to immigration and refugees resonated with broader themes found within the Protestant mainline, before the SBC's decided turn toward the Christian Right by the end of the century. Examining Southern Baptists alongside mainline groups also allows this book to broaden its regional scope, factoring in more southern and southwestern history. Add to this the fact that one president during this period, Harry Truman, identified as Southern Baptist, and it becomes imperative that the SBC be included alongside leading mainline denominations in order to better grasp the Protestant impulse of the time.

Historians of twentieth-century American Protestantism often find it a challenge to distinguish between the views of the clergy and laity. Frequently, historians find that the liberal to moderate nature of mainline denominations was indicative of leadership, while the masses of church members were usually more conservative, if not evangelical.[19] Simply to assume that mainline denominations went the way of modernity and liberalism does not acknowledge Protestant polity and the decentralized, congregational nature of churches, where more traditional norms were maintained. But one must also avoid going to the other extreme and assuming that a stark chasm separated religious leaders and rank-and-file Protestants. Historians cannot afford to overlook the role of ideas in religious groups and the diffusion of principles that occurs over time among theologians, religious leaders, and church members.[20]

If one is to understand Protestant orientations toward culture and nationalism, home missions must be taken into account. Despite a broad spectrum of doctrinal differences, leading white Protestant denominations shared similar forms of immigrant ministry. While backing foreign missionaries around the globe, each Protestant denomination also sponsored home mission departments during the twentieth century that carried out domestic agendas. They organized departments that ministered to "foreigners," "immigrants," specific foreign-language groups, or different nationalities. In addition to denominational programs, there were several interdenominational groups that arranged work among immigrant groups in America. Most notably, the FCC (as note above, renamed the NCC in 1950) organized mainline Protestant work in America at the start of the century, establishing the Home Missions Council and the Council of Women for Home Missions. Later, Church World Service, also sponsored by the NCC, helped to coordinate refugee resettlement following World War II and during the Cold War. Such work was a composite of evangelism, benevolence, various forms of social ministry, and often political advocacy.

Nineteenth-century efforts to share the gospel to an increasing populace as the United States extended its western border helped to lay the foundation for home missions, which focused not only on migrant white settlers, but on Native Americans and African Americans. By the late nineteenth century, the temperance movement often came under the wing of Protestant home missions, along with other social causes promoting a moral society. Meanwhile, pervasive industrialization and urbanization created a context that demanded that denominations respond to the needs of urban populations. Denominations began constructing settlement houses in major urban centers across the nation in order to meet the spiritual, material, and educational needs of the working class, often comprised of immigrants.[21] By the early twentieth century, the social gospel movement encouraged home missionaries to move beyond just providing benevolent relief and more toward social activism. More liberal Protestant figures began recognizing that sources of injustice and poverty must be addressed. By the mid-twentieth century, Protestant home missions represented a diffusion of social gospel and traditional evangelistic aims, thus producing a robust wing of American Protestantism that advocated national and spiritual regeneration.

Under the umbrella of "Home Missions," most Protestant denominations continued to work among immigrants after 1924. Though the legislation passed six years earlier had drastically reduced immigration to the United States, the North American Home Missions Congress, a gathering of Protestant missionary leaders, in 1930 reported, "The Restriction Law has largely changed the immigrant situation in the United States. It should be remembered, however, that over ten million people of foreign birth have made this country their permanent home and are becoming more and more an integral and formative part of its political, social and industrial life." The Congress concluded: "Home missionary efforts among these people should be continued."[22] Thus, even after the Immigration Act of 1924, Americans were convinced the fate of the nation was still tied to immigrants. This book also situates Protestant denominational responses to immigration within the historical context of midcentury global affairs. Protestants believed home and foreign missions were intertwined and work among immigrants represented a synthesis of these two forms of Christian ministry. As a result, what happened overseas informed Protestant responses to foreigners within the United States.

Home mission sources shed light on a broad swath of church life and provide insight into the work of people who were not simply denominational elites. Much of the home mission work conducted at the grassroots level suggests that progressive sentiments were slowly making inroads among some church communities. At the same time, by virtue of their involvement in church leadership and denominational work, home missionaries still held sentiments removed from the majority of churchgoers less active in church structures who were less inclined to promote the welfare of immigrants and generally supported restriction. Still woefully understudied by historians, the topic of home missions offers valuable avenues for researching American society and culture.[23]

Midcentury denominational home mission programs vacillated between adjusting to the times and aiming to maintain the "historic faith." This sentiment is evident in a 1952 Presbyterian article describing the denomination's home mission work: "The automobile has replaced the horse for these traveling ministers; the motion picture and the wire-recorder give new wings to the old words. The message remains the same."[24] Often the history of American Christianity is that of culture and religion shaping each other. Denominations continued to stress the importance of evangelization; nevertheless, spiritual priorities are hardly ever divorced from temporal concerns. The history of Protestant home missions to ethnic communities in the United States speaks to a constant interplay between religious work and cultural transmission. Americanization programs and citizenship classes demonstrate Protestant attempts to do more than simply meet the spiritual needs of immigrants. Cultural assimilation was often the aim, though cultural accommodation was a common outcome of such ministries.[25]

While a more traditional, evangelical impulse remained in most Protestant denominations into the twentieth century, there nevertheless was a diffusion of social gospel sentiments that reflected a progressive impetus within mainline Protestant denominations. In short, the social gospel was a distinct emphasis placed on Christian social ministry, otherwise known as "applied Christianity," that began absorbing certain tenets of liberal, modernist theology during the late nineteenth century in an effort to Christianize a nation succumbing to rampant industrialization and urbanization. The social gospel movement reached its apogee of institutional advancement in the formation of the FCC in 1908 and its Social Creed of the Churches declared that same year, which outlined progressive ideals on labor and justice agreed upon among member institutions.[26] The social gospel was closely tied to the progressive movement in America and represented more distinct liberal trends of the age, though, in keeping with broader progressivism, it failed to mount significant opposition to racial injustice. Among proponents of this form of social Christianity, a shared terminology developed, most often linked to the concepts of the brotherhood of man, fatherhood of God, and postmillennial stress on the kingdom of God. Mainline Protestantism's increasingly moderate stance toward immigration reflects in part these social gospel tenets that were making inroads among more Protestants by the mid-twentieth century.[27]

Home missions and social gospel sentiments helped to mold the political viewpoints of many mainline luminaries. As they encountered diverse cultures and tongues, white mainline Protestants were forced to reconsider the nativist political positions inherited from earlier generations. As we will see, the American public interpreted in various ways the politics surrounding immigration law during the twentieth century.[28] According to historian Roger Daniels, the Constitution "provided no particulars, so that naturalization has been a kind of political litmus test of the national climate of opinion about immigrants and immigration."[29] White Protestant opinion is a central component of this "litmus test," as this demographic has maintained a disproportionate amount of influence within American society and politics. As the social gospel encouraged political confrontation in the legislative arena, Protestant denominations actively responded to evolving immigration policy. Such activism can be traced back to concern over the 1882 Chinese Exclusion Act but became more concerted by the time Congress implemented the 1924 quotas and Japanese exclusion. The legislation of that year remained a point of contention for many Protestant leaders for the next several decades. By 1952, when Congress passed the McCarran-Walter Act that continued the controversial quota system, mainline Protestants had become even more vocal against immigration policy they perceived as racist. Protestant leadership frequently appealed to members of Congress for immigration reform, and in 1961 the NCC hosted the convention noted above where Protestant ministers and multiple politicians spoke on the shortcomings of US immigration policy. But the political history of mainline Protestants and immigration is not simply a story of increasingly progressive rhetoric. Protestant appeals for immigration reform often paused to consider the impact immigration would have on America and how capable the nation was to absorb more immigrants. All the while, historic nativist concerns still reverberated among many of the Protestant rank and file.

Confrontation between white Protestants and immigration is nothing new. Throughout colonial and nineteenth-century American history,

Protestants were at the forefront of fierce nativist movements.[30] As historian Ray Allen Billington asserted in his 1938 book, *The Protestant Crusade*, nativism and anti-Catholicism were intimately linked during the nineteenth century.[31] Many Protestants during the twentieth century continued to draw from this legacy as they defended a white, Anglo-Saxon, Protestant identity for America, but they did so with much less militancy. An increasing number of them, often steering the course of denominations and ecumenical organizations, began challenging racist visions of the nation that promoted 100% cultural assimilation. Liberal Protestants even contributed to a decline in nativism through their eventual cooperation with Jews and Catholics, groups that had earlier triggered strident anti-immigrant protest. Moreover, efforts to evangelize and minister to immigrants through home missions checked nativist tendencies as they instead fostered a more compassionate spirit. Many home missionaries drew inspiration from the earlier social gospel movement and its emphasis on brotherhood and fraternity.

This book teases out the fate of nativism among mainline Protestant groups in America during the twentieth century. While they were not vehemently nativist, mainline Protestants often considered soberly the economic and cultural import of immigrants and refugees, and forms of paternalism and assimilationist agendas continued. As historian Erika Lee has demonstrated, xenophobia is not an episodic phenomenon within American history, but rather an ever-present response that takes various forms at different times in history.[32] Mainline Protestants never fully exorcised the demons of nativism, but they were more inclined than previous generations to welcome immigrants into the nation—while at the same time hoping and assuming that these foreigners would join Protestant churches. While many leading Protestants of the early to mid-twentieth century grew more comfortable with cultural pluralism, they were unwilling to let go of their vision of a Protestant Christian nation. In short, they had not unshackled themselves entirely from earlier nativism.

That lingering nativism manifested itself in many ways. Despite progressive gestures toward a more diverse American, inherent in mainline Protestant visions for the nation were clear categories of what defined a "true" American. Historian K. Healan Gaston puts it best when she notes, "Indeed, every conceivable definition of a nation's religio-political culture will involve more and less subtle and costly acts of inclusion and exclusion."[33] This confluence of inclusion and exclusion is apparent throughout midcentury mainline Protestant agendas concerning immigration policy. When lobbying for immigration reform, liberal mainliners made it clear that they did not believe it was in the best interest of the nation to increase immigration, but rather better to remove a quota system that favored some immigrant groups over others. Moreover, while they decried Asian exclusion, they were slow to realize the racist implications of the quota system itself. And during the 1930s and 1950s, white Protestants largely overlooked the government's repressive policies of deportation and repatriation targeting Mexican Americans. As historians have stated, the notion that America was a "nation of immigrants" that came into vogue during the twentieth century still often excluded Latino and Asian immigrants and assigned to them a marginal status in American society on account of race.[34] Mainline Protestants were not immune to such sentiments.

This history also contributes to a better understanding of racial thought during the era of immigration restriction.[35] A definition of race premised on scientific attempts to categorize a supposed natural, biological hierarchy of humanity was already in vogue by the 1920s. Madison Grant's *The Passing of the Great Race* in 1916 drew the public's attention to what he believed were the deleterious effects immigration had on the racial makeup of America. Grant warned that the "altruistic ideals" and "maudlin sentimentalism that has made America 'an asylum for the oppressed,' are sweeping the nation toward a racial abyss. If the Melting Pot is allowed to boil without control, . . . the type of native American of Colonial descent will become extinct."[36] While mainline leaders often frowned upon such racist sentiments, the prevalent racial marginalization within society often meant that groups such as African Americans, Native Americans, and Mexican Americans were included alongside European, Asian, and Latin American immigrants in home mission programs focused on racial "outsiders" in need of Protestant attention.

As historian Matthew Frye Jacobson has persuasively argued, racial categories changed during the twentieth century in light of continuing immigration and the burgeoning civil rights movement. American society expanded the racial categorization of "white" so that it included European immigrant groups as racial discord between white and black

Americans increased by midcentury. Overall, race was an amorphous concept during the twentieth century, never following consistent categories and often used loosely and synonymously with nationalities and ethnicities. Liberal Protestants generally frowned upon blatant racial prejudice in society and claimed that all people were equal before God. But as the century progressed, discrepancies evolved between white Protestant agendas concerning Asian, Mexican, and European immigrant groups. Protestant progressives were quick to note the racial discrimination inherent in Asian exclusion, but never advocated for significant increases in Asian immigration. Meanwhile, the restriction of southern and eastern Europeans flew under the radar of most mainline Protestants until midcentury, around the same time that European immigrants became "white" within society at large. And Mexican immigrants remained a racialized group that never received the same level of advocacy from mainline Protestant reformers. The following chapters help shed light on the progression of racial categorizations among liberal Protestant reformers and how their understanding of race helped to shape their approach to home missions and immigration policy.[37]

Changing perceptions of race were also tied to current events. The rebirth of the Ku Klux Klan in 1915, racism in Nazi Germany and the ensuing Holocaust, the formation of the United Nations and its defense of human rights, and entrenched segregation in the US South shaped the way mainline Protestants considered immigrants and helped inspire those who stood for racial equality. As the civil rights movement advanced in the 1950s, it provided a great impetus for Protestants to combat the racist components of immigration policy. The injustice other marginalized groups endured was now brought under scrutiny. Much of the effort to liberalize immigration policy by midcentury trailed the work of African Americans advocating for desegregation and voting rights.[38]

In addition to institutional Protestantism, politics, and race, this book also addresses gender dynamics. Both immigrant and native, white Protestant women are key actors within this story. As Donna Gabaccia, Martha Gardner, and other historians have shown, US government policy regulating immigration and naturalization had gendered implications, and immigrants themselves maintained definitions of gender norms as they settled into their new surroundings.[39] Home mission programs also communicated white Protestant notions of marriage and family to incoming immigrants.[40] As historians have noted, women contributed extensively to the newly formed field of social work by the turn of the twentieth century, and this correlated with strong home missionary endeavors and social gospel efforts on the part of white Protestant women.[41] Examples of this fusion of social reform and missions include the work of Jane Addams, Georgia Harkness, Thelma Stevens, and Una Roberts Lawrence, among many others. As historian Gale L. Kenny demonstrates, mainline women espoused cosmopolitan ideals in their home mission programs during the interwar period while struggling to maintain such programs. These women embraced roles in home missions at a time when Protestant institutions were still largely under male control, often resorting to the formation of separate auxiliaries, boards, or departments to find some semblance of autonomy.[42] Meanwhile, female missionaries transmitted what they believed to be traditional gender and culture norms to immigrant women through Americanization programs sponsored by home missionary societies. This book offers further insight into these seemingly contradictory orientations of women active in Protestant programs. In the end, mainline Protestant women balanced both traditional cultural and gender roles with active leadership in missions, thus reconciling their own marginalization alongside efforts to inculcate white Protestant customs among the ethnically marginalized.

Organization of the Book

The following history of mainline Protestant responses to immigration is divided into five chapters and a conclusion that investigate the overall progression of home missions and mainline political positions on immigration policy during this period. Over the course of these 40 years, it becomes evident that mainline Protestants subscribed to a form of cosmopolitanism and cultural pluralism, while still reticent to support religious pluralism. This particular orientation toward pluralism reflected an inherent tension between consensus and pluralism within Protestant positions.

Though the chapters follow each other chronologically, the first two chapters generally stress the ideological and theological basis of ministries to immigrants inherited from the earlier social gospel, while the later chapters place more emphasis on the political responses of mainline Protestants and the contemporary developments that shaped their views on immigration. Adhering to chronological order helps us to relate their home mission programs and political lobbying to domestic and international developments between the years 1924 and 1965 (e.g., the Immigration Act of 1924, the Great Depression, World War II, the Cold War, etc.) and to identify certain elements of continuity during this period, such as the assimilationist goals and desire for a Christian nation that Protestants maintained. In sum, assessing the cultural import of mainline Protestant views helps elucidate how a significant segment of the US population cultivated a concern for moderate immigration reform by the latter half of the twentieth century, while also accounting for Protestant efforts to reconcile pluralism with the ideal of a Christian nation.

Titled Settling into Restriction, the first chapter examines home missions during the latter half of the 1920s and Protestant responses to congressional legislation. This chapter identifies the social gospel's influence on mainline Protestant ministries among immigrant and ethnic communities, in addition to providing a survey of Americanization programs during the 1920s. Settlement houses facilitated much of this work among immigrant communities, and Protestant women were often at the forefront of these ministries. Through an investigation of home missions, it becomes evident that earlier social gospel sentiments were being diffused among regular churchgoers, resulting in a synthesis of evangelism and social concern among mainline Protestants. This chapter also identifies Protestant reactions to the Immigration Acts of 1921 and 1924 that limited eastern and southern European immigration and excluded Japanese immigrants entirely.

The second chapter, The Trying Thirties, continues to assess home mission programs and traces the diffusion of the social gospel within traditional, evangelistic ministries among mainline Protestants. Meanwhile, denominations were forced to retrench their budgets for home missions during the Great Depression. The economic crisis and rising fascism in Europe during the 1930s provide a global backdrop for assessing domestic concerns over the "foreigner." Both of these developments influenced the way Americans considered immigrants and their supposed political and economic liabilities. Mainline Protestants responded by striving to make the United States a Christian nation, a theme that permeated their home mission work.[43] Another critical topic in this chapter is the growing reluctance of some Protestants to advocate Americanization and their increasing acceptance of cultural diversity, even while efforts to assimilate immigrants continued in various forms. Finally, this chapter highlights the continued work of mainline Protestant leaders to challenge Asian exclusion and their responses to legislation Congress considered during 1936 (the "Kerr-Coolidge" bill) that aimed to assist undocumented immigrants.

Chapter 3 covers the World War II era and early Cold War period. This chapter, The Huddled Masses the War Produced, concentrates on the domestic and international implications of the war for Protestant missions to immigrants. During this period, home missionaries often promoted an "American Way of Life" while attending to Asian immigrants, bracero workers, Japanese Americans in internment camps, and refugees. Nevertheless, such programs reflected a measured respect for cosmopolitanism and cultural pluralism, though they were by no means universal sentiments among American Protestants. The Second World War also encouraged various social sensibilities among white Protestants as it pertained to race, diversity, gender roles, and family values. This chapter focuses on an increasing Protestant critique of racial discrimination inherent in the immigration quota system, especially as church leaders called for reinstating Chinese and Indian immigration. It was during and immediately after the war that mainline leaders in the FCC began an aggressive push to overturn Asian exclusion once and for all, though with mixed results.

Strangers in Mayberry, chapter 4, provides a closer look at how white Protestant Americans interpreted increasing pluralism after World War II. As America set itself apart from foreign powers whose ideology was considered "godless" (i.e., Nazi Germany and the Soviet Union), home missions and evangelization of immigrants remained imperative. Cold War ideology channeled fears toward the threat of global communism and stressed the importance of keeping the country Christian. This chapter considers the continuity of earlier home mission impulses while also examining white Protestant support for postwar refugee resettlement. Following the Refugee Relief Act of 1953, many denominations sponsored resettlement programs that provided living accommodations and employment for thousands of refugees fleeing political instability in other parts of the world. The chapter describes the manifold programs and pamphlets Protestants produced to address the postwar refugee crisis and promote resettlement of Cold War refugees, culminating in widespread support for World Refugee Year sponsored by the United Nations in 1959, while the Cuban refugee crisis was unfolding. Assisting refugees provided an opportunity for American Christians to deliver humanitarian relief, promote their denominations, and counter communist revolution overseas. In their attention to refugee relief, Protestants were quick to note the international role of the United States and its obligation to defend freedom. All the while, these refugee sponsorship programs resulted in displaced people being relocated among white Americans not familiar with foreign ways.

The fifth chapter, Paving the Way for Pluralism, recounts mainline Protestant communication with political representatives and testimony before congressional committee hearings, culminating in the Immigration and Nationality Act of 1965, which ended the discriminatory quota system. During this time, mainline groups affiliated with the NCC increased their protest against the federal government's racially biased immigration policy, as seen in their continued criticism of the discriminatory quotas established in 1924 and their response to the 1952 McCarran-Walter Act. In their attempts to challenge restriction, liberal Protestants encountered pushback from conservative Protestants and anti-communist figures during the Second Red Scare of the early 1950s. Despite occasional opposition, however, mainline Protestant leaders often advocated a more liberal immigration system that confronted racial discrimination in the spirit of the civil rights movement and elevated America's stature internationally.[44] In addition, it was during this time that sociologist Will Herberg argued that the nation was becoming a "triple melting-pot" for Protestants, Catholics, and Jews; nevertheless, many Protestants continued their drive for a Protestant Christian nation, despite growing pluralism and increasing religious tolerance. Finally, this chapter concludes by exploring how Protestants aligned themselves in 1965 when Congress finally overturned the immigration quota system based on national origins.

The conclusion considers what this history reveals about the place of Protestantism in America and its varied responses to pluralism. As the twentieth century progressed, white mainline Protestants slowly came to witness their hold on American culture slip in the face of ethnic and religious diversity. Unlike other periods of American history, however, Protestants did not resort to staunch nativism, but instead worked to assist foreigners and incorporate immigrants into the nation. Mainline Protestants arrived at a pluralistic bargain whereby they accepted cultural pluralism and immigration reform, while thinking they could still manage a Christian nation. Instead, they inadvertently contributed to increasing immigration and religious pluralism, which would ultimately undermine their position in American society. Despite trying to support cultural diversity while also reinforcing a Judeo-Christian identity for the nation, mainline Protestants ultimately failed to sustain this vision as an increasing acceptance of religious pluralism in the United States and rising numbers of immigrants practicing religions outside of mainline Protestantism outpaced their hold on the nation. Such an arrangement helped to reconfigure US society and culture by the twenty-first century. Finally, this history provides context for statements religious leaders have made during the late twentieth and early twenty-first centuries regarding the government's immigration and refugee policies. Many of Donald Trump's religious critics and supporters are products of midcentury Protestant orientations to immigration, pluralism, and America's global presence.

1

Settling into Restriction

The church in its Americanization work has a sacred duty
to perform. It must build in the immigrant the ideals which
will make him a true citizen of America, and in a higher
sense a citizen of the Kingdom of God.
—Georgia Harkness, *The Church and the Immigrant*

In 1926, Henry Goddard Leach, editor of the popular journal *Forum*
based out of New York City, published an article reflecting on America's recent past and near future. Leach took the intellectual and cultural
pulse of his day and determined that the United States was entering a
period in history when much was in flux following the trauma of the
First World War. When assessing the international scene, Leach noted
America's new place in the world and the dramatic political changes
taking place in Europe. Though the 1920s were supposed to be a time
of isolationism, he quipped, "The world has contracted and we have
expanded."[1]

Immigration was a visible manifestation of this contraction and
expansion for the United States. It was certainly a cause for concern
for Leach. "After a century of unthinking hospitality," Leach wrote in
reference to recent legislation, "America has recently closed her gates
abruptly to the tide of immigration. We Americans are taking count of
stock. We are girding up our loins for a new day. We are heeding the sign
'Stop! Look! Listen!' in our national life." Leach then resolved, "A new
American consciousness is dawning in this post-war period." Leach was
convinced that immigration restriction allowed the nation to assimilate
its recent additions. Later in the article, Leach concluded, "The closing
of the Immigration door is an insurance for a new and compact national
consciousness. Who knows but we will melt and fuse into some distinguished expression of our national purpose as noble as our health and
our energy."[2]

For Leach, as his essay's title suggested, "The Next Forty Years" were going to be a formative period for America. But history rarely follows one's predictions, even someone as eloquent as Leach. During the next 40 years, a "national consciousness" did coalesce at various points, but the overall trajectory of American culture was one of further fragmentation, aided in part by past immigration and the continued, though drastically reduced, entrance of more people from overseas. The "melting" and "fusing" that Leach hoped for, an allusion to Israel Zangwill's 1908 play *The Melting Pot*, would never be complete, and despite efforts to restrict immigration, foreign-born people and their children continued to make America a more plural nation.

By the early twentieth century, significant numbers of immigrants had come to the United States from southern and eastern Europe, Asia, and Mexico. Many Americans worried that these immigrants threatened time-honored political, cultural, and religious institutions. Immigrants during the late nineteenth and early twentieth centuries were considered "foreigners" in every sense of the word. They came speaking little or no English and worshiping foreign faiths, and Americans feared these more recent immigrants would not assimilate according to American ideals, as had earlier immigrants who came from northern and western Europe.

It was the perceived threat these "new" immigrants posed to traditional American culture that troubled many within the native-born population. The vicissitudes of World War I only compounded the issues, and a desire for "normalcy" in the aftermath of conflict led many Americans to support their government's decision to restrict immigration. Reflecting public concerns, Congress passed stringent immigration legislation in 1917, 1921, and 1924. The 1917 law established a literacy test for incoming immigrants, expanded Asian exclusion, and forced Mexican immigrants to pay a head tax in order to immigrate. The 1921 Emergency Immigration Act set up a temporary quota system based on the total population in 1910 of each European nationality in America, allowing for 3% of each nationality to enter. Then the 1924 law pushed the baseline back to 1890 and lowered the percentage to 2%, an intentional effort to limit immigration from southern and eastern Europe. The 1924 quota law also excluded Japanese entirely.[3]

Native-born white Protestants, the majority affiliated with either the FCC or the SBC, responded to increasing immigration and its sudden demise in 1924 as citizens of both the Kingdom of God and the United States. With 20,052,781 constituent members in the FCC as of 1921 and 3,524,378 church members aligned with the SBC by 1926, white Protestants represented a significant portion of the population, with an even greater hold on American culture.[4] When confronted with rising immigration, they maintained vibrant home mission ministries that sought to bring immigrants into the Christian fold while also introducing them to American ideals. Moreover, Protestant leaders responded to legislative proposals during the 1920s in a manner that reflected theological and missional positions. Along the way, Protestant political concerns and home mission programs designed to ensure the spiritual, cultural, and material well-being of immigrants helped temper nativism among church members.

Protestant Ministry among Immigrants

During the first two decades of the twentieth century, America witnessed the arrival of more than 14 million immigrants.[5] Protestants rose to what they perceived to be the challenge of this increasing immigrant population. They decided the foreign-born must hear the gospel message and experience the warm charity of American Christians blessed with the means to aid men, women, and children rendered listless from long travels.[6] Most Protestant denominations had some form of organization charged with the task of home missions, and these departments usually included work among "foreigners," as immigrants were often called. By the early twentieth century, Protestants realized the world was coming to America. A speaker announced at a Methodist Episcopal women's convention in 1923, "I can give a foreign missionary . . . as large a field for his entire life work in any one of fifty American cities, as he could adequately reach in any European, Asiatic, or African field."[7] A booklet produced by the Protestant Episcopal Church (PEC) likewise noted that its work was "Foreign Missions at Home."[8] Another publication printed a poem in 1924 titled "God Is Sending Them" that demonstrates this spirit of missions that many Protestant denominations acted upon:

> God is sending now the peoples
> By the million to our shores;

They are coming from all nations,
    They are knocking at our doors.
Shall we send the gospel message
    To the souls across the seas,
And neglect the heathen with us
    Who have needs as great as these?

It is God who in past ages
    Hath controlled the tides of men;
And our God in his high heaven
    Doth control today as then.
It is God who calls his children
    With command both loud and clear:
Haste, O haste, my faithful workers;
    I have sent the nations here![9]

Many denominations, while retaining their own home mission departments, also combined their work and planning through ecumenical organizations. During this period of time there appeared a rising tide of ecumenism among mainline Protestantism, leading most noticeably to the creation of the FCC, the Home Missions Council (HMC), and the Council of Women for Home Missions (CWHM) in 1908. The HMC served as a clearinghouse for Protestant work among immigrants, with more than 40 denominational organizations aligned with the HMC by 1920. The HMC fostered missions to immigrants that included work among ports of entry, Americanization, and vacation Bible school programs for immigrant children, along with sponsoring the Interdenominational Council of Spanish-speaking Work.[10]

Ellis Island became the site of numerous efforts to minister to incoming immigrants. Despite setbacks during World War I, when immigration through Ellis Island came to a halt, ministry at the island was in full swing during the early 1920s. Just as immigrants poured into the port looking for a new start, a multitude of Protestant organizations claimed Ellis Island as their base of operation, where they could provide benevolence to the newcomers. The proliferation of ministries that claimed Ellis Island was at times staggering. In an effort to consolidate these ministries, the General Committee of Immigrant Aid was organized to coordinate all agencies working on Ellis Island. By 1922, this included 19 organizations, 12 of which were Protestant. While assistance at this port came in many forms, a prominent piece of Protestant missions on the island was mediation. A Congregationalist worker on Ellis Island recognized, "The missionary or social worker is a buffer between the immigrant and the Government agencies which he many times misunderstands and which do not always understand him."[11] The Congregational Home Missionary Society (CHMS) sponsored a kindergarten and upper-level schooling for children on the island.[12] The Foreign-Born Americans Division of the PEC claimed, "Successful work is being done in meeting, commending, and following up immigrants entering this country through Ellis Island. About 2,000 Anglican immigrants have been commended to the care of our clergy in various parts of the country."[13] Providing benevolent assistance and reaching prospective church members defined encounters between the native- and foreign-born at Ellis Island.

Angel Island in the San Francisco Bay served as the West Coast's counterpart to Ellis Island, and Protestants made sure workers were present and ready to provide Christian support, despite strong regional political and social resistance to Asian immigration. Often their work offered cultural and religious resources. A 1922 article in *Woman's Home Missions* described Christmas festivities on the island. The event was clearly an attempt to introduce immigrants coming to the West Coast to both the gospel and American patriotism. The list of gifts given during the Christmas celebration is telling. "There were gifts for all: Christmas cards with John 3.16, and an American flag for each one, various other things including handkerchiefs, toys, games, and dolls, an American doll for each Chinese woman—a gift which transports her to the topmost peak of happiness."[14]

Geographically located between both Angel and Ellis Islands, southern Methodists sponsored work among immigrants at the port of Galveston, Texas. There John E. Reifschneider worked under the auspices of the Woman's Missionary Council since 1913. In their work at Galveston, Methodists often had to provide services to immigrants scheduled to be deported, and in some instances home missionaries would counsel deportees on how to reenter once they were allowed to immigrate again. For those immigrants who were admitted, home mis-

Figure 1.1. Home missionary Katharine R. Maurer sharing stereoscopic slides with children at Angel Island. Courtesy of the General Commission on Archives and History of the United Methodist Church, Madison, NJ.

sionaries helped them comprehend the naturalization process and find employment. Reifschneider witnessed firsthand the challenges of immigration processing at ports of entry and recognized that more restrictive legislative measures would help deter immigrants from leaving their homeland who would only be turned away if they came to the United States. Methodists were invested in the work at Galveston to such an extent that the District Director of Immigration at the port applauded the ministry of Reifschneider and southern Methodists, particularly in their work with deportees who were being held in local county jails.[15]

Faith-based community centers were another important institution Protestants used to minister to the needs of immigrants. These centers were a direct descendent of the settlement houses in vogue during the earlier progressive movement at the turn of the century.[16] Denominations often sponsored multiple community centers that ministered in a variety of ways. The Northern Baptist community center in Hammond, Indiana, named Brooks House, is a good example. Under the ambitious administration of John M. Hestenes, the center strove to transform the local immigrant community. Brooks House offered a plethora of programs, including recreation for adolescents, laundry facilities, a library outfitted with literature to help Americanize the newcomers, medical services, a room for meetings, and, Hestenes noted with racist condescension, a "kindergarten filled with little tots of every degree of tint from African duskiness to Saxon peaches-and-cream." According to one observer, Brooks House helped transform "a dozen different European races . . . united and working harmoniously together in the interests of better social and moral conditions." Hestenes's vison for urban reform through the ministry of Brooks House demonstrates the staying power of social gospel aspirations during the 1920s. "Two years ago," according to an article covering Brooks House, "this section of the city had housed a sullen mass of suspicious, clannish, ignorant foreign-born with neither the will nor the knowledge to improve their conditions; living in dirt and squalor; torn by petty hatreds, the prey of Bolsheviks, unscrupulous politicians and the money lust of a soulless industrialism." But no more. All the while, Brooks House maintained evangelical commitments; a description of the center affirmed that "souls are reached with the chief message . . . contained in John 3:16." Brooks House was just one of 34 community centers Northern Baptists operated as of 1924.[17]

Other Protestant work directed toward immigrants was made available through the pioneering Bureau of Reference for Migrating Peoples. Formed in 1922 by the HMC and CWHM, this organization helped connect American churches to new immigrant arrivals. The Bureau, under the leadership of Episcopal worker Raymond Cole, relied upon the World Alliance for Promoting International Friendship Through the Churches for names of immigrants likely to come to America. The Bureau then provided the immigrants' names to religious institutions in towns where they awaited the arrival of the immigrants. The Bureau peaked at 15,000 assignments in 1926 but had to close operations three years later because of financial constraints. Such an operation demonstrates the frequent transnational nature of home mission work. The Bureau of Reference also reflects a commitment to sectarian identity, as the Bureau only sought immigrants who were Protestant and coordinated with specific denominations based on the religious background of the foreign-born.[18]

The work of the Presbyterian Church in the United States of America, Protestant Episcopal Church, Congregational Christian Churches, and Southern Baptist Convention each provide useful glimpses into denominational efforts to minister to immigrants at this time. The Presbyterian Church in the United States of America (PCUSA) in 1918 identified its goals: to publish material on immigration work, cooperate with other denominations, and promote community center work. Its area of influence stretched across the nation, extending from New York to California. A 1918 report noted that the denomination spent a total of $86,000 for immigration ministry in 20 cities, four iron and coal regions, and rural areas in Texas and California.[19] The Presbyterian Board of Church Erection also tabulated ten buildings that were maintained for work among foreigners between 1920 and 1921 at a cost of $60,595, along with two new buildings for Mexicans totaling $9,600 and eight new community centers at $36,250.[20] By 1929 the PCUSA was sponsoring 55 churches, 12 settlement houses, and four medical centers among Mexican American communities, along with three boarding schools and seven day schools.[21] Presbyterians were also convinced that they would need to educate future home missionaries for immigrant ministry. The Presbyterian seminary at Dubuque University in Iowa educated prospective ministers who would "meet the demand of a ministry for the foreign-speaking population of our country."[22]

The Episcopal Church also sought to reach immigrants through various means. This portion of its home mission work was organized through the Foreign-Born Americans Division established in 1919.[23] A 1922 Episcopal manual on immigration identified various immigrant groups in need of Episcopal assistance, including Italians, Poles, Hungarians, and Mexicans. According to the manual, the Catholic background of these particular groups made them prospects for the Episcopal fold. The manual went on to outline other ethnic and national groups that either already were a part of the Episcopal Church in America or were candidates for cooperative endeavors, including Japanese, Chinese, "Hindus," Jews, Czechs, Slovaks, Scandinavians, Russians, Greeks, and Armenian and Assyrian Orthodox. The 1922 manual was generally sympathetic to the special challenges immigrants faced while being processed on Ellis Island and the subsequent urban living conditions they endured. Even as late as 1922, Episcopalians in immigrant work were still drawing from precedents set by the earlier progressive movement; the manual even cited the work of Jacob Riis. While the handbook recognized that some immigrants were not assimilating, and thus posed a threat to the nation, this was rather the fault of Americans not reaching out and demonstrating "Christian neighborliness." Episcopalian leadership acknowledged the importance of Americanization, but ultimately identified "religion—'the knowledge and love of God through Jesus Christ our Lord,'" as "the most important factor of all, without which true democracy cannot stand; without which all so-called Americanization must fail; and that which it is the Church's God-given responsibility to supply." Alongside this evangelistic program, Episcopalians also sponsored childcare, neighborhood houses, and cultural "refinement." Occasionally, such efforts included ministers and workers who had been immigrants themselves, particularly among Italians.[24]

Another Episcopal pamphlet titled *How to Reach the Foreign-Born* continued to outline their work. Published in 1924, it called upon local parishes to be hospitable to immigrants, reminding its readers that their "approach to these, our neighbors, should always be not as foreigners but as friends." It challenged local parishes not to treat immigrants as "curious exhibits to be looked at, nor creatures of a lower order to be avoided." Instead, Episcopalians should realize that the foreign-born are "just the same sort of men, women and children as the rest of us." The pamphlet even acknowledged a level of diversity within the nation, admitting that the "glory of the American type is that it is a rich composite." In addition to the services listed in the 1922 manual, the 1924 pamphlet also mentioned other ways Episcopalians reached out to local immigrants, including night schools, clubs, hospital visits, children's camps, financial advice, cooperation with Orthodox churches, assistance with "the intricacies and official discourtesies of naturalization," and helping men find "skilled work." The program referred to Episcopal efforts to publish spiritual material in foreign languages, including printing prayer books that incorporated "their" prayers. The evangelistic mission of the Episcopal Church resonated in the pamphlet's concluding prayer:

> O Saviour of mankind, who didst send Thy disciples unto every nation bidding them feed Thy sheep, and Who in these later times hast brought from many nations a multitude to dwell in our land; Grant that our

Church in America may prove faithful to the trust that Thou hast laid upon her, and may have grace and power to feed by Thy appointed means these people of many races and tongues; through the same Jesus Christ our Lord. Amen.[25]

Like other mainline efforts, the Episcopal Church offered a comprehensive approach to ministering to the foreign-born that united spiritual counsel with social services.

By the 1920s, Congregationalists also sponsored robust home mission programs directed toward immigrants.[26] The CHMS implemented a multifaceted program that included a school on Ellis Island and preaching in 21 languages. Just prior to the implementation of restriction, Congregational home missionaries acknowledged that they were undersourced when it came to immigrant work: "Open doors call for double our present expenditure. This is our problem of foreign missions at home."[27] According to a 1924 report, the CHMS sponsored 266 "churches and missions among the foreign-born" and 29 "English-speaking churches doing work among the foreign-born."[28] The American Missionary Association (AMA) also guided Congregational work in California among Filipino immigrants and in Utah among Japanese.[29]

The Ellis Island school, led by Jennie F. Pratt, was an attempt to facilitate cosmopolitanism under the auspices of Christian witness, "helping the children of twenty languages and twenty different racial inheritances to live together and develop harmoniously." In her daily work, Pratt spoke multiple languages. On the island, Congregational workers bathed the children, taught them English, instructed girls in sewing and knitting, and provided outdoor activities, toys, crafts, and music, all while the children's parents worked with immigration officials to gain entrance into the United States. In the meantime, Congregational home missionaries reinforced American patriotism among the immigrant children, with such tunes as "Red, White and Blue, We All Love You!"[30]

Spiritual and social commitments also defined Southern Baptist immigrant work during the early twentieth century. Southern Baptist work among what they often referred to as "foreigners" began during the late nineteenth century, including work at the port of entry in Baltimore and among Chinese on the West Coast. By the start of the twentieth

Figure 1.2. Teacher Jennie F. Pratt in front of a classroom of children on Ellis Island. American Missionary Association Photographs, 1887–1952, Amistad Research Center, New Orleans, LA.

century, the Home Mission Board and the Woman's Missionary Union were often at the forefront of immigrant work among Southern Baptists. Southern Baptists adhered to a strong evangelistic ministry but never discouraged providing relief for the dispossessed in society.[31] Though the South is not usually considered a haven for immigrants during the early twentieth century, Southern Baptists begged to differ. A 1923 publication calling for pledges for the SBC's Home Mission Board pointed out immigrant populations among Southern Baptists. With the headings "Foreigners at Our Door" and "Vast Groups in Cities and Rural Sections Present Duty to Provide Them With the Gospel," the piece called attention to large populations of Italians, Mexicans, "French-speaking people," Bohemians, Greeks, and Russians situated in various cities of the South. To stress its point, this call for funds also noted that 37,700 foreigners lived "in Kansas City within eight or ten blocks of where the Southern Baptist Convention held its session last May."[32] According to a Southern Baptist report describing their ministry to immigrants during the 1923–1924 year, 11,894 sermons and addresses were given, 30,141 visits conducted, and 824 people baptized, along with progress made in the area of church construction and repairs.[33] With hopes to raise future ministers for immigrant work, one description of the Baptist Bible Institute in New Orleans suggested, "New Orleans, with its 400,000 population, consisting of divers nationalities, affords an unsurpassed opportunity for the study and solution of both Home and Foreign Mission problems."[34] Good Will Centers, having much in common with other Protestant community centers, were established by Southern Baptists in urban areas to meet the spiritual and social needs of incoming immigrants. Southern Baptist women often provided the early impetus for immigrant ministry, but as historian Melody Maxwell has demonstrated in the case of a Good Will Center in Birmingham, Alabama, their efforts were eventually appropriated by male leadership.[35]

Southern Baptists were also aware of increasing Mexican immigration that the restrictive congressional legislation of the 1920s, which focused on European and Asian immigrants, largely overlooked. The 1924 "Report of Committee on Mexican Work" produced by the Baptist General Convention of Texas suggested half a million Mexicans lived in Texas. It recognized some Mexicans were in Texas to work temporarily while others planned to stay. As for the latter, the report noted that they "should be reached as citizens who are to help make this a great state, or else hinder its program by being a financial and social burden on our people." Either way, evangelization was the ultimate answer. "Kind treatment, fair dealing and frank conversations about religion would result in winning many of them to Christ." And if some immigrants returned to Mexico, taking their Protestant faith back with them, Texas Baptists were getting a two-for-one deal. The report also demonstrated concerns over education. It pointed out that Mexicans struggled to attain public education and called upon Baptists to intervene by either supporting public education for Mexicans or offering Baptist elementary education instead. The report ultimately recognized much work remained to be done and that Baptists were "touching the huge task with only our finger tips."[36] Commenting on Mexican immigration, Texas minister J. M. Dawson concluded in 1927, "Our future is so bound up with theirs that we cannot refuse to think of them, cultivate them, work with them and together strive for the worth while things in civilization. Will the churches default with this responsibility?"[37] Southern Baptists and most other Protestant denominations worked to follow through with this perceived "responsibility" as the century progressed.

The Social Gospel Inheritance and Its Challenges

Through the work sponsored by denominations and parachurch groups like the HMC, many Protestants in America believed immigration placed opportunities for missions on their doorsteps. While there were many fronts to this advance of home missions, most Protestant home missionaries shared a similar inspiration for their work, the social gospel. A thriving movement espoused by many mainline Protestant theologians, clergy, and home missionaries at the turn of the century, it sought to apply the love of Christ to society and replace oppressive institutions and systems with social justice instead. Most historians agree that by the 1920s the social gospel was losing momentum as a cohesive movement. Many of its early spokesmen had died, and it continued to face resistance from evangelical and fundamentalist Protestant quarters. Nevertheless, the principles of the movement persisted and became diffused among the more rank and file of Protestant churches. Many young Protestant men and women making their first forays into home missions during the 1920s had been fed a steady diet of social gospel precepts by their earlier mentors.[38] This in turn led to a diffusion of social gospel imperatives with more traditional evangelistic hopes, what the AMA recognized in 1924 as the "evangelization and social redemption of our country."[39]

Social gospel rhetoric clearly survived the waning of the movement. Expressions such as the brotherhood of man, Fatherhood of God, and Kingdom of God were important concepts among progressive Protestants at the turn of the century, and these terms continued in the parlance of ministers and home missionaries into the later twentieth century. While references to the Kingdom of God evidenced the postmillennial optimism of social gospelers, the brotherhood of man and Fatherhood of God were semantic inheritances from late nineteenth-century social reformers and liberal theology. The notion of the brotherhood of man in particular succumbed to various interpretations both secular and sacred during the late nineteenth century and into the twentieth in America.[40] At the School of Applied Ethics in Plymouth, Massachusetts, in 1892, both Jane Addams and Henry C. Adams tied the idea of brotherhood to democracy and suggested it was a key element of social work. Addams perceived the budding idea among the younger generation: "I think it is hard for us to realize how seriously many of them are taking to the notion of human brotherhood, how eagerly they long to give tangible expression to the democratic ideal."[41] The concept appears to gain prominence a year later as a term celebrating religious pluralism and world peace at the Parliament of the World's Religions held during the Chicago World's Fair.[42] After she attended the World's Fair, Katharine Lee Bates incorporated the sentiments of brotherhood into a poem the religious periodical *The Congregationalist* published in 1895. Now enshrined as a patriotic standard of the United States, the poem became the lyrics of "America the Beautiful." Though "brotherhood" was not included in the original 1895 version, by 1904 Bates had published the poem with the refrain laden with the familiar missional, and imperialistic, appeal: "America! America!; God shed his grace on thee; And crown thy good with brotherhood; From sea to shining sea."[43]

At about the same time, the nascent social gospel movement began to coopt the notion of the brotherhood of man, and by the early twentieth century it was given an evangelical twist, as the concept "Christian Brotherhood" was commonly used. Though some Protestant leaders still supported the international peace and religious pluralism implied in the idea, the term indicated a growing toleration for ethnic difference and ecumenical cooperation, as opposed to sectarianism.[44] In his book on home missions published in 1917, while discrediting the predominant racism of his day, southern Presbyterian Samuel L. Morris wrote, "Upon the scientific fact of blood relationship, Philanthropy bases the brotherhood of man. Upon the revealed fact of redemption by the blood of Christ, Christianity grounds the brotherhood of believers."[45] It was no coincidence that the spokesman of the social gospel movement Walter Rauschenbusch formed an organization named the Brotherhood of the Kingdom, and along with Washington Gladden and others, social gospel leaders advanced the ideas and rhetoric of the brotherhood of man.[46] In his 1919 text, *The Social Gospel and the New Era*, John Marshall Barker offered no finer definition of the social gospel and its relationship to brotherhood:

> Just as he [Jesus Christ] is the life of the vine, and the branches derive their life and fruitage from him, so the various social activities and institutions are giving expression in a larger and ever-increasing degree to

Christian principles of conduct, and to the divine ideal of the brotherhood of man. . . . The essential essence of the Kingdom is an abiding
divine power in the world which is gradually but surely giving form and
direction to the existing social order.[47]

Such rhetoric would infuse home mission work among immigrant
and ethnic communities during the first two decades of the twentieth
century. Howard B. Grose commented in his book *Aliens or Americans?*
published in 1906 that the "hope of America's evangelization is increased
by the fact that the pure religion of Jesus Christ is so essentially democratic in its fundamental teachings of the brotherhood of man, of spiritual liberty and unity." Grose then noted, "The immigrant comes into a
new environment, created alike by civil and religious liberty, and cannot
escape its influence."[48] Later in 1921, an Episcopal manual made clear: "If
we are to win our new neighbors to constructive participation in our national life we must show them that Americanism aims at nothing more
or less than liberty, equality, justice and the brotherhood of man under
the guidance and protection of God and in accordance with His laws."[49]
The AMA, led by Congregationalists, announced that its goal was to
aid the "unprivileged groups of America—particularly the American
Highlander, the Negro, Indian, Chinese and Japanese, Porto Rican [*sic*],
Mexican and Hawaiian. It remains, as it began, a crusade of Brotherhood standing in a day of race friction and class discrimination for the
undiluted application to human relations of Jesus' way of life."[50] Though
an often vague ideal, Protestant home missionaries frequently employed
the idea of the brotherhood of man in their immigrant ministries as they
pressed for toleration of other ethnicities and tried to incorporate immigrants into American churches.

The diffusion of social gospel principles with active home mission
programs helped temper nativism among some quarters of the white
Protestant community. Many denominational leaders decried the prejudice they witnessed within the nation; nevertheless, it is probable that
much of the Protestant laity, and many clergy, harbored similar prejudices and fears that were prevalent among society at large. As scholars
have noted, white leaders of the social gospel movement at the turn of
the century did not fully grasp or tackle structural racial injustice, leaving it up to the newly formed National Association for the Advancement

of Colored People and black proponents of the social gospel to challenge discrimination.[51] This lacuna explains in part the hesitation still found among liberal Protestants toward immigrant groups during the early twentieth century. A 1917 editorial published in *Christian Century* demonstrates a concern over rising immigrant numbers that were outpacing the "native population," suggesting that the "birth rate is nearly twice as high among the foreigners" and favored the increase of Catholicism. (This obviously overlooks the fact that the children of non-Asian immigrants born in America are by law citizens and thus should be considered a part of the "native population.") Nevertheless, the editorial expressed hope that more recent immigration birth rates would level out. "They will lose their group formation in our population," the editorial posited, "and eventually be absorbed in the American life, as doubtless the ten tribes of the Israelites were absorbed in the east."[52]

On occasion, more strident voices surfaced within Protestant publications criticizing the impact immigration had on America. Richard H. Edmonds, a prominent Baltimore journalist, wrote to Southern Baptists in 1924 encouraging their home mission work that bolstered the formation of a New South. For Edmonds, the "foreign element" had weakened the North and the West and was threatening America. Edmonds surmised that the "future of this country is in the hands of the South, to be saved or lost according to what the Anglo-Saxons of the South may do," in part because it is a region where the "foreign element is still comparatively small."[53] This more blatant appeal to Anglo-Saxon aspirations, a concept laden with racial, ethnic, and cultural biases, was common stock during the 1920s, an age when many whites appealed to "one hundred percent" definitions of what it meant to be American. While the Baptist publication that printed Edmonds's letter did not provide an editorial response, the decision to publish it without comment tacitly acknowledged his concerns.

Elsewhere, other Protestant voices were also less than sanguine about immigrants in America, especially when it came to Mexican immigration that continued outside the quota restrictions. In 1924, Arizona Presbyterians expressed concerns over immigration from Mexico. In their minds, immigration was linked to drinking, gambling, dancing, and "kindred vices of the underworld," and so the Presbytery of Southern Arizona wrote a resolution calling on the US and Mexican governments to close the border after 8 p.m. and requiring that a dry zone be implemented south of the border.[54] A Presbyterian pamphlet by Charles A. Thomson published in 1929 identified multiple arguments against Mexican immigrants prevalent in Anglo society, including racist stereotypes such as the inherent criminality of Mexicans and their dependence on welfare. While the author worked to dispel such myths and encourage his readers to extend friendship to Mexican immigrants, it is likely many of his Protestant constituency held such views. Moreover, even the author recognized the challenges a migrant lifestyle posed for assimilation and noted the low numbers of naturalization among first-generation Mexican immigrants.[55] Other home mission endeavors among Mexican immigrant communities during the 1920s elicited paternalistic responses. One YWCA executive in her account identified "child-like" characteristics of Mexicans and concluded that their immigration "placed us of America in the position of teachers of an awakened race."[56] Such sentiments reflected broader public concerns that, in the eyes of the federal government, justified the formation of the Border Patrol that same year.

In the end, the restrictive legislation Congress passed in 1924 did not set Protestant minds at ease. "They are liabilities or assets to the community," according to an Episcopal booklet printed in 1924. "These people are our future political and economic rulers. As they will be, so will our country become. We cannot afford to close our eyes any longer to this obvious fact. Restriction of immigration does not remove the overwhelming numbers already here. It has not even stopped the crowds smuggling themselves over our borders."[57] In 1926, the *Independent* lambasted Methodist Bishop Adna W. Leonard and his criticism of New York governor, and soon to be Democratic presidential candidate, Al Smith, who was not only Catholic, but also second-generation Irish. According to the article, Leonard proclaimed, "I am one hundred per cent Anglo-Saxon. America is a Protestant nation and always will remain so." He continued, "We never will surrender our priceless American heritage to the hands of the foreigners who trample on our flag."[58] Another Methodist, Erdmann D. Beynon, expressed concern over the possible threat immigrants posed to rural churches. "That the immigration from eastern and southern Europe has created a direct challenge to the Protestant churches of America is now generally conceded. Though our quota law has greatly curtailed the immigration from these regions," Beynon noted, "still it did not become effective soon enough to eliminate the problem. The 'foreigner' is with us—in vast numbers—and as he moves here and there across the cities and villages of our country, he leaves in his wake a trail of abandoned Protestant churches." For Beynon, this was a task for home missions and presented a challenge for more con-certed efforts by local churches to reach their immigrant neighbors.[59] Such comments suggest Protestants brought together concerns over the well-being of American society and the nation's supposedly Protestant identity when considering immigration.

Pluralism vs. Americanization

Many Protestant home missionaries remained hopeful that immigrants would still benefit the nation and the church. This hope was often bound up with efforts to Americanize immigrants and tolerate limited forms of cultural pluralism. This is clearly seen in the "Melting Pot" narrative of American history that playwright Israel Zangwill popularized in 1908. According to this interpretation, throughout history disparate groups of people had come to America and contributed to its distinct culture. Earlier social gospel leaders and settlement house workers often grap-pled with cosmopolitan aspirations and assimilationist expectations. Josiah Strong, both an outspoken social gospeler and nativist, recog-nized in 1911 the tension between pluralism and Americanization when he asked, "How shall such a heterogeneous multitude be transformed into Christian Americans—made one in loyalty to Christ and coun-try?"[60] According to historian Rivka Shpak Lissak, Jane Addams and other settlement house workers respected cultural differences among the foreign-born they worked with while still promoting Americaniza-tion.[61] Finding the proper balance between cosmopolitanism, cultural pluralism, and assimilation, however, would prove elusive for Protestant home missionaries over the next several decades.

One of the most prominent scholars to write on cultural pluralism during the early twentieth century was Horace Kallen, a scholar at the New School for Social Research in New York City who had earlier emi-grated from Germany. As we saw previously, in his work Kallen took up the subjects of pluralism and American democracy, reaching the conclusion that America could withstand, and actually benefit from, diverse cultures within its national borders. Rather than adhering to the assimilationist expectation that immigrants accept Anglo-Saxon ways, Kallen believed ethnic diversity could be maintained. Writing in 1915, he asked, "What do we *will* to make of the United States—a unison, singing the old Anglo-Saxon theme 'America,' the America of the New England school, or a harmony, in which that theme shall be dominant, perhaps, among others, but one among many, not the only one?" Kallen hoped for "a multiplicity in a unity, an orchestration of mankind," what he referred to as a "symphony of civilization."[62] By the 1920s such an interpretation of cultural diversity appeared periodically among home missionaries as they strove to aid immigrants of varied cultural backgrounds and integrate them into the Protestant church. And on occasion, a few Protestant leaders even acknowledged that cultural pluralism could bolster the nation.[63]

In addition to advocates of more cosmopolitan ideals were Protestant leaders who recognized a limited form of religious pluralism in America. This growing toleration for faiths outside of Protestantism had been developing since the late nineteenth century among liberal ministers and reformers, as historian David Mislin has pointed out, often drawing from the principle of the brotherhood of man. By the 1920s, some mainline Protestant leaders acknowledged that America was a nation in which Protestants, Catholics, and Jews all contributed to the religious landscape.[64] In fact, religious services, replete with pipe organ accompaniment, organized by the General Committee of Immigrant Aid on Ellis Island during the 1920s, came in the form of Protestant, Catholic, and Jewish.[65] In 1926, Presbyterians also took part in a conference sponsored by the American Jewish Committee to address government policy concerning deportations and immigration registration.[66] In their acknowledgment of religious liberty, even more traditional Protestant groups, such as Southern Baptists, recognized the place of Jews and Catholics in America. Speaking from the steps of Congress in 1920, George W. Truett reminded his Southern Baptist audience that despite their faith being "the very antithesis" of Catholicism, a "Baptist would rise at midnight to plead for absolute religious liberty for his Catholic neighbour, and for his Jewish neighbour, and for everybody else."[67] Of course, such claims by white Protestants were easier to make while they remained in command of American culture.

A fierce dialectic, however, defined Protestant thought on national identity and immigration by the early twentieth century. With timid acceptance of cultural pluralism and religious pluralism for Jews and Catholics, white Protestants were also products of their time and demanded that immigrants assimilate according to American cultural norms. As churches worked to evangelize and minister to immigrants, many believed they had the additional responsibility to inculcate American ideals and voice their political views. Often at the nexus of this "duty" for "God and Country" was the work of Americanization. Several denominations devoted entire programs and commissions to the task.[68] Most Protestant Christians felt America was a land of opportunity and liberty and that its values and culture must be preserved; thus, those whom Protestants identified as "foreigners" would need to accept this way of life as well. Consequently, Americanization became an important platform for Protestant work among immigrants. Historian Derek Chang, in his study of American Baptist home missions during the late nineteenth century, labels the product of such efforts as "evangelical nationalism."[69] Even though society in large part dismissed Americanization programs by 1920 and aimed instead for outright restriction, as historian John Higham contended, Protestants remained strong advocates of assimilation into the 1920s.[70]

Americanization proved to be an amorphous term, allowing various groups to coopt it for manifold purposes. Kallen begrudgingly defined Americanization as a two-pronged agenda. At one level, it was cultural and "appears to denote the adoption of English speech, of American clothes and manners, of the American attitude in politics." At another level, Kallen was concerned that the notion of Americanization was premised on race. "It connotes the fusion of the various bloods, and a transmutation by 'the miracle of assimilation' of Jews, Slavs, Poles, Frenchmen, Germans, Hindus, Scandinavians into beings similar in background, tradition, outlook, and spirit to the descendants of the British colonists, the Anglo-Saxon stock."[71] With such a fluid term, Protestants readily formed their own application of the term.

Numerous publications espoused such principles. One author affiliated with the CWHM went so far as to title her 1913 book *America,*

God's Melting Pot.[72] One Protestant writer even composed "A Hymn of Christian Americanization."[73] The leading "textbook" for Protestant Americanization programs during the 1920s was Charles Alvin Brooks's *Christian Americanization: A Task for the Churches.* The publication of this text was a testament to the ecumenical spirit of the early twentieth century. Brooks, affiliated with the American Baptist Home Mission Society, published the book under the CWHM and Missionary Education Movement of the United States and Canada. The HMC distributed this book with the hope that it would educate adult church members on Americanization. Brooks recognized the social import of Americanization, but for him the spiritual was never far from the social. Indeed, the book was promoted alongside a compilation of Scripture passages titled *The Bible Message for the Stranger Within Our Gates* by Ida Harrison.[74]

In his book, Brooks argued that World War I served as a reality check for advocates of Americanization. He suggested that Americanization "was supposed to be an automatic process. Was not America a 'melting pot'? . . . The war has cured us of absurd optimism." In his consideration of Americanization and the church's role, he defined what the principle was not. It was not tied to the war, race, the English language, American culture, or militant nationalism, nor was it nativism. Instead, Brooks argued that Americanization was something more sublime.[75]

> America is not a "melting pot." It is something far more human and vital, more divine and spiritual than that. What we need to keep steadily in mind is that the process of Americanization is not the reduction of all to a common denominator but the elevation of all to the highest possible plane; to consider that each race reacts upon the other to the enrichment of all; and to endeavor to realize that the various racial stocks, thus contributing, lose their separate and distinct identity in the building of a new entity, a new race, which shall be a demonstration, in this day of grace, of the blood brotherhood of all men and the spiritual oneness of the sons of God.[76]

For Brooks, Americanization was spiritual, but not in the evangelical sense. The spiritual mission of Americanization was more transcendent. His position was not far removed from the social Darwinism defined by Herbert Spencer during the late nineteenth century, though Brooks emphasized cultural transformation rather than racial characteristics. According to Brooks, Americanization would, through an evolutionary process, produce a robust national culture out of a diverse population.[77]

Many denominations took such ideas to heart and sponsored Americanization programs within home missions. The editors of the *Missionary Voice*, a periodical of the Methodist Episcopal Church, South (MECS) announced in 1923: "One of our great tasks is the evangelization and assimilation of large groups of foreigners. . . . It is our business to help establish the Kingdom of God on earth."[78] Yet, this was not simply a responsibility relegated to denominational staff. The Episcopal Church reminded its congregants that organized work went only so far. It announced, "Yet better and more efficient than paid advisers, is ordinary Christian neighborliness of ordinary men and women. . . . This is the real foundation of true Americanization, and the lack of it has been the root trouble. Have you been neighbors to your neighbors?"[79] For Brooks, Protestants were largely stalling Americanization because they did not open up their homes to immigrants, and in the process "lost invaluable opportunities for interpreting America." Despite the rising tide of nativism, Brooks remained hopeful, concluding, "To democratize and Christianize our contacts is to become a radiating center of the American spirit."[80]

Despite Brooks's admonition, Americanization in many ways reflected nativist concerns current within society at large. This is evident in a 1922 article published in the *Woman's Home Missions*, a publication of the Methodist Episcopal Church (MEC). The author began her essay by stating, "One cannot talk long on immigration without Americanization for they go hand in hand." She recognized the difficult conditions immigrants faced. With cosmopolitan flair, she also conceded that in America, "we are all immigrants." Her empathy turned to concern, however, by the end of the article. She noted, "The United States has been called the melting pot of all nations. The trouble is not all who fall into the pot melt."[81] The southern Methodist *Missionary Voice* was even more blunt, announcing that when an immigrant "comes to America to live he ought to be required to be an American to the extent at least that he will respect and obey our laws and in some measure conform to our customs. If he is unwilling to do this he has no place here."[82] In a piece titled "A Hyphenated Allegiance," the *Presbyterian* suggested that maintaining citizenship in more than one country was just as bad as Christians who leave the world behind and join the church, but do not "burn the bridge behind them. No more than in the days of our Lord's mission can any man, in Church or State, serve two masters." In other words, the immigrant must wholeheartedly convert to American ways. The continued presence of immigrant communities with strong ethnic identities worried white Protestants who expected Americanization to occur naturally.[83] Southern Methodists shared similar sentiments: "More and more these Mexicans are being assimilated by the Americans around them, and if the Church will do its full share by them, they will become Christian citizens and a valuable aid in making America Christian, otherwise they will become a menace to our civilization."[84] Such perspectives reflect previous decades of foreign missions predicated on cultural imperialism and a vaunted view of a supposed American civilization.

For Southern Baptists, the immigrant problem and Americanization were closely linked to two other groups that begged careful attention, African Americans and Roman Catholics. One report declared that prospects for African Americans in southern urban centers were not promising since the "great congested masses of negroes in our big Southern cities are thrown . . . with the great congested masses of foreigners who know nothing about the negroes and many of whom know far less about American ideals and American Life than the negroes." As for Catholicism, the report suggested the immigrant population in the urban South served as a wellspring for Catholicism. According to the Southern Baptist report, the "twofold problem of foreigners and Catholics" reflected the "Americanization problem and the evangelization problem." The report then suggested, "Whoever helps to solve the problem of the foreigner in our midst helps also to solve the problem of Roman Catholicism and vice versa. They are indissolubly linked together."[85] The solution for Southern Baptists was evangelism, which only reinforced American principles. An article in the *Baptist Standard* on Italian immigrants reflected this dynamic, warning that not ministering to the foreign-born was a dereliction of a "great duty." It was, according to the article, "a double sin against God and against our beautiful land of America."[86]

Race and assimilation took on complex and paternalistic forms in the South, where home missionaries often organized ministries around racial and ethnic groupings. Home missions to "Negroes," "Orientals," "Italians," and "Mexicans" reflect the southern Protestant vantage point of races in need of Christian influence, social uplift, and Americanization, within the confines of a distinct southern economic context. "With the migration of the Negro to the North," noted the secretaries of the Home Department of the MECS, "we may expect the Mexican and the Italian, the Greek and the Bohemian, and other foreign-speaking peoples to come into the South and take their places on the farms and in the trades." But the cultural challenges this phenomenon posed were equally great: "Unlike the Negro, these people know little about our American customs and less about our type of religious life."[87] In the eyes of some home missionaries, immigrants and African Americans were opposing forces in the South.[88] While racial categorizations were often conflated with ethnic and national groups, southern Methodists still adhered to the stark color line of black and white in the segregated South. When conducting settlement house work, the MECS sponsored Wesley Houses for white patrons and Bethlehem Houses for the black community. Demonstrating the often liminal racial status of immigrants, Mexicans were directed to Wesley Houses, even though home missionaries still questioned their whiteness.[89]

Congregationalists also grappled with assimilationist aims in their work in New Mexico. At the Rio Grande Institute in Albuquerque, home missionaries implemented a complicated assimilationist agenda. The school was meant to meet the educational needs of Spanish-speaking children from first through eighth grades in the Southwest. But a report in 1927 noted that Anglo students were also admitted to assist with this process. The institute was referred to as an "experiment in a bi-racial and bi-lingual school," and included 138 students as of 1928. Congregationalists also sponsored what were known as "plaza schools" that combined education, medical assistance, evangelism, and other settlement house tasks in the southwestern parts of the United States. In such work, Congregational home missionaries promoted forms of Americanization among immigrants.[90]

While most Protestant home missionaries embraced the logic that Christianity and Americanization reinforced each other, some contemporaries both without and within Protestantism were more skeptical about the notion of Christian Americanization. In 1920, representatives from the FCC and Central Conference of American Rabbis met in New York City to work through Jewish concerns about Protestant Americanization. The final statement they agreed upon recognized the responsibility to "disclaim, and deplore, the use of the term 'Americanization' in any case where it is made to mean, or to imply, that there is no distinction between the words 'Americanization' and 'Christianization,' or carries the implication that Jews, or people of other religions and other races, are not good Americans." This did not mean, however, that Americanization was undesirable. The Jewish and FCC representatives agreed "to co-operate with each other, as brethren, in all efforts for Americanization and for promoting righteousness in the American people."[91] In this instance, mainline Protestant leaders were willing to stretch their definition of Americanization to include the concerns of the Jewish community.

Americanization sometimes found detractors among more conservative Protestants who were not as optimistic about Christianity's ability to redeem the social order. Conservative and fundamentalist Christians believed in the power of individual conversion, and groups like Southern Baptists, while supporting Americanization, were not as vocal on legislative reform. Americanization, if it entailed using Christianity primarily for social ends, drew criticism from some Protestants. Writing in 1923 while teaching at Princeton Theological Seminary, J. Gresham Machen, a Presbyterian fundamentalist with a strong aversion to modernism, big government, and social gospel activity within his denomination, noted with a tinge of sarcasm the reception given to immigrants by a government and populace claiming Christianity. He stated, "We have attacked them by oppressive legislation or proposals of legislation, but such measures have not been altogether effective." With tongue in cheek, Machen pondered, "It may be strange that a man should love the language that he learned at his mother's knee, but these people do love it, and we are perplexed in our efforts to produce a unified American people." Thus, Christian social workers were left with few options: "So religion is called in to help; we are inclined to proceed against the immigrants now with a Bible in one hand and a club in the other offering them the blessings of liberty. That is what is sometimes meant by 'Christian Americanization.'"[92] Clearly, some conservative Protestants did not support Brooks's form of Christian Americanization, and others instead stressed evangelism rather than using religion for what they believed was a form of social control. And for Jews, Catholics, and other non-Protestants in America, the Americanization work that home missionaries promoted could appear threatening.

Congress and Immigration Restriction

While most Protestant denominations in the United States continued to support Americanization, Congress passed legislation restricting immigration in 1917, 1921, and 1924 in part as a response to strong currents of nativism within American society. White Protestants were often caught between staunch nativists and immigrant communities. The Protestant response to the 1917 law and the literacy test it created was cool at best. According to Brooks in *Christian Americanization*, the literacy test could have unforeseen consequences. For Brooks, literacy and intellect did not guarantee that desirable immigrants would enter America and assimilate. "Some very brilliant men and women of foreign birth have proved rather dangerous and with all their native capacity seem not to have assimilated the American spirit to any marked degree."[93] The *Presbyterian* voiced similar concerns: "A man may be able to read and speak many languages, yet be a rogue; while another may not be able to read and yet be an industrious, thrifty, valuable citizen." The article concluded that the literacy test "may increase the sharp devils and reduce the plain, honest men."[94] At least two Baptist publications, however, *The Baptist and Reflector* and *The Home Field*, did publish material between 1915 and 1916 supporting a literacy requirement.[95]

Through the Emergency Immigration Act of 1921, Congress established a temporary annual quota that admitted only 3% of the total population of each European nationality in America as of 1910. Similar to the 1917 legislation, this law did not garner much of a response from Protestants. The *Christian Century*, one of the leading mainline Protestant publications, did not address the law in its issues for May, when the law passed, or June.[96] The *Christian Advocate* did mention the law's passage, but without commentary.[97] G.B.F. Hallock vaguely referenced immigration restriction in an article published in the *Presbyterian* a month prior to the bill's passage. He suggested, "If the whole body of good people prayed as earnestly as Abraham did for Sodom, we would not have to exclude foreigners. We would evangelize them. We would break the power of unrighteousness."[98] Hallock's comment was more of a critique of American Christianity than it was a response to the quota law. The most strident support for the restrictive legislation came from the southern Methodist press. A 1923 editorial in the *Missionary Voice* outlined the threat it believed unrestricted immigration posed. The piece acknowledged that the 1921 legislation targeted some nationalities over others. Its editors concluded, "This provision was intentional. Immigrants settled this country and established this Government but they were immigrants from Northern and Western Europe." The editors then warned: "If the gates are opened and the tides of immigration permitted to run at full height nothing can save our cherished institutions and customs."[99] The 1921 law escaped much attention because Protestants in large part supported the idea of a quota system and believed that some form of restriction was necessary in light of recent immigration. The 1924 legislation, however, drew more criticism from Protestant circles.

The legislation passed in 1924 outraged many Protestants, not because of the more stringent quotas it established targeting southern and eastern Europeans, but because it excluded Japanese immigrants entirely, what one Congregationalist report described as an "unchristian act."[100] Problems surrounding Japanese immigration had already been brewing for several years. Japanese immigration to the West Coast at the turn of the century brought workers that many Americans believed threatened labor, and anti-Japanese movements began, including efforts to segregate schools. The Gentlemen's Agreement between President Theodore Roosevelt and Japan implied that Japanese in America would have access to public education and in turn Japan would decrease emigration to America. Anti-Japanese sentiments continued, however, and the Supreme Court even ruled that Japanese were ineligible for citizenship based on race in 1922. The 1924 quota law affirmed that ruling by excluding Japanese immigrants entirely.[101]

Japanese immigration had also been a topic of discussion within Protestant circles prior to the passage of the 1924 law. Sidney Gulick was a key Protestant figure on this subject. He had previously served as a university professor in Kyoto for seven years and also helped form the National Committee for Constructive Immigration Legislation and the Commission on Relations with Japan. With his international expertise, Gulick contributed to the immigration debate in America and even proposed a quota system as early as 1914. By 1917 he advocated an immigration quota policy that would restrict immigration based on each nationality's ability to assimilate, rather than on race.[102]

Gulick also served as secretary of the FCC's Commission on Relations with the Orient. Under Gulick's leadership, the Commission kept close watch on international relations with Asia and offered legislative proposals. The Commission even had the opportunity to present its recommendations to President Woodrow Wilson and the Foreign Relations Committee in 1917. By 1920 the Commission produced a report calling for various reforms to be made to US immigration policy. It recognized that Japanese immigration was a national issue, rather than a matter that should be left to the state of California to settle. The report declared that the previous Gentlemen's Agreement that tacitly discouraged Japanese immigration should be discarded, and it also denounced any "race discrimination" in standards for selecting immigrants from different nations. The report, however, did acknowledge that immigration "should not exceed the number of that people that we can assimilate, Americanize and steadily employ." Moreover, the report called for reforming naturalization requirements and discarding laws discriminating against Chinese immigrants.[103]

The report then went on to describe the proper Christian response. It argued that Christians must be concerned about discriminatory laws, as they frustrated Japanese whom Christians were trying to reach. Christians must also incorporate the principles of justice and morality into the debate. The report, however, included the caveat that it was incumbent upon *individual* Christians and ministers to apply principles of justice, instead of churches openly proposing legislation. Reflecting social gospel sentiments, the report concluded, "The Golden Rule must be applied. Christ's teaching of brotherhood and its actual practice can alone solve the grave problems of races and nations that are ominously looming up before us."[104]

The Commission and its secretary, Sydney Gulick, eventually struck a nerve among nativist groups. A 1921 brief produced by the Japanese Exclusion League of California announced, "The plea of Sidney Gulick, and a number of his Christian friends, that we make citizens of the Japanese and then trust to making good citizens of them by Christianizing them, advocates an experiment dangerous in the extreme." The author then argued that Christianity did not offer much hope, for even if Japanese accepted Christianity, Japanese immigrants would still retain their former Shinto beliefs. This report also discredited arguments that exclusion would hinder home and foreign missions to Japanese. In this instance, Gulick and Protestants who advocated his moderate restriction clearly parted ways with nativists who called for the outright exclusion of Japanese immigrants.[105]

Many Protestant groups criticized the Immigration Act of 1924 once they read about its treatment of Japanese immigration.[106] Based upon the principles articulated by the FCC's Commission on Relations with the Orient in 1920, it is no surprise that this act drew outrage from various corners of American Protestantism. There were several facets to this frustration. First, Protestants remained concerned that the law would have a deleterious effect on home and foreign missions. William Axling, a former Northern Baptist missionary to Japan, argued, "This legislation has in tragic fashion put Christianity on trial in Japan. . . . It has raised great question marks against such central Christian truths as a divine Fatherhood, world brotherhood, justice, fair play and good will. It has struck the Christian movement in the Japanese empire a staggering blow."[107] Second, the principle of the brotherhood of man inspired many liberal-minded Protestants to espouse international harmony and oppose racial discrimination. Proponents of this principle believed the legislation violated this ideal by singling out Japanese for exclusion and disregarding the sovereignty of Japan.

Finally, those who criticized the 1924 legislation because of its treatment of Japanese immigration feared that Japan might pose a threat to international peace. Such thinking dovetailed with the push for disarmament during the early 1920s. No one wanted to see the world at war a second time. According to the *Presbyterian*, "Nothing could be more unwise than to alienate further the great Mongolian peoples at this hour of coveted peace. It would be hostile to all our professed principles of Christianity and statesmanship."[108] In another issue, the *Presbyterian* suggested the 1924 legislation "forced [Japan] to look for an enlargement of their race and commercial opportunities elsewhere," thus further perpetuating aggressive expansion.[109] The AMA in 1924 combined both missional and diplomatic concerns when it concluded that its home missions addressed "not merely a domestic race problem but the most critical of international relations depends largely on proving that Christian brotherhood is practicable."[110] These fears would prove to be prescient as Japan invaded China during the next decade and attacked Pearl Harbor 17 years later.

The Northern Baptist Convention (NBC) provides a good example of a Protestant denomination that protested the legislation in 1924. One editorial in the *Baptist* argued that while nations are entitled to concerns over assimilation, aggressively pursuing national agendas only encourages war. Instead, the Baptist editorial suggested, "In the family of nations there must be the interchange of common courtesies if good-will is to be preserved." Instead, Congress chose to exclude Japanese immigrants without consulting the Japanese government. The editorial concluded that "it seems to us ill-advised to slap Japan in the face. . . . By the action of congress a problem that was largely sectional may become international and set in motion a long train of difficulties which will seriously set back the progress that was begun by the disarmament conference in Washington in 1922."[111] Northern Baptist protest, however, was not confined to editorials alone. The president of the NBC, Corwin S. Shank, was in Japan at the time Congress considered the legislation.[112] He returned to America and passionately condemned the legislation in his annual address to the convention, declaring that a Christian America must embrace the principle of brotherhood. His speech was followed by a "deafening and prolonged applause."[113]

Of course, such efforts to engage politics caught the attention of some observers who feared that institutional religion and politics were mixing. Massachusetts Representative George H. Tinkham decried the petitions the FCC sent to legislators criticizing the legislation and argued that they abridged the separation of church and state. Speaking in defense of the FCC, General Secretary Charles S. Macfarland responded that the church must not renege on its responsibility to advocate justice. In fact, Macfarland claimed that the 1924 immigration legislation "runs counter to the efforts of the churches to maintain social justice." Associate General Secretary Samuel McCrea Cavert went on to frame the issue as such: "The Administrative Committee of the Federal Council was in effect taking the position that all of the Church's talk about international morality and brotherhood would be rendered sterile if it were to acquiesce" to the violation of Japanese sovereignty and previous treaty obligations. For FCC spokesmen, the church's moral duty required that it speak to political concerns while not tampering with legislation.[114]

What is telling is that Protestants did not challenge the underlying rationale for a quota system established in the 1921 and 1924 laws, but rather focused their attention on Japanese exclusion. In 1922, the Methodist Episcopal *Woman's Home Missions* recognized that the quota law passed in 1921 "favors immigration from the northern Protestant countries of Europe," but the journal did not provide further reflection on this observation.[115] An editorial in the PCUSA women's *Home Mission Monthly* suggested that the 1921 legislation should be extended so that the nation could "[select] the type of immigrant that is needed and can be most readily absorbed."[116] Positions published in the southern Methodist *Missionary Voice* a few months after the legislation was passed echoed similar sentiments, arguing that while restriction was necessary, exclusion of Japanese was hasty. Instead, Japanese should be assigned a quota (which would be "negligible") and allowed naturalization.[117] While mainline Protestant leaders opposed outright racial discrimination toward Japanese, they did not attack the prejudice toward southern and eastern Europeans in the quotas established in 1924.[118] This suggests Protestants generally believed restriction across the board was necessary, and were only willing to offer resistance when certain nationalities were targeted for outright exclusion. Writing in the *Reformed Church Review* in July 1924, E. H. Zaugg admitted, "I would not like to be taken as an advocate of unrestricted Japanese immigration. The admission of a large number of Japanese into our country would doubtless create a very serious race problem. But all that the Japanese desire is that they be treated on an equality with other nations."[119] Former Hawaii pastor Albert Palmer even admitted in the *Christian Century* that "until America has solved her race problem in the South, it would be folly to invite another one on the Pacific Coast."[120] For many American Protestants the total immigration during the last several decades was staggering, and the predominantly Catholic and Jewish backgrounds of many of these immigrants did not set Protestant minds at ease.

The Aftermath

The 1924 Immigration Act stirred Protestant concerns and signaled a level of political commitment over immigration not seen since 40 years earlier when some Protestant leaders expressed concern over the Chinese Exclusion Act of 1882.[121] After Congress passed the 1924 law and codified Japanese exclusion, American Protestant leaders continued their opposition and were inclined to keep a close eye on legislation.[122] In December 1925, the FCC passed a statement on Japanese exclusion, continuing to criticize its diplomatic ramifications and racial basis. The Federal Council statement expressed the conviction that the "dictates of humanity and the welfare of the world demand the recognition by all governments of the brotherhood of man and the inherent right of all nations and races to treatment free from humiliation." Despite these lofty claims, however, the statement still conceded the "need of restriction of immigration in order to conserve American standards of labor and living," and argued that Asian immigrants should simply be held to the same quota, which would allow a paltry 350 Asian immigrants to enter the country.[123]

Denominations also continued to protest the 1924 legislation. The PEC went on record in 1928 noting that "present immigration and naturalization laws discriminate against oriental nations and are therefore not only a hindrance to missionary work but also a barrier to good will between ourselves and these nations."[124] Even Southern Baptists, ever reluctant to address political matters, voted at their 1925 convention to condemn Asian exclusion, noting their desire to "prove our Christianity by exercising the spirit of brotherhood toward our Chinese brethren." Though it acknowledged the need to restrict "undesirable immigrants," the Southern Baptist statement concluded, "The Committee regrets that the recently enacted Immigration Law did not treat the citizens of China and Japan, as they did other nations."[125] In 1927, the Commission on Inter-Racial Relations at the National Council meeting of Congregational Churches promoted the "revision of our naturalization laws as will make eligibility for naturalization dependent upon demonstrated capacity to fulfill the duties of citizenship worthily rather than, as at present, upon the accident of race."[126] Even as late as 1934, the General Council of the Congregational Churches continued to criticize Asian exclusion, arguing instead that Asian nations should be included in the quota system.[127]

Meanwhile, home missions to immigrant communities and ethnic Americans continued. Efforts to evangelize and Americanize immigrants persisted, as mainline Protestants recognized the large foreign-born population still within the nation inherited from earlier immigration. While most of the nation embraced immigration restriction, Protestants continued to support the principle of Americanization in their ministries to foreigners; it remained a viable solution for what they saw as America's immigration problem. Often the work took on forms of paternalism, whereby, in the words of one southern Methodist, Protestant home missionaries should serve as "Big Brother to the nations of the world."[128] In the crucible of home missions, white Protestants encountered varied forms of cultural and religious pluralism. The coming decades would serve as a key period for Protestants as they continued to formulate their approach to pluralism. If the presidential election of 1928 and its Catholic candidate Al Smith provided any indicator, white Protestants were still far from embracing a religious pluralism that included Catholics and Jews.[129] Even cosmopolitanism was still held in question as the nation emerged from World War I with a patriotism premised largely on Anglo-Saxon culture norms.

Conclusion

"America now has achieved almost complete isolation, by her high tariff wall, her more than half closed gates, and by her refusal to join the League of Nations," concluded Christian professor and former immigrant Edward A. Steiner in 1929. "America is not to be any more the dumping-ground, refuge, or war ally of Europe. She has chosen to be her sovereign self; but no nation lives to itself or dies to itself, and her influence upon the future of mankind will continue to be a blessing or a curse, as she herself decrees."[130] As Steiner and others observed, the United States would never be able to carry out its isolationist agenda following World War I; continued immigration and vibrant ethnic communities made this abundantly clear. Most Americans did not find this cause for celebration, but rather concern. Protestants at the time the 1924 Immigration Act passed were not knee-jerk nativists hell-bent on keeping foreigners out of the country, but neither were they immune to nativist ideals. They demanded Americanization and accepted the quota system that put immigrants from southern and eastern Europe at a disadvantage. At the same time, however, some Protestant leaders were vocal advocates of justice, as seen in their defense of Japanese immigrants following the passage of the 1924 law. Protestants often coupled this hope for justice with their Christian duties. This fervor for home missions and social gospel ideals tempered potential nativist inclinations among Protestant groups.

Too often historians use the 1920s as a convenient capstone to developments in American culture. Protestant fundamentalism falls to its knees in Dayton, Tennessee, the rebirth of the Ku Klux Klan comes to an end by 1925, and the Immigration Act of 1924 marks the dissipation of concern over immigration. Yet, Protestant fundamentalism survived the 1920s by developing its own subculture, and while the Klan lost political momentum by 1925, it continued as a fragmented organization and reared its racist head again during the midcentury civil rights movement.[131] Furthermore, the legislation Congress passed in 1924, while limiting immigration, did not end public discussion over the foreigner in America or fully close off the nation to immigration. Over the course of the next 40 years, mainline Protestants continued their home mission work among immigrants and ethnic Americans and remained attentive to forms of pluralism. All the while, they struggled with how best to maintain their privileged status in a nation they desperately desired to be Christian, while still accounting for the diversity immigrants brought to the nation. This became further complicated as economic and political crises of global proportion created new challenges for the nation over the next several decades. As Steiner had predicted, isolationism was never really a viable option for the United States during the interwar period, but its role on the international stage would continue to be ambiguous as long as its national identity remained contested.

2

The Trying Thirties

But the "melting pot," which for so many years bubbled merrily, now only simmers. . . . The first period of our national life comprised years of pioneering. The next was one of assimilation. The immediate future will be years of stabilization. That period has already started. America, in the homely parlance of the housewife, is beginning to "jell."
—Louis I. Dublin, "The American People: The Census Portrait"

The United States closed its gates in 1924, resulting in restriction for the next four decades. Five years after Congress passed the Immigration Act, Edward Steiner published *The Making of a Great Race*. Clearly meant to upend Madison Grant's racist screed *Passing of a Great Race* published 13 years earlier, Steiner averred that racial diversity was no threat to America. In his book Steiner focused on American religion and the nation's ethnic and cultural makeup inherited from earlier immigration. Though acknowledging the persistence of diversity, Steiner was confident in the nation's ability to produce a "cultural homogeneity." He concluded, "This culture will be influenced less by what the immigrant brings than by what he finds and into what he can grow."[1]

Meanwhile, other Americans were less certain that the nation could truly absorb recent immigrants. Nine years later, as America trudged through a Great Depression that left one out of every four working-age Americans without a job and dismantled the nation's financial institutions, the President General of the Sons of the American Revolution announced over the radio that hard economic times necessitated continuing immigration restriction. He commented on the high number of legal and undocumented immigrants and stated bluntly, "American jobs should be for Americans." He also declared that much work was still needed in the area of assimilation. He concluded, "Until they have lost their hyphens they are not assimilated."[2] Despite restriction and the supposed closure it brought to concerns about immigration, foreigners, soon joined by refugees, remained in the public eye.

Many mainline Protestants had to grapple with the competing visions of Steiner and the Sons of the American Revolution. Rather than drop immigrant mission programs entirely following the 1924 Immigration Act, Protestant home missionaries continued to focus on immigrant communities during the 1930s. While fewer immigrants entered the country, the millions of foreign-born who came since the late nineteenth century were a noticeable presence in American society. White Protestants considered this a missional challenge that must be met.[3] Oftentimes white Protestants responded to immigrant and ethnic communities through a robust home mission program that represented a diffusion of social gospel ideals with evangelistic aspirations, resulting in an often ambivalent attitude toward pluralism. Social gospel principles from prior decades beset societal prejudices and beckoned a vision for brotherhood that for some Protestants included the immigrant, and commingled with these social gospel aspirations was the traditional gospel message of a relationship with Jesus Christ. The denominational ministries of Northern Baptists, Methodists, Presbyterians, Episcopalians, Congregationalists, and even Southern Baptists, to an extent, reflected these dynamics.[4]

Home Missions and Social Concern

Christian home missions offered a point of contact between white Protestants and immigrant communities that joined social work with the evangelical mainstays of evangelism and religious education. Christian missionaries on the home front believed their message resonated with the immigrant. One missionary, after spending time with a Greek immigrant who had obtained a collection of Bible stories, recalled, "The first one is of Abraham making a home in a new country for his family. She appreciated that for she too was a stranger in a strange land."[5]

The social gospel inheritance was a central component of Protestant home missions during the interwar years, including programs directed toward "strangers." The mainstays of settlement house work and port-of-entry ministries remained strong into the 1930s. The HMC sponsored

533 community centers employing 1,240 staff by 1935.[6] The PEC maintained settlement houses in 17 locales, including centers in Alabama, Los Angeles, Chicago, and New York.[7] Episcopal women continued their efforts on Ellis Island, and Methodists on the West Coast conducted similar programs on Angel Island.[8] Social gospel language also permeated Protestant endeavors. References to the "brotherhood of man," or at least its implication, reflect the continued presence of the social Christianity prevalent during the Progressive era. The Episcopal Church in 1931 declared, "Essentially, a democracy is the political expression of the spirit of human brotherhood. It ought, therefore to mean, always, a development of the sense of social and community responsibility and duty."[9]

Hermann N. Morse, a Presbyterian home missionary and leader within the HMC, also challenged the practice of racially and ethnically segregated churches on the basis of the "universality of Christian brotherhood." As a prominent mainline spokesman for home missions, Morse played a vital role in promoting immigrant ministry at the time. He served the PCUSA's home mission department starting in 1912 and later became the chairman of the Five-Year Program of Survey and Adjustment sponsored by the HMC, CWHM, FCC, and Community Church Workers. Morse was a dauntless advocate for home missions and was convinced that the fate of the nation was tied to Protestant efforts. He later edited *Home Missions Today and Tomorrow*, published in 1934. The report, a product of the Five-Year Program, provided a detailed analysis of home mission work among immigrant groups in America. Throughout his work, Morse linked a strong missionary ethic to social gospel principles.[10]

But Protestant work among immigrants diffused these social gospel ideals with the traditional evangelistic message that had always been at the heart of Protestant missions. At the forefront of Protestant denominations who sponsored evangelistic missions were Southern Baptists. Often Southern Baptists prioritized evangelism well above social ministry. One report asserted, "Social programs will not rebuild the world. If we turn our holy faith into a social gospel, . . . we turn our backs on . . . the fearful and universal fact of sin and man's desperate need for redemption."[11] Southern Baptists, however, were not alone in stressing evangelism. The Episcopal Church and MEC both sponsored Commissions on Evangelism, and most other mainline Protestant denominations continued to stress a message of conversion. The FCC even maintained a department devoted to evangelism.[12]

By the 1930s most Protestant interpretations of evangelism included a social component. A report sponsored by multiple mainline home mission organizations acknowledged in 1934 that New Testament forms of evangelism were essential. But rather than resort simply to sharing the gospel message by word of mouth, the report called for a multifaceted interpretation of evangelism and stressed the social significance of personal salvation.[13]

> Christ expected that from a redeemed personality would come a redeemed society, that the love which He awakens in the heart of the individual will always express itself socially. . . . There is no conflict in New Testament Christianity between personal regeneration and social regeneration, between evangelism and social service. They must go together in the program of the Christian Church if the Kingdom of God is to come into the life of the nation and into the life of the world.[14]

Such an interpretation of evangelism reflects the gradual spread of social gospel aspirations to the lower reaches of the Protestant church. Social concern had always been part and parcel with the evangelistic agenda of Protestants in America, but during the first half of the twentieth century, notions of evangelism alongside more concerted, structural social reform took new forms. A diffusion of social gospel tenets with the traditional gospel message was occurring. No longer did social gospel ideals remain the domain of theologians distant from the average Protestant in the pew, nor were social gospel tenets only the refrain of groups at the forefront of social protest. In many respects, what historian Susan Curtis identifies as the commodification of the social gospel had been realized by the 1930s, and the notions of advancing the Kingdom of God through social reform and brotherly love were repackaged for the regular Protestant church member during the interwar period.[15]

Matthew Bowman's insightful work in *The Urban Pulpit* helps to clarify the history of mainline Protestants during the early twentieth century. Bowman asserts that rather than a simple divide between modernists and fundamentalists, a third group, "liberal evangelicals," largely constituted American Protestantism. By examining Protestants in New

York City during the early twentieth century, he describes a class of Protestants that favored innovative methods corresponding to a changing culture, while still maintaining the primacy of Christian conversion and spiritual formation. Bowman states, "Liberal evangelicals were those who came to believe that evangelicals could have it all: aid to the poor and their conversion, communion with Christ through rather than instead of social reform." The mainline subjects of this book largely fall within this categorization.[16]

This hybrid form of home mission was ubiquitous among Protestant denominations during the 1930s, especially within their work with immigrants. A section of a Presbyterian program that considered Mexican missions demonstrated this diffusion of the social gospel with traditional evangelism when it noted, "The soul of man must be saved. But how, if the body and the spirit of the man are crushed by a cruel and heartless social and industrial order?"[17] Another Presbyterian also considering work among the Mexican American population pondered, "And so throughout the Southwest, the message of Christ is forming and re-forming individual lives, is leavening entire communities."[18] Even with a more overtly evangelistic emphasis, Southern Baptists did not avoid social concerns.[19] They tied to evangelization the notion of a "Christian America," sponsored Americanization among immigrants, and recognized that home missionaries were not only religious but were also cultural interpreters to foreigners who came to America.[20] This missiology was often manifested through the community center work directed toward immigrants, where religious and social concern went hand in hand. Morse recognized that the work of Protestant community centers drew upon the earlier settlement house movement, but he asserted they were "much more definitely and avowedly religious."[21] Clearly, at the level of home missions, the social gospel promoted at the turn of the century had not displaced the evangelical task of sharing the gospel, contrary to the fears of fundamentalist Protestants at the time. Instead, evangelism continued, but with broader perceptions of its social significance.

While this melding of the social gospel with evangelistic missions was a component of the Protestant home mission programs, this missional orientation was also the result of immigrants who practiced traditional forms of Christianity while settling in America. This process reflects the trends historian Philip Jenkins identifies by the end of the twentieth century whereby southern hemispheric Christianity and its traditional, more conservative theology and religious practice were returning to western nations and shaping Christianity there.[22] This process was already occurring incrementally by the early twentieth century as arriving immigrant groups were practicing more traditional forms of Christianity at a time when American mainline leaders were turning to more liberal theology and progressive agendas. According to mainline reports, Protestant "evangelical" work among Italians was largely an internal affair. A report produced by the Survey Committee on Italian Evangelization acknowledged: "the fact that the initial drive came very largely from the awakened purpose and passion of the Italians themselves has led to the conclusion that what we have is an Evangelical Movement among Italians and not a missionary project thrust by Americans from outside on an unreceptive population."[23] This process largely explains the evangelistic nature of work among Spanish-speaking groups in the Southwest and elsewhere. Later in 1961, it is telling that Spanish-speaking churches in New York City threatened to leave the city's Protestant council because of white Protestant disregard for collaboration and the "liberal morality" among English-speaking mainline churches.[24]

Much of the work Protestants conducted among immigrant communities occurred through denominational channels. Southern Baptists facilitated a sweeping home mission program, working among Spanish-speaking populations, Italians, Chinese (particularly in the Mississippi Delta), Jews, and immigrants in urban communities as far north as Illinois. Despite being based in the more rural South, and thus with less of a context for immigration, Southern Baptists claimed they had before them "nearly five million foreigners from twenty-nine countries."[25] By the 1930s, Southern Baptists, like most other denominations, employed immigrants themselves to help facilitate their work. Joseph Gartenhaus, a convert from Judaism and immigrant from Austria, led Southern Baptist work among Jews, a predominantly immigrant group at this time.[26] Another example was Donato Ruiz, who worked for the Southern Baptist Home Mission Board in Texas. Earlier in life, he had a Protestant conversion while in Mexico and was temporarily jailed due to connections he had with two American missionaries believed to be spies, but he was later released, remarkably on account of a man who took his place and was eventually executed. Once free in the United States, Ruiz conducted expansive missions work in the central Texas town of San Angelo. He broadcast a radio program three nights a week in which he preached in Spanish, and his wife led the San Angelo Mexican Baptist Church choir. The radio program reportedly reached as far as El Paso and northern Mexico, blurring the boundaries of foreign and home missions.[27]

Perhaps the most prominent Southern Baptist home missionary who promoted immigrant work was Joseph Piani, who trained for the Catholic priesthood earlier in life at a Salesian seminary in northern Italy. He later traveled to Brazil as a Catholic missionary, but there began to doubt his Catholic faith and chose to become Baptist. He then immigrated to the United States in 1906. While his brother eventually became the Archbishop of the Philippines, Piani remained Baptist and eventually changed his name to Plainfield when he was naturalized. He would go on to study at Southern Baptist Seminary in Louisville, Kentucky, where he completed a doctoral thesis in theology in 1911. With his particular background, Plainfield offered valuable insight for Southern Baptists seeking to reach their immigrant neighbors. Plainfield completed a manual by 1938 for Southern Baptists on missions work to immigrants, titled *The Stranger Within Our Gates*.[28]

Within this text Plainfield called for both concerted evangelism and Americanization, whereby he, as a Southern Baptist, was an "interpreter of the Gospel and of America to the foreigners." While his evangelistic agenda far outpaced many mainline home missionaries, his appeal to Americanization was not far removed from other Protestant contemporaries. Plainfield quoted from Charles A. Brooks's *Christian Americanization* and Hermann N. Morse's work, while occasionally using the vocabulary of his social gospel contemporaries. Plainfield believed immigrants posed a challenge in the form of a "conflict of interests." For Plainfield, the solution was home missions: "It can be done largely by training the foreigners and their children the obligations of American citizenship over and above any other foreign obligation, and by teaching all Americans to be patient, sympathetic and kind to the foreigners in their midst. It is peculiarly a Home Mission task."[29]

Former immigrants were not the only ones able to attain leadership within Southern Baptist home mission networks. On this front, women also claimed key roles in such work. In the case of Southern Baptist work among Italians in Kansas City, ethnic and female leadership merged by 1940. This ministry was led by Lewis DiPietro, a former Italian immigrant, and his American wife Mary Ruth, starting in the 1930s. According to one account, the DiPietro's ran a successful mission program, one in which Mary Ruth "had to bridge the gap between her American rearing and ideas" and her husband's Italian background. As of 1940, the local political machine that controlled much of the Italian community came to an end, and the home missionaries believed an opportunity was at hand to reach Italians with the gospel and American ideals. To aid the DiPietro's, the Kansas City Woman's Missionary Union sponsored a female worker to join them. Tenette Lavender applied for the position, having recently graduated from Southwestern Baptist Seminary. Correspondence concerning her application reveals the high expectations and concerns for immigrant ministry at the time.[30] While seeking recommendations, one denominational leader wanted to know the following of Lavender:

> Do you think she can adapt herself to the viewpoint of a foreign people? Does she have qualities of mind and heart and disposition that lead you to believe she could work well with Italians? . . . no Italian is easy to work with. Does Tenette have a happy disposition and the ability to throw off worry and adjust herself as she will continually have to do? Is she devout in temperament? Do you think she can really depend upon the Lord and yet be aggressive in her own program of work?[31]

The opportunities Lavender encountered provided women with the opportunity to pursue "aggressive" tasks that would not have been available in other forms of ministry at the time.

Northern Baptists, much more comfortable with ecumenical and progressive Protestantism than their southern counterparts, also sponsored multiple fronts of missions work among immigrants. These included foreign-language churches and associations, mission centers, and settlement houses. One report claimed that as of 1933, Northern Baptists maintained 101 centers for Slavic people, 46 for Italians, 31 for Magyars (Hungarians), and 69 for Mexicans. These endeavors were often led by immigrant ministers themselves, particularly among Italians.[32] In a speech before the Italian Baptist Association in Brooklyn, the Baptist Reverend A. Di Domenica outlined an expansive Baptist movement among Italians in New York in recent decades, including industrial classes, Sunday schools, evening English classes, street preaching, Christian centers, and stereopticon slides. Di Domenica observed, however, that many programs were steadily declining, largely owing to reduced immigration and increasing competition with other social service providers (e.g., public schools). Yet, he acknowledged that Protestant work among Italians was still fruitful: the immigrants who returned to Italy carried with them their Protestant faith; Italian Protestants were less prone to commit capital crimes; they "enrich[ed] American churches"; and Protestant work among Italians strengthened home life and reduced divorce rates. And in his remarks, Di Domenica advocated an evangelistic approach, "following the method of Jesus in dealing with individuals and not with the masses as the lovers of cold statistics would wish to see."[33]

In many respects, women were at the forefront of Northern Baptist missions to immigrants. They channeled this portion of their work through a ministry formed in 1919 that they labeled Christian Americanization, renamed Christian Friendliness in 1936. By 1928, the group claimed 3,000 volunteers. Christian Friendliness missionaries strove to meet the perceived spiritual and physical needs of immigrants while working according to the guiding principle: "For active good will, mutual understanding and Christian fellowship between individuals and groups of different national background." While denominationally supported, the organization was structured in a way that allowed for more local involvement and leadership, with a special emphasis on personal engagement indicative of the evangelical heritage of Baptists. Christian Friendliness executive secretary Mary Martin Kinney outlined their work in a book aptly titled *The World at My Door* published in 1938. Her description reflects both an optimistic penchant for social reform and continued stress upon personal conversion as they worked with immigrants.[34]

The PCUSA also worked diligently among immigrant communities under the umbrella of its National Missions program. During the interwar period, Presbyterians recognized a miniscule increase in immigration, but noted the real challenge was in assimilating the children of former immigrants who came over before World War I. Their work stressed the importance of generational awareness and language aptitude, and they sponsored work among Italians, Hungarians, Jews, Mexicans, Chinese, Japanese, and Filipinos. Through their missions endeavors, they held out hope that foreign language churches would eventually become "self-sustaining," despite the challenges they faced. Like most of their other Protestant counterparts, Presbyterians also promoted neighborhood houses. A neighborhood house conference hosted by Presbyterians in 1937 described the breadth of their work, which included "the experience of a polyglot neighborhood in Baltimore along with that of a Russian community in San Francisco, and a home of neighborly service in a congested Mexican quarter of Los Angeles." Between 1935 and 1936 alone, Presbyterians budgeted $505,280 for their work among the foreign population.[35]

The Episcopal Church ministered to immigrants in ways similar to its fellow Protestants, and the 1930s proved to be a period of continued focus on immigrant communities. There remained an Episcopal missionary active on Ellis Island to reach out to immigrants and refugees coming from Europe. The New York Diocese that sponsored Ellis Island work reported in 1934 that 927 immigrants were assisted that year.[36] But Episcopalians also recognized newer sources of immigration. In 1935, the Episcopal Church conceded, "Only recently have we begun to realize that our Church has some responsibility for evangelization of the Orientals in America. The Chinese, Japanese, and Filipinos, most of whom live on the Pacific coast, constitute a problem of national importance." The Episcopal Church then noted, "We are beginning a work with the Mexican people who are coming across the border in large numbers." With these foreign populations now residing in their nation, Episcopalians felt it was their national and Christian duty to help them assimilate.[37]

The Methodist Episcopal Church remained committed to ministering to immigrants as an extension of its home missions. In 1932 Methodists noted the urban tensions created by earlier immigration: "The American city is a cross-section of all nationalities. . . . In these situations and until the process of amalgamation has been completed, race prejudice and hatred constantly appear." Determined to address this challenge, Methodists conducted work among several immigrant groups. During the 1930s, Methodists sponsored home missions on several fronts among Japanese

Figure 2.1. The Plaza Community Center sponsored by the Methodist Episcopal Church as a site where Mexican Americans in Los Angeles could receive social and religious services. Courtesy of the General Commission on Archives and History of the United Methodist Church, Madison, NJ.

and Chinese Methodists on the West Coast. A 1932 report noted that work among Japanese "stresses aggressive evangelism, self-support, buildings and equipment, second generation work, and international relations, contemplating a revision of the unjust exclusion act." A Chinese Home in San Francisco assisted 35 young female residents and 125 kindergarten students. Methodists also focused on the Spanish-speaking population, Filipinos, Italians, and the fruits of American imperialism, Hawaii and Puerto Rico. Indicative of contemporary conditions, Methodists in 1932 did choose, however, to discontinue publishing foreign-language material in light of immigration restriction, the Great Depression, and the fact that more immigrants were using English.[38]

Like most mainline Protestant denominations, Methodists also sponsored robust social work among immigrant communities. Methodists ran schools, clinics, settlement houses, and community centers, including locations in Colorado, Utah, Wyoming, and Pennsylvania, to "teach American ideals and Christian citizenship to the foreign-born" working in local mines. The Methodist Woman's Home Missionary Society reported that "[a]ll settlements contribute to the training in Christian citizenship of the foreigner in our country." Among the Society's many programs was assistance to immigrant girls arriving at New York, Boston, and Angel Island on the West Coast. Methodist church life and social services offered to immigrant populations were also fostered by what were known as Churches of All Nations. With congregations in Boston, New York City, Philadelphia, Chicago, Denver, and Los Angeles, Methodists worked to provide church services devoted to different immigrant languages, while also serving as a locus of assistance for their respective immigrant neighborhood. (According to one account, during his time in New York City in 1917, even Leon Trotsky frequented a Church of All Nations.) And during the 1930s, Churches of All Nations began focusing more of their attention to meeting the needs of second-generation immigrants.[39]

Before combining with their northern Methodist Episcopal counterparts in 1939, the Methodist Episcopal Church, South, also promoted home missions to various immigrant groups through a variety of denominational initiatives, including community center work in Birmingham and New Orleans.[40] As of 1930 the MECS organized work among Mexican immigrants under the Texas Mexican Mission and Western Mexican Mission. Under their respective regional governance, Methodist home missionaries sponsored multiple education initiatives among Mexican children, including boarding schools, Sunday school, and vacation Bible schools. Several of these institutions offered instruction in English and Spanish. In San Antonio, southern Methodists ran the Wesleyan Institute to offer ministerial training for Mexican men, and in Laredo, Texas, they managed the Holding Institute, a boarding school that enrolled 357 students. Among the Mexican population, southern Methodists also carried out social center work, where they offered various educational and health initiatives. As was common at other settlement houses at the time, services offered often reflected gendered patterns, with girls receiving training in sewing, cooking, and childcare, and athletics being stressed among boys. Meanwhile, southern Methodist work among the Mexican immigrant populations aimed to combat the Catholic Church's "strangle-hold." In addition to their time with Mexicans, southern Methodists also worked among the Italian, Cuban, and Greek populations in southern Florida, particularly those employed in the cigar or sponge industries. This home missions initiative was collectively referred to as the "Latin Mission," and workers encountered difficult economic and social contexts in this area, including the recent Florida real estate boom and bust and bootlegging.[41]

The MECS also conducted home missions among Asian populations on the West Coast under their California Oriental Mission. Among Asian immigrants, southern Methodists focused much of their attention on Koreans. In keeping with home mission trends, this work included religious education, social services, and evangelism, which at times included reinforcing a Christian faith that some Korean immigrants brought with them. Methodist home missionaries prioritized the Korean language in their work, even printing a Korean Methodist periodical. And education for Korean children incorporated both English and Korean to enhance the missional reach of their work and hopefully reach the first generation. In the process, southern Methodists acknowledged the importance of Korean culture. "Our Korean schools," one MECS report noted, "do not only create a sympathetic understanding and a good relation between the parents and the children through teaching them the Korean language, but also instilling in them a true Korean spirit." In addition to their work among Koreans, southern Methodists also ministered to Japanese immigrants who came before the 1924 exclusion act, which often meant focusing efforts on reaching the second generation.[42]

Despite the continuity of mission and practice among denominational programs, some denominations claimed that they were in a better position to serve certain immigrant church networks in the United States than other Protestant organizations. Presbyterians, historically Calvinist, maintained that they were well-suited theologically to assist members of the Reformed Church of Hungary who had moved to the United States.[43] The Southern Baptist preacher Plainfield concluded that Baptists also supported a distinctive mission to immigrants: "Being the champions of religious freedom and democracy, professing no allegiance of the soul to any human authority, and recognizing no creed formulated by man, Baptists with the Bible can make a very strong appeal to the conscience of the foreigners."[44] American Protestants, despite the ecumenical spirit of the age, still retained denominational identities.

The Episcopal Church demonstrated a strong affinity to various Orthodox groups in America, including the Russian Orthodox Church,

Greek Orthodox Church, Serbian Orthodox Church, Armenian Apostolic Church, and Polish National Catholic Church.[45] This relationship reflected a trend during the 1920s and 1930s among the Episcopalians' counterparts across the Atlantic in the Church of England. Anglican leaders during the interwar period aimed to facilitate ecumenical ties with Orthodox leaders displaced by developments in Russia, eastern Europe, and the Middle East. Meanwhile, the FCC even stood in defense of the Patriarch of the Orthodox Church during Atatürk's secularization programs by calling on a US ambassador and the Secretary of State in 1922.[46] The Episcopal Church considered itself a steward of these transplanted Orthodox churches in America. This was demonstrated when the Armenian Archbishop Leon Tourian was assassinated in New York City in 1933. One Episcopal report commented that "the Protestant Episcopal Church lost a sincere friend and the Armenian Church a gifted leader." The Episcopal cathedral in New York City provided its sanctuary for the funeral service, for which the Episcopal sponsors had to open up the nave, crossing, and choir sections inside the church for the 15,000 people who attended the Armenian Archbishop's funeral.[47]

While Protestant denominations maintained specific ministries within their own organizations, oftentimes during the interwar period, mainline Protestant denominations conferred with one another on home missions. Ecumenical Protestant work, centered in the FCC, provided much momentum for mainline American Protestantism by the 1930s.[48] A conference of Christian social workers held in Chicago toward the end of 1932, referred to as the Interdenominational Conference on the City and the Church in the Present Crisis, serves as an example. The HMC, CWHM, Chicago Church Federation, and FCC all sponsored the event. More than 400 people took part, and the conference included multiple scholars, prominent ministers and church leaders, a Chicago attorney, dean of the Rockefeller Memorial Chapel at the University of Chicago, and the social gospel stalwart Jane Addams, who spoke on the challenges of diversity in the city, having just received the Nobel Peace Prize the year before. The continuity and diffusion of the social gospel with evangelistic missions were manifested at this conference. The final conference reports proclaimed, "Preaching which thus bases itself upon human need, and endeavors to bring men and women to seek the consolation and power of the Christian gospel, is evangelistic in the very best sense." The conference agreed, "In our work with individual New Americans we recognize two methods of approach,—the religious and social service, as complementary to each other, and as very practical and effective."[49] Overall, the conference incorporated a social science approach to ministry inherited from the earlier days of the social gospel, alongside the mission to share the gospel of Christ.

Whether denominational or ecumenical, most home mission programs during the interwar period were adjusted to account for generational dynamics Protestants perceived were at work among recent immigrants. By the 1930s, often at the center of home missions among immigrant communities was a strong focus on the children of immigrant parents. The Methodist General Conference declared in 1936, "The children of the second and third generations of the immigrants are now accessible to the gospel of Jesus Christ as they have never been before."[50] For Southern Baptist home missionary Una Roberts Lawrence, the later immigrant generations had proven their national loyalty during World War I. Speaking of Mexican immigrants along the southern border, Lawrence commented, "Like them, the Mexican boy was unconscious of any national or racial peculiarity. He was simply an American, eager to do his part, willing to die if need be for his country. Many of them did die. Many came back with wounds that make them living sacrifices to their country's call."[51] Reflecting the contemporary theory outlined by the scholar Marcus Hansen, Protestants had faith that the second generation was consistently learning English and accepting American cultural norms.[52] Thus, many programs targeted immigrant youth less inclined to use their parents' native tongue, and Protestant home missionaries either assumed the second generation was already proficient in English or provided English instruction to facilitate further assimilation.[53] Kinney repeatedly noted the legacy of succeeding generations of immigrants. She observed, "Living in two worlds, attempting to make of two cultures something finer than either, keeping one's roots in the old while still having as many contacts as possible with the new, is far from easy. These are the youth who need the confidence and encouragement that older Americans can give, if they will."[54] According to mainline Protestants, as the second and third generations assimilated and learned English, there was less of a need for separate churches.[55] "Twenty years ago we began to give large and worth-while emphasis to the foreign-language peoples.

We now must definitely turn to the English-speaking children of these people. This cannot be done solely with foreign-speaking churches."[56] Within the complicated process of immigrant settlement and accultura- tion, Protestants believed the younger generations were dislocated and in need of religious guidance. The 1932 Chicago Conference lamented that many immigrants "have lost interest in the faith of their fathers"; thus, mainline Protestants felt they had a mandate to "mak[e] religion more effective in the life of New American youth."[57]

While the second generation provided its own challenges, the cata- strophic economic crisis of the 1930s also tested Protestant home mis- sions. Retrenchment became necessary among institutional Christianity as the nation experienced unprecedented unemployment rates and a depressed economy. As Franklin D. Roosevelt unveiled his ambitious New Deal programs in 1933 to counter the challenges labor, industry, and agriculture faced, a dynamism was unleashed that inspired innova- tive means. The social welfare programs of the New Deal were in some respects a culmination of earlier social gospel aspirations, notably in the progressive ideals of Harry Hopkins, who managed the Works Progress Administration, and Frances Perkins, who as Secretary of Labor worked especially hard to admit German Jews fleeing Nazi oppression.[58] Mean- while, the nation grew more wary of immigrants and the purported threat they posed to American labor, leading federal and local govern- ments to seek to deport Mexican immigrants. Moreover, many potential immigrants recognized opportunities were limited in the United States, so that between 1932 and 1935, the nation actually witnessed a deficit in immigration numbers as large numbers migrated back to their home- lands or moved on elsewhere.[59]

The Episcopal Church began to retrench spending and divert more responsibility to local dioceses. The denomination's Foreign-Born Americans Division was dissolved in 1930, probably due in greater measure to declining immigration, though its funding was already di- minishing at the start of the Great Depression. In 1924 the Episcopal Domestic and Foreign Missionary Society spent $47,011 on work among the foreign-born. By 1930 when it was closed, this was nearly cut in half to $27,566.[60] Southern Baptists had their hands tied during the 1930s because of increasing debt during the 1920s and the embezzlement of more than $900,000 by the Home Mission Board's treasurer in 1928. The

Depression only compounded these issues. In 1927, the combined total of Home Mission Board spending for ministry to immigrants, Native Americans, and African Americans was $104,839, but by 1935, this was reduced to $38,055.[61] By 1932 the MEC had to combine several departments conducting work among immigrant groups to help with funding and to cut down on the number of superintendents employed by the denomination. The Methodist Board of Home Missions and Church Extension also reassigned some immigrant ministries to district superintendents. In keeping with trends among other Protestant denominations, total disbursements for Methodist Home Missions and Church Extension fell from $2.5 million in 1928 to $1.03 million in 1935.[62] Congregationalists, in their ties to the AMA, also encountered hard times. In planning their 1933 budget, the AMA had to cut $150,000, and even sell their Rio Grande Institute to the Catholic Archbishop of New Mexico.[63] For many Protestant groups, the economic challenges of the 1930s only heightened the need for more ecumenical work.[64]

Despite the economic setbacks, home missions continued. The global context of the interwar period made international matters more prescient, and Protestants were keen to note the close relationship between home missions and foreign missions. This became a demographic reality between 1932 and 1935, when there were more emigrants leaving the United States than immigrants entering; many home missionaries saw the opportunities of return immigration.[65] As America's global role increased, the domestic and foreign were further conflated. Kinney noted, "The quality of life which the Christian religion can produce here in the midst of class and race friction, nationality antagonisms and group ambition, will determine in large measure how convincing Christian missionaries can make their message everywhere."[66] Such logic helped temper nativist dispositions. One Southern Baptist missions program announced, "A person has no love for foreigners in other lands—no matter how much he may profess it—if he despises the foreigners in this land. (I John 4:20)."[67] As Americans witnessed the rest of the world inching closer to another world war, national life and missions, both home and foreign, were made all the more pertinent. The Episcopal Church concluded, "We now dedicate ourselves to the task of winning America for Christ that America may fulfill her mission to the world."[68] This argument would become more frequent among Protestants as the twentieth century progressed and the United States assumed global leadership, and framers of US foreign policy worked from a similar logic.[69] Occasionally mainline Protestants, particularly home missionary women, cultivated the notion of being "world citizens" and critiqued the former missionary impulse that patronized other nationalities and people of color.[70]

Interpreting National Identity

As the 1930s presented both domestic and global challenges, mainline Protestants in the United States turned to a national identity grounded in a common religious identity. Morse concluded in 1935, "In the attempt to create a national unity on the basis of a common allegiance to Jesus Christ and a common acceptance of the righteousness revealed in him, is perhaps the greatest significance of home missions as a service of the church to our nation."[71] As the 1930s brought economic trials and international tumult, the "evangelical nationalism" of the late nineteenth century, identified by historian Derek Chang, remained.[72]

Whether ecumenical or denominational, most forms of home missions by the 1930s reflected strong overtures to the nation's well-being, often envisioning a Christian nation. One Methodist denominational leader declared that domestic Christian work is "committed to the composite purpose of making the mind and heart of America truly Christian."[73] Episcopalians acknowledged that their church "must do her part to make America Christian."[74] Playing off of the New Deal efforts to alleviate agricultural woes, a Southern Baptist missions report declared, "The trouble with America is not soil erosion, but soul erosion. . . . A genuine revival of character based on a new birth from heaven through faith in the Lord Jesus Christ is the only thing that will create the kind of citizen that will build the right type of national life."[75] While conservatives opposed to the New Deal, as described by historian Kevin Kruse, heavily promoted the idea that America was a Christian nation at this time, the notion that the nation had a Christian identity was also the product of robust Protestant home missions.[76] It was only a small step to connect these national ideals with immigrant ministry. "We owe it to the alien in our midst as well as to our country," reported the Episcopal

Figure 2.2. An Americanization class on the structure of Congress held at the Marcy Center in Chicago. Courtesy of the General Commission on Archives and History of the United Methodist Church, Madison, NJ.

Church in 1935, "that he be trained with a Christian purpose for the responsibilities of citizenship."[77]

In some home mission circles, the assimilation, or Americanization, of immigrants remained a vital goal well into the 1920s and early '30s. The first two decades of the twentieth century witnessed concerted efforts among Protestant home missions to incorporate immigrants into the national framework through English and citizenship classes, with the hope that the supposed melting pot would do its work. Some Protestants, however, feared that assimilation was not working. While not repudiating the legacy of immigration, the Chicago social worker conference in 1932 paused out of concern when it considered urban immigrant populations and America's future. "The wholesale change in racial stock or national background has profoundly altered the psychology of our urban life and is therefore of the deepest significance to the urban church. Moreover, it has seriously disturbed the spiritual foundations of America, foundations as laid during the 300 years, particularly the last 100 years, before 1890."[78] And while sympathetic to the plight of Mexican immigrants, the HMC did note, "If, however, there is again a considerable increase of Mexican immigration, the new group will not only present a constantly recurring problem, but will also retard the assimilation of those who are already here."[79] For those Protestants who held firm to Americanization, they were still set apart from the public wave of nativism that resulted in the 1924 Immigration Act. The Southern Baptist minister Plainfield noted, "No foreigner can truly become Americanized who is not Christianized. Christianity is the golden gate. The task falls upon the churches." Yet, Plainfield warned against "ramming the American flag down the immigrant's throat and forcing him to foreswear all his traditions as well as his political allegiance."[80]

Much of the work conducted by Protestant home missionaries hinged on the importance of ministering to immigrant women and reinforcing traditional gender roles, domestic responsibilities, and definitions of family life.[81] Settlement houses often provided classes based on a gendered division of labor, most notably sewing classes for girls. St. Mark's Community Center, a southern Methodist site in New Orleans, offered various clubs, including a Home Maker's Club, that would "enable them to be better wives and mothers." In keeping with the trend of more women entering the workforce, however, the center also sponsored a Business Girls' Club.[82] Southern Baptist Tenette Lavender, who worked with Italians in Kansas City, organized Wednesday and Friday "women's circles," group sessions that provided meals, a devotional, and attention to childcare and nutrition.[83] Northern Baptist Mary Kinney provided a detailed account of how Christian Friendliness ministry reinforced cultural expectations of American women. "Mothers in the foreign families were often more seriously handicapped than the men and children," observed Kinney. Women did not have the same opportunities to learn English, as did the men while at work and the children at school. Kinney noted that Northern Baptist women also encountered other needs in their work: "There was the Mexican wife whose husband wanted her to find out how to make American pie. Then there was the mother who said in bewilderment, 'Babee—no grow—no seeck—jus no grow.'" Overall, this focus on immigrant women reflected the hope that if immigrant mothers were reached, the rest of the family might also come to church.[84]

On occasion home missionaries worked to circumscribe more paternalistic forms of ministry as they worked alongside immigrant women.

One booklet recounted to its Protestant readers an example of mutual assistance, whereby local Anglo and Mexican American women in an unnamed community offered insight into each other's domestic households. "There was sharing of interest between the best of the two groups, through that institution which comes closest to life. Cooperation succeeded where paternalism failed."[85] Rather than becoming the "Lady Bountiful bestowing knowledge," Kinney warned her Baptist counterparts, "The kind of courtesy most acceptable is not that which *does* for people; it is the courtesy that makes it possible for friends to *do things together*." But efforts to counsel immigrant women in "baby care," while well-intentioned, reflected forms of paternalism by attempting to inculcate supposedly American childrearing practices. Kinney noted that Christian Friendliness workers often used the *Well Baby Primer*, a text written by Caroline Hedger that was meant to aid Americanization work through English instruction and, according to one review, teach "American standards of baby health."[86] Protestant women involved in home mission work often aimed to meet the immediate needs of immigrant women, and in the process propagated various gender and cultural norms.

By the 1930s some Protestant social workers began to entertain hopes that assimilation had run its course. A 1936 Methodist report believed immigrants were slowly assimilating: "the solid foreign-speaking sections of our cities are steadily being reduced," in part because of the "decline in the use of the old-country tongue, as the children are American born."[87] For many denominational leaders, a perceived decline in the use of foreign languages was a strong indicator of assimilation. In his report for the HMC, Morse remarked, "From a practical standpoint, language is a first concern in the approach to the New American. It opens the door as well to his cultural background."[88] And for those ethnic churches and home mission programs still using languages other than English, it was only a matter of time before they embraced English. The endgame was to merge foreign-language churches into native congregations. Yet, on occasion, a few home missionaries were more flexible and realized that using foreign languages was necessary for home missions and for training immigrant pastors.[89]

During the 1930s Americanization programs began to taper and lose some of their earlier appeal as some mainline Protestants moved toward a more cosmopolitan position. Mabel A. Brown wrote a scathing critique of Americanization efforts in an article that the *Christian Century* published in October 1930. Reflecting on her settlement house work among Italians, Brown contested, "Tastes, both in aliens and in apple pies, differ, and to those who have actually assisted in applying the veneer of American civilization to the newly-arrived immigrant, misgivings occasionally occur—not about the motives of those who promote the work, nor about the technique of the process of Americanization, but about the effect of this process on the alien." She critiqued American standards expected of immigrants that stripped them of their cultural traits and left them "sacrificed on the altar of Americanism."[90] It is telling that in 1936 Northern Baptist women chose to rename their Americanization program, calling it "Christian Friendliness" instead. Their caution with using the word "Americanization" is evident in Kinney's frank admission: "For the naturalized citizens, for the American-born second and third generations, for the Orientals born abroad who cannot be naturalized, the word 'Americanization' seemed inadequate."[91]

In place of Americanization was a more favorable approach to national diversity and a limited amount of respect for cultural and religious pluralism. In his home missions report for the AMA in 1929, Fred L. Brownlee recognized the missions had moved past earlier assumptions with such questions as "Are you a purveyor of a 'superior' culture or do you consider it a composite produced by the best in the customs and experiences of all races, nations and classes?"[92] The HMC acknowledged in 1934 its aim for "[c]ontinued appreciation of the background and culture of the various races which are becoming a part of the New America."[93] In a 1933 pamphlet, the Chicago Presbytery proudly listed the names of workers within its Church Extension Board who represented more than 30 different nationalities.[94] A Methodist community center in Portland conducted a wedding for a Japanese woman that "was a combination of American and Oriental custom." The same center also promoted a program for boys that brought in Protestant, Catholic, and Jewish lecturers.[95] And in New Orleans, St. Mark's Community Center hosted a biennial fair highlighting various nationalities. Center workers even received support from foreign consuls in the city. In the end, the fair was intended to help encourage "friendship and fellowship among the nationals living in our midst, and . . . contribute something to the cause of peace between nations."[96]

Una Roberts Lawrence's text, *Winning the Border*, on Southern Baptist missions to Spanish speakers in the Southwest, further demonstrates growing cultural sensitivity. At first glance, more predictable themes are found, including evangelism, descriptive analysis of the border region, aversion to Catholicism, and even the common Protestant ambivalence toward the Mexican Revolution and its suppression of the Catholic Church during the prior decade. But in her examination of border history and missions efforts, Lawrence attempted to display sympathy for her subjects and their culture, contrary to the nativist inclinations of many of her contemporaries in the South. She instructed her readers on how to pronounce "Mexico," as "May-heé-coh." Lawrence also commented on using the term "Americans" in the context of the United States. "In using that name as an exclusive and distinctive designation we lay ourselves liable to the just charge of arrogance and self-conceit. . . . [W]e are fully conscious that 'American' belongs alike to all the peoples of the twenty-two nations of the two Americas." Concerning race prejudice, Lawrence concluded, "The history of missions shows that war and race prejudice are enemies of the Kingdom of God."[97]

Increasing respect for immigrant culture among some Protestant home missionaries came in the form of what historian Robert Fleegler labels "contributionism." This concept taught that America's history was closely tied to the immigrants who helped contribute to the nation's cultural identity.[98] Northern Baptist home missionary Kinney communicated this principle while observing the challenges the foreign-born faced: "Living in two worlds, attempting to make of two cultures something finer than either, keeping one's roots in the old while still having as many contacts as possible with the new." Kinney believed, "The migration of the forty million people to the United States during the past one hundred years means for this country the opportunity which few new countries have had, a chance for a many-sided culture to which most of the world has contributed."[99] Moreover, in his 1929 pamphlet on Mexican immigrants, Presbyterian Charles A. Thomson encouraged his readers to recognize "what contributions his group can make to your church and community."[100] In essence, this appeal to a "many-sided culture" was a tacit acknowledgment of cultural pluralism.

But even amidst overtures for cultural diversity, the earlier paternalistic threads of Americanization and assimilation were still prevalent by midcentury. During one social event hosted by Northern Baptists that recounted American history and displayed a picture of the mythic female figure of Columbia, a procession of people reflecting various nationalities was led by an "American child holding by the hand two little Japanese children, and on the other side two little Chinese children!" According to the account, "It made an unforgettable picture. . . . Nationality seemed to be forgotten as mothers and fathers talked with one another."[101] Such notions of American superiority and nationalist ideals would never fully disappear from Protestant discourse, even after some mainline Protestants gradually grew more comfortable acknowledging the nation's diversity.

Evangelistic and social aspirations promoted by mainline Protestantism were made more important, if not problematic, in light of the diversity that immigrants had brought to the nation by the 1920s. An understanding of American religious pluralism that acknowledged that the nation would always retain a sizable demographic of Catholics and Jews was prevalent among many mainline Protestant leaders by the 1930s.[102] How did home mission programs square with such a pluralistic reality? Largely, Protestant home missionaries acknowledged the place of Catholics and Jews in America, but they still worked from a paradigm that interpreted the nation as Protestant and attempted to bring Catholics and Jews into the Protestant fold. The HMC acknowledged the complexity of "Inter-faith Relations," noting that the nation consisted of four distinct non-Protestant faiths: Catholics, Mormons, Jews, and "the comparatively small numbers of adherents of other religious faiths like Buddhism or the original religions of the American Indians." The report articulated the concern that many people of various "races" were "adrift" and recognized the importance of evangelizing groups outside of Christianity. While commenting on Catholicism's failures, the HMC still held out hope that its work would encourage reform within the Catholic Church. The report ultimately called for "spiritual unity," not in "doctrine or polity" but in "objectives and controlling points of view."[103]

Such an outlook on religious pluralism reflected a Protestant hubris that often led to misinterpretation of other faiths. Despite attempts to work with its Catholic counterparts, the HMC report took a dim view of Catholicism. This led to a misinterpretation of the Catholic Church and its relationship to immigrant communities. The HMC noted that Protestant churches served as centers of local community for immigrants, while Catholic churches were simply locations for worship. Clearly, Protestant home mission leaders did not understand Italian Catholic immigrant communities and the resources that the Catholic Church provided immigrants as they settled in America. Instead, Protestant home missionaries resorted to the common perception that Catholicism was not "enlightened Christianity," but rather a staid institution.[104]

With such an ambivalent interpretation of pluralism, in addition to the diffusion of social gospel and evangelistic aspirations, Protestant home missions entered a liminal period during the interwar years. Should home missionaries aim to convert immigrants, or respect their native faith and accept a religiously plural nation? Were home missionaries duty bound to expect immigrants to Americanize upon accepting Protestant Christianity, or rather celebrate the nation's cultural pluralism? A debate surrounding a book published in 1933 helps shed light on these questions. A sociology professor at Columbia University, Theodore Abel, published a book titled *Protestant Home Missions to Catholic Immigrants*, a project sponsored by the Institute of Social and Religious Research. Abel declared in his preface that Protestant work among Catholic immigrants "represents an aspect of the struggle of Protestantism to retain its religious supremacy in this country" and "is carried on with the aim of promoting Americanization and breaking down the isolation of immigrants from American society by bringing them into the fellowship of the Protestant church." And in his conclusion, Abel noted, "The evangelization of Catholic immigrants was undertaken by the Protestant churches in the belief that the ideals and principles of government and social life in America were derived from and supported by the spirit of Protestantism."[105]

Little did this social scientist realize the storm he would create with these conclusions. A HMC report in 1934 cited Abel's work negatively and contended, "Such an ulterior purpose is true neither to the genius of Christian missions, nor to the historical development of the new mission among immigrants; it is not the thing for which ministers and lay workers on the field unselfishly poured out their service." Instead, Protestant home missionaries ministering to Catholic immigrants "were engaged in something far different; to share experience, to be a good neighbor; to help all immigrants to become and to live as Christians; to assist them in making their adjustments to American life; to aid them in establishing churches for Christian fellowship and service and for the worship of God in a language which they could understand."[106] While Abel's book concerned the HMC, its most strident critics were home missionaries on the front lines. Frank A. Smith, representing the American Baptist Home Mission Society, circulated a copy of Abel's book among fellow Baptist workers and asked them for their thoughts. What has survived is a flood of sometimes lengthy book reviews by upset Northern Baptist missionaries engaged in local work across the country. In their correspondence with Smith, the home missionaries, often representing various nationalities, communicated an evangelistic focus, serious misgivings with Catholicism, reticence toward Americanization, and reluctance to embrace Abel's strictly social scientific perspectives.[107]

Many of those who responded to Smith's request refused to acknowledge that Protestants were out to steal converts from Catholic churches. Rather, those immigrants who became Protestant were already outside the Catholic fold. One worker with the Hungarian Baptist Union of America, Jos Matuskovits, noting he was a former Catholic, argued that the Catholics Protestant missionaries reached were not Catholic in the first place but were anarchists who threatened both society and the Catholic Church itself. The Italian Ministers Association of Greater Chicago wrote challenging Abel's assertion that home missionaries were trying to impose "Protestant supremacy." Rather, the Italian association stated that sharing the gospel message was its primary concern, asserting that "evangelical Christianity has something to offer to 'Catholic Immigrants' which they have not in Roman Catholicism, namely: a knowledge of the Bible, a vital, closer, and friendly relationship with Jesus Christ, the founder of Christianity, and a better, more practical appreciation of the ethical values of His teaching." Edwin Dolan, Field Secretary of the Massachusetts Baptist Convention, also denied any intent for "supremacy"; instead, Baptist missions were "governed by the sincere desire to bring the Gospel message to a neglected and needy people." Home missionaries on the West Coast involved in work with Mexicans also chimed in, acknowledging the legitimacy of their work in light of evangelistic principles. One respondent bluntly noted, "The trouble has been that our Protestant leaders have been too willing to soft pedal anything that looked like anti-Catholicic [sic] propaganda." Throwing caution to the wind, the writer linked Catholic immigrant children to crime and concluded, "As you say in your letter, it is grist from the same mill that furnishes criticism of missionary work among the Jews and advocates the same point of view expressed in the Laymen's Report on Foreign Missions about not proselyting Hindus or Mohammedans."[108] The responses of Northern Baptist workers to Abel's suggestion that they were simply vying with Catholics to increase membership and proclaim America a Protestant nation demonstrate a commitment to evangelism and lingering reproach of Catholicism that curbed their enthusiasm for a religiously plural nation.

Other respondents criticized Abel's assertions concerning Americanization and home missions. In a 16-page review, Antonio Mangano, minister of an Italian Baptist church, denied Americanization was the end goal, arguing instead that it was only the natural result of evangelization. Mangano wrote, "Had Prof. Abel dug down below the surface of his subject, he would have discovered that Protestant church membership and Americanization were the inevitable by-product of communicating the gospel message to these people." Mangano deduced that Abel did not perceive the spiritual element, for "[i]t cannot be grasped by the scientific social investigator." Frank L. Anderson, one of the denominational faithful with a long career in home missions in Chicago who later served as president of the International Baptist Seminary in New Jersey, wrote another scathing response to Abel's book. Concerning Abel's comments on Americanization, Anderson concluded, "The patriotic motive is over done. . . . Missionary boards or their representatives have rightly made Americanization one of the talking points, but the religious motive, namely, that of having men and women come into direct relationship to Jesus Christ as their Lord and Saviour, has been the supreme, dominating motive." While Americanization had become passé among some Protestant home missionaries, the earlier notion that Protestant Christianity and assimilation reinforced each other endured during the 1930s.[109]

Political Statements and World Crisis

While continuing to foster home mission work among immigrants, some Protestant leaders also turned to political matters. In its denominational reports, the MEC continued to challenge the 1924 Immigration

Act. The Methodist Woman's Home Missionary Society declared in 1932, "Unjust discrimination is a disturbing element to international understanding and world peace, therefore, we endorse the action of the General Conference of 1928 that we urge all Christian citizens to unite in removing such legislation as restricts immigration and the rights of citizenship on grounds of race and color." That same year, the Methodist California Conference even sent a Japanese delegate to the General Conference, and a Methodist Preachers' Meeting of Southern California called for revision of the immigration act and naturalization laws.[110] By 1936 Methodists concluded, "We appeal for such modification of the present Immigration Act as will place Orientals on the same quota basis as now governs immigration from European countries."[111] Methodist leadership was convinced that the "immigration law has still its evil effects between our two nations; and it must be evident to you all that it compromises the Christian spirit. . . . Over against racial discrimination we Christians must stand before the people of the Orient."[112] In Protestant circles, the issue of Japanese exclusion was not going away any time soon.

While Asian exclusion remained a travesty for mainline Protestants, another crisis of political and humanitarian magnitude unfolded much closer to home. But unlike Asian exclusion, this event went largely unnoticed.[113] During the early 1930s, federal and local officials conducted a series of deportations and repatriation efforts throughout the Southwest that forced half a million Mexicans and Mexican Americans, including many US citizens, to return back across the border. In the midst of the Great Depression, long-standing racism and socioeconomic concerns led many white Americans to support such efforts. Since many repatriation drives at this time were local, rather than federal, they often went unnoticed by many mainline Protestants who were apt to more closely follow federal immigration policy. Caught up in the wave of nativism, many mainline Protestants were either ignorant or looked the other way as countless immigrants were forced back into a Mexico still reeling from the Mexican Revolution of the previous decades.[114]

Many Protestant mainline leaders supported limiting Mexican immigration during the Great Depression. The more progressive Congregational Commission on Inter-Racial Relations sponsored a conference in 1929 that concluded that restriction was necessary, though the Congregational church should still seek to minister to Mexican immigrants living in the United States. "As we must deal with the Mexican for better or worse, we urge our people and our churches to cultivate friendly relations with these people in every possible way."[115] A 1930 editorial in *Christian Century* further articulated the outlook of mainline Protestants at this time. Referring to legislation Congress was considering that would have applied the quota system to Mexican immigrants, the *Christian Century* editors recognized this would perpetuate a system that discriminated against select groups of people, reflected in the "unfortunate precedents made in dealing with oriental immigration." And yet, the editors acknowledged, "A good case can be made for the wisdom of placing restrictions on Mexican immigration." Thus, they proposed instead that all Latin American immigrants be given a quota. This would in turn limit Mexican immigration while also not singling them out.[116]

While the deportation and repatriation of Mexican Americans went unaddressed, mainline Protestants continued to advocate for immigration reform on other fronts. In 1933, President Franklin D. Roosevelt assembled a commission to consider naturalization policy and advise Congress, and FCC leaders took note. The mainline Protestant dignitary Sidney Gulick, the indomitable voice on matters of immigration during the 1910s and 1920s, remained active in the area of immigration policy as Executive Secretary of the FCC's Department of International Justice and Goodwill. In 1933 he wrote to immigration officials in the Bureau of Immigration (under the Department of Labor), the Department of Justice, and the Secretary of State. In his letters, he continued to oppose Asian exclusion and the threat such restriction posed to international diplomacy. Gulick wrote to the Secretary of Labor concerning the government's decision to deny naturalization to Asian Americans on account of race, pointing out that Native Americans and African Americans could become citizens.[117] Besides Gulick, another important voice at this time for mainline Protestantism was Walter Van Kirk, who had been serving in the FCC's Department of International Justice and Goodwill since 1925. Van Kirk wrote in 1933 to immigration officials concerning the requirement that when immigrants applied for citizenship, they must also be willing to serve in the US military if needed. FCC officials found this requirement onerous and a violation of an immigrant's rights of conscience.[118]

In addition to Gulick and Van Kirk, the FCC's Executive Committee also recommended to the Department of State several revisions, including bestowing naturalization to immigrants who were conscientious objectors to military service and providing citizenship to immigrants who had applied for naturalization prior to *Ozawa v. United States* (1922), the Supreme Court case that barred Japanese from attaining citizenship because they were not considered "white." The FCC proclaimed, "Such action will remove the stigma inflicted on other great races by our present race-discriminatory naturalization laws. It will also at the same time enable the Government and people of the United States to resume their moral leadership of the world in the recognition of the inherent dignity of humanity and the rights of man as man." The FCC assured the State Department, "These suggested changes are needed for the true welfare of the United States and also of the world."[119] Such efforts, however, would prove fruitless in changing current immigration policy at this time.

Then in 1936, Congress considered legislation known as the Kerr-Coolidge bill that would have extended grace to undocumented immigrants without a criminal record, particularly those whose family members were legal immigrants living in America.[120] This meager overture to liberal immigration reform caught the attention of mainline Protestant leadership, along with other religious groups such as the National Catholic Welfare Conference, Young Women's Christian Association, and National Council of Jewish Women. FCC officials believed this bill would "humanize our immigration laws, and especially avoid unnecessary breaking up of families of immigrants of good character," while also continuing to deport aliens who posed a threat to the nation. FCC officials wrote to the recently formed Immigration and Naturalization Service (INS) within the Department of Labor. Their hope was that the government would act on the Kerr-Coolidge bill before March 1, 1936, when nearly 3,000 immigrants were scheduled to be deported. The INS Commissioner, D. W. MacCormack, evidently concurred, even assuring, "Today we have the support of every important religious group in the United States, without regard to creed or denomination. . . . For a long time it did not appear to me that the public generally were taking any interest in this problem, but I am now advised by members of Congress that they are receiving many communications in support of the bill."[121]

In the meantime, the FCC contacted ministers across the nation, soliciting their signatures for a statement approving the Kerr-Coolidge bill. The statement was signed by 2,208 ministers from 48 states, though representing only 29.7% of the total number of people the FCC originally contacted. The Joint Statement produced was a compromise of sorts, acknowledging that the Kerr-Coolidge bill "would make stricter provision for the deportation of criminal aliens and at the same time remove certain hardships to which aliens of good character and their innocent families in this country are now subject."[122] Such efforts proved futile, however, as the bill was never passed.

By the end of the 1930s, Protestant denominations soon encountered a development that tested their devotion to the church and nation and signaled a new challenge for home missions. When theologian Paul Tillich spoke at New York City's Riverside Church in October 1936, he described an opportunity for Protestants to challenge the understanding that national identity was premised on racial and ethnic composition. This opportunity came in the form of increasing numbers of refugees fleeing Europe. Tillich, a German refugee himself, instructed the ministers in his audience that "support of emigres is a support of this prophetic protest against the demonic energy of religious nationalism," a force he was all too familiar with while living in Nazi Germany. Tillich appealed to his Protestant audience to assist the developing refugee crisis and left them with a haunting question. If emigration repeatedly defined the Christian experience and Protestant churches were instead becoming enmeshed in "occidental civilization," Tillich wondered, "Are they prepared for it or have they become so immovable, spiritually and practically, that the wild stream of coming history will overflow them or throw them away?"[123]

Refugee relief came in two forms. Concerned Americans could either send financial relief overseas or resettle refugees in America. Much energy was committed to the former, though the latter was not without precedent. In 1922 the FCC recognized the continued oppression of Armenian and Greek refugees in Turkey. Much assistance was sent in the way of relief overseas, but the FCC also recognized the possibility of resettling refugees in America. At the same time, FCC officials acknowledged that the quota system in place through the Emergency Immigration Act of 1921 should be respected, in order "to guard against breaking down the principle of restrictive legislation on immigration." The FCC concluded that Armenian and Greek refugees should be allowed to enter "in excess of quota" when they had family already in the United States, a position the FCC communicated to Congress in December 1922 while Congress considered legislation. Tragically, resettlement efforts were never offered at this time.[124]

As the Nazi regime began its systematic oppression of Jews and dissidents during the 1930s, some mainline Protestants turned their attention to this crisis. The American Christian Committee for German Refugees was formed by 1934 to try to raise financial relief, though the funds raised were meager. Ecumenical Protestants including S. Parkes Cadman and Harry Emerson Fosdick helped promote its work.[125] Halford E. Luccock, a Methodist professor at Yale Divinity School, believed the United States should admit 100,000 German immigrants in 1939, roughly the equivalent of Germany's quota for four years, and then suspend immigration from Germany for three years. This proposal would have allowed the quota system to remain intact and a greater number of Jews to flee to the United States.[126] And while serving as the Foreign Secretary of the FCC, Henry Smith Leiper argued that concerns over the impact refugees would have on American jobs was baseless and that the United States should receive refugees fleeing Germany on moral and economic grounds. "Ignoring completely the inhumane and un-American aspects that would be involved in complete immigration stoppage," Leiper reasoned, "it would also, from a strictly utilitarian point of view, be bad business for America not to avail itself of the refugee talents now available."[127]

Beginning in 1939, Northern Baptists and Episcopalians began to turn their attention to Christian and Jewish refugees fleeing Germany.[128] Led by the Diocese of Southern Ohio in 1938, the Episcopal Church formed a Committee for European Refugees, whose aim was to assist other organizations such as the American Committee for Christian Refugees, to educate parishioners, help refugees with affidavits, and facilitate resettlement. In December 1938, the Episcopal Woman's Auxiliary noted, "At this Christmas Season when we remember a Jewish family for whom there was no room in the inn at Bethlehem, we are sorrowfully aware of the countless numbers of their race who are today seeking shelter for themselves and their children," and the Woman's Auxiliary appealed to Episcopal women to advocate for the refugee. But rather than abide by Tillich's admonition and justify their work solely on the ground of Christian mission, their response to the refugee crisis was rather a fusion of national mission and Christian purpose. An Episcopal report pointed to "a realization that all of these refugees, whether Christian or Jewish, were symptoms of a world revolution striking at the basis of Christianity and democracy."[129]

Conclusion

Published in 1939, *Christ in Concrete* is a novel about an Italian immigrant family in America coping with the tragic loss of their father who died on the job while working as a bricklayer. Rivaling John Steinbeck's *Grapes of Wrath*, also published that year, the popularity of *Christ in Concrete*, written by second-generation Italian Pietro di Donato, reflects the persistence of America's immigrant heritage in the public eye.[130] Public attention to immigration never dissipated following the restriction of the 1920s. The history of Protestant home missions to immigrants offers further insight into these developments and demonstrates the various ways that Protestant figures considered pluralism. They were beginning to arrive at the pluralistic bargain, in which they tried to juggle both greater acceptance of immigrant cultures and the ideal of a Christian nation.

By the beginning of World War II, a potent diffusion of evangelistic hopes and social gospel ideals meant that Protestant home missions remained a primary concern when approaching ethnic Americans and immigrant communities. By 1940 the Episcopal Church recognized the opportunities at hand. "This matter of Christianizing America has assumed a place of vital importance in these days of world turmoil and world disaster. . . . In a world of rapid changes like the present, it is quite conceivable that the American Continent may become an oasis of Christian culture and the sole hope of Christian survival."[131] Such an "oasis," according to Protestant thinking, required home mission programs that continued to reach out to immigrants. In *Toward a Christian America*, published in 1935, Morse, drawing from his service for the HMC, considered the relationship between home missions and national unity. He believed this was accomplished in part by missions among immigrants.

Morse suggested Protestant missions were tasked with the work of "interpretation" and "practical assistance to the alien in helping him to negotiate the transition from old world to the new and to break through walls of prejudice and misunderstanding which, if permitted to stand, would make us not a unified people, but an aggregate of contrasting and conflicting groups."[132]

Such thinking proved to be a potent blend of nationalism and religion as America emerged from a period of self-induced isolation. The next decade would witness such perspectives further define America's position in a world threatened by fascism and communism. America was entering a period when foreign ideologies, rather than religions or races, were the primary threat.[133] Noting the international context, one Southern Baptist in 1938 concluded, "The rivals of Christianity today are not Buddhism, Confucianism and Mohammedism but communism, nationalism and humanism."[134]

3

The Huddled Masses the War Produced

> If ever the world needed the principles of Christ exemplified
> in the democratic ideal of our churches, the ideal of broth-
> erhood in social life, the foundation of stewardship in the
> economic world and a gospel which has at its heart the spiri-
> tual and the personal regeneration of men, it is this hour in
> which we now live.
> —Southern Baptist Convention, 1942 *Annual*

In his book *Protestantism's Hour of Decision*, Baptist Justin Wroe Nixon claimed that America in 1940 was entering tumultuous times and argued for the advancement of Christianity and democracy. Nixon inherited grand visions for American society from one of the foremost leaders of the social gospel movement, having studied under Walter Rauschenbusch earlier in life and later served with him on the faculty of Rochester Theological Seminary. By the start of World War II, Nixon melded his social gospel upbringing with American democracy. Writing on the eve of America's entrance into the war, Nixon appealed to "true brotherhood" and argued that "American Protestantism has an obligation to the world." Nixon believed America's "democratic way of life" was in a precarious position, "engaged in a struggle for existence. Can we Protestants remain mere spectators of that struggle?" As Nixon confronted a world spiraling into chaos, he appealed to his Protestant readers, "There they stand, Protestantism confronting democracy, each like the side of an arch, hardly able to stand alone."[1]

For Nixon, America's European immigrant past contributed to the nation's democratic legacy. Past immigrants brought with them both Protestant faith and democratic ideals. "Here the representatives of the most virile European stocks came together, under favorable material conditions and under the influence of ideals which emphasized the worth of the individual and the equal rights of men to share in the processes of government."[2] As Nixon demonstrated, the "democratic way of life" captured the imaginations and agendas of many Protestants during the World War II era and infused their work among the nation's immigrants. Historians Philip Gleason and Robert Fleegler note that this form of nationalism created an environment in which both toleration and unity were expected. Despite the apparent contradiction, many mainline Protestants elevated both ideals while fostering denominational and ecumenical work among immigrants. Immigrant ministries continued much the same, but Protestant home missionaries began placing more stress on social and racial harmony, despite the challenges the war produced. White Protestant leaders promoted an "American Way of Life" during the global upheaval of World War II while also working to respect different cultures and races.[3]

As the Second World War erupted, American Protestants turned to the founding principle of their earlier immigrant work, Christian brotherhood, and stressed universal dignity and humanity in response to the racism witnessed overseas.[4] The SBC concluded in 1948, "Our homeland has been called the racial meltingpot of the world because we have all races in our citizenship. This furnishes us, as no other nation is furnished, the material for a clinic in working out the Christian principle of brotherhood."[5] Earlier concerns over immigrant hordes coming to dilute the Anglo-Saxon racial order in America dissipated as political ideologies were seen as the primary threat. And for the racism that remained, some white Protestants began challenging racist assumptions many Americans took for granted. One Presbyterian appealed to a spiritual brotherhood in his ministry that transcended race: "They say blood is thicker than water, but I believe love in Christ is thicker than blood and we must prove it."[6] Concerns both foreign and domestic collided by 1939 as war erupted in Europe. The always close relationship between domestic and foreign missions was heightened during this time. This translated into continued concern over immigration policy as it affected foreign missions and shaped overseas perceptions of the United States. In turn, mainline Protestants through the ecumenical FCC remained active in the political sphere, working to ensure America served as an "arsenal for democracy."

Foreign Wars, Domestic Missions

As war began in Europe, Protestant home missionaries, often through community centers, continued to minister to the foreign-born and try to mold them into the nation's future citizenry.[7] Ministry to Asian communities was especially acute at this time, and the increasing numbers of Latin American immigrants also took precedence in mainline Protestant programs. The social gospel tenet of the "brotherhood of man" and evangelism continued to direct much of home missions. But running throughout the 1940s was a sense of imminent change and mounting challenges. A Methodist report in 1940 highlighted these themes. "Christianity's attitude toward, interest in, love for, and ministry to these various national and family racial groups who have come here from every-whither, as your people and my people came, to make this their home, their country and their flag, is bound to determine the character and the quality of future American citizenship." The report continued, "However important it may be to make the world safe for Democracy, it is absolutely imperative to develop Democracies that are safe for the world." The means to this end were what this Methodist report identified as the "fundamental teachings of Christianity: the Fatherhood of God, the Saviorship of Jesus Christ; the Brotherhood of Man; and the infinite value of human life, regardless of national or racial considerations."[8] As the war raged on, Protestants believed the hour was at hand when they must reaffirm America's providential purpose in the world, both outside and within the nation's borders.

In this climate, Protestants, and American culture at large, promoted an American Way of Life that many believed was at stake. This notion was rife with cultural and religious expectations, and it only reinforced the decision to continue Americanization within home missions.[9] One booklet published by the PCUSA recognized that "its ministry to the peoples of diverse language and racial groups has had a considerable part in this Christian Americanization process" still at work by the 1940s.[10] Oftentimes, the theater for American ideals was the community center or neighborhood house.[11] A Maryland Southern Baptist report commenting on Americanization efforts noted the threat immigrants posed who "care less for our American way of life."[12] Protestant home missionaries were convinced that their best chance for inculcating the

American Way of Life within immigrant communities was through assimilating the second and third generations.[13]

Home missionaries remained diligent in working with earlier European immigrant groups, including Italians and eastern Europeans, but there was also increasing attention to newer groups, such as Asians and Latin Americans.[14] As of 1940, Methodist work in California proliferated among Chinese, Korean, Filipino, and Japanese populations, aided by the institutional merger of the MEC and MECS in 1939. The Methodist merger, while maximizing resources, however, consigned Asian Methodists to separate "missions" or "provisional" conferences, often with the long-term plan to integrate these groups into the larger, white annual conferences as they assimilated to American culture. Such segregation, however, was in keeping with the decision at the time to also organize black Methodists within a separate annual conference within the denomination for the time being.[15] Protestant home missionaries also turned their attention to Filipinos. A territory of the United States until 1946, this status gave residents in the Philippines the opportunity to migrate to America outside of Asian exclusion. As population centers developed along the West Coast, Protestants redirected home mission work. In addition to Methodists, the Episcopal Church also sponsored work among Filipinos during the 1940s, even re-utilizing buildings formerly used in Japanese missions for Filipino programs following Japanese relocation after 1942.[16] In their work among Asian immigrants, Protestants especially tailored their programs for the second generation. This often came in the form of English language services, though in the case of several Presbyterian centers, workers did try to educate the second generation in their own ethnic language and culture in order to ameliorate the concerns of the first generation and equip the younger generation to find employment in immigrant communities.[17]

The challenges missionaries encountered at this time in missions work among Asian immigrant communities are evident in the experience of Southern Baptist home missionary Margaret Jung. Following graduation in 1939 from the training school of the Woman's Missionary Union, Jung planned to serve as a missionary in China. Once Japan seized much of East Asia, and with the onset of World War II, however, Jung had to change her plans, and instead went to work with the Chinese community in Phoenix, Arizona. She encountered a difficult task in Phoenix, where first-generation Chinese immigrants resisted American culture and Christianity and where Buddhism and Confucianism remained prevalent. But she was not without hope. She believed the "[c]hief method of approach is through the little children," whereby they "softened the hearts of the Chinese elders toward Christianity." To accomplish these ends, Jung ran a Sunday School program that eventually enrolled 50 people.[18]

Mainline Protestant home mission programs also focused increasingly on Mexican immigrants at this time. Despite setbacks due to repatriation efforts during the Great Depression, Mexican immigration resumed during the war, in large part as a result of the Bracero Program initiated in 1942 between the US and Mexican governments. This initiative authorized migrant laborers to enter the United States and work in the agricultural sector during the labor shortages of World War II, which remained an official policy until 1964. Mexicans, other than incoming bracero workers, who had immigrated earlier were by the 1940s beginning to establish distinctly Mexican American communities.[19] Many denominations replicated the efforts of Presbyterians, who by 1943 conducted multifaceted work among Spanish-speaking populations, including day schools and health care.[20]

Often this work melded social and evangelistic ministry with patriotism during the war years. One Southern Baptist survey of Mexican churches along Texas's southern border during 1943 applauded the patriotism of Baptist Mexicans in the region. The report declared, "It was gratifying to see how truly American our Mexican friends are." The report described kindergarteners who saluted the flag and noted the absence of Mexican men who were away loyally fighting in the war.[21] Later, Southern Baptists purported that Latino immigrants who converted to Christianity became better workers, improved local public health, and made the nation Christian. Indeed, the report claimed, "If we are ever to have a Christian America from the political standpoint, in the Southwest at least, it is imperative that the Spanish-speaking voting populace be evangelized."[22] And as soldiers fought the Axis powers overseas, some Protestants continued to wage spiritual war against the Roman Catholic Church. Southern Baptists frequently acknowledged resistance they faced among Catholic clergy in local towns, and one Presbyterian report noted the challenges Catholicism and Pentecostalism presented to its work among the Portuguese in Massachusetts.[23]

During the 1940s, Protestants continued their time-honored form of settlement work, often referred to as community centers. The Caspian Community Center operated by Presbyterians in a polyglot iron mining region in Michigan demonstrates the maintenance of home missions to immigrants during the war. Described as "unselfish social service with a deeply religious background," the center provided numerous cultural and social resources to the local community, including clubs, Sunday school, music, Boy Scouts, sports, drama, and film, in addition to opportunities to participate in programs sponsored by the National Youth and Works Progress Administrations. As the seasons changed, the center was there to reinforce American culture among its disparate groups, including "bobbing for apples" for Halloween, skating during the winter, and singing carols for Christmas, including "God Bless America," for the nearby village to hear. According to the title of one article describing its work, the Caspian Community Center was "Where the Melting Pot Bubbles." As the rest of the world succumbed to racial and religious divisions, Caspian maintained a peaceful disposition among such diverse elements as "Catholic or Protestant, Jew or Gentile, white, black, red or yellow. For all are sons of God and brothers of Christ, trying to live in love and charity with our neighbors as true Americans." The center combined the goals of home missions and settlement work in an effort to "foster tolerance, both religious and racial. It combats caste pride and an exalted sense of nationalism wherever they crop up. It is trying to build a 'sense of community,' which is prerequisite to any lasting peace." A commixture of American ideals, Protestant beliefs, and communion with nature made Caspian a vital center for Presbyterian work in an area sequestered from the raging global turmoil overseas.[24]

While many Protestants were confident that evangelization and assimilation would run their course, some were still wary of the effect the immigrant had on the nation if evangelization did not occur. An SBC Home Mission report in 1948 declared, "The races and nationalities and religions of all the countries of the world will in the future be coming to our land and will more and more affect our national, social and religious institutions and life unless these alien races are evangelized."[25] Southern Baptists were concerned about the growing pluralistic nature of America, but hoped to take advantage of the opportunity while the immigrant generation was supposedly still impressionable. One report suggested, "This is the crucial generation of so-called Americanization when the people are amenable to new concepts. They are changing to new things and in religion what they come to be will depend on what they have to choose from. They cannot choose Christ unless we preach the gospel to them."[26] Baptists demonstrated an urgency in their ministry that reflected both national and spiritual concerns.

Other Protestants were also less than sanguine about the impact immigration had on America. Some members of the Episcopal Church kept a watchful eye on immigrant demographics and how their numbers affected church membership. The Joint Commission of the General Convention on Strategy and Policy published Walter Herbert Stowe's *Immigration and Growth of the Episcopal Church* in 1942, though with the disclaimer that it did not reflect everyone's views. Stowe suggested various cultural, social, and religious factors were responsible for limiting Episcopal growth during the denomination's history. "But the one enormous handicap," concluded Stowe, "which it could not overcome until after 1930—and the one most responsible for the slowing up of its rate of growth since 1846, and more especially since 1890—was immigration." Now that immigration was stabilized, Stowe believed foreigners would gradually assimilate, the nation could achieve "assimilation" and "homogeneity," and the Church would recover its losses. Stowe was certain that now following the restriction of the 1920s, the Episcopal Church was in a better position to consolidate its position in America. While the year 1920 was a "low water mark," Stowe believed "the dawn came with the Johnson Act of 1924." (Stowe recognized in a footnote, however, that he still opposed the Asian exclusion of that law, in keeping with the common position among mainline Protestants that while quotas were necessary, Asian exclusion went too far.) By the end, Stowe remained hopeful that European immigrants from prior decades would contribute to the nation. "The unchurched among this foreign white stock is one of the Episcopal Church's frontiers of the future and its opportunity."[27]

Whether they remained skeptical or hopeful, Protestants dedicated to home missions were drawn to the international implications of their work at a time when America was a rising superpower. Protestant attention to home and foreign missions during a century of global turmoil led them to take seriously the international reputation of America. "To the

Latin American nations," claimed a 1946 SBC report, "the things we do here in the States as a people are speaking much louder than all that our missionaries in their own countries can say."[28] Baptists were aware that their treatment of minorities would hinder or help their work overseas and also shape outside perceptions of America. The SBC later recognized in its 1949 convention reports that foreign missions could only begin after the foreigner in America was reached.[29]

This confluence of the international and domestic was an inevitable by-product of the Second World War, and Protestants often imbibed the spirit of the times.[30] A year before America entered the war, Methodists acknowledged that their "missionary task is characterized by both home and foreign field environments, problems and service opportunities." Their aim was to bring together "peoples from every part of the planet, who are resident in and potential citizens of the United States, almost the only remaining country in the world, where oppressed and persecuted contingents of humanity have anything like a fair chance for the normal pursuit of their happiness and welfare."[31] Episcopal leadership in 1945 likewise used the theme "The Christian Fellowship: International and Interracial Understanding" for one of their programs that year.[32]

Tolerance and internationalist themes during the World War II era reinforced a limited respect for cultural diversity, even while home missionaries still promoted the notion of an American Way of Life. A Northern Baptist drama written for churches titled "Mrs. Mayflower and Mrs. Quota Talk It Over" demonstrates these convergent aspirations. The play includes a character named Mrs. Mayflower who attends Pilgrim Church located on Washington Avenue. The plot involves Mrs. Mayflower paying a visit to Mrs. Quota, an Italian American. The drama portrays Mrs. Quota as an eager, sincere Italian immigrant who speaks broken English and whose son is off fighting in the war. The drama admires Italian cultural identity and even provides footnotes with Italian pronunciations to aid English readers unfamiliar with the language. During the course of the play, Mrs. Quota discusses the difficulties she faces in raising her second-generation daughter who is determined to become more American and less Italian. Mrs. Mayflower later instructs Mrs. Quota's daughter on the importance of her Italian background, stating, "But really the American way that we talk so much about is something that has grown and been added to as each new group of immigrants came to our shores." While a cosmopolitan outlook and cultural pluralism are acknowledged, American cultural expectations are still present. During the course of their visit, Mrs. Quota describes the assistance she was receiving from another Northern Baptist woman, Miss Friendly, who was active in immigrant work and refugee relief. Friendly taught Mrs. Quota to use English, boil milk for her infant, make apple pie, add butter to her vegetables, and shop for dresses, while also preparing Mrs. Quota for her citizenship test. Overall, the play holds immigrants to a standard that allowed for ethnic cultural retention while still promoting a form of melting pot assimilation.[33]

Conditions the War Produced

The United States officially entered World War II on December 8, 1941, the day after Japanese pilots bombed Pearl Harbor. Over the next several years the war unleashed a host of challenges on the domestic front. Protestant home missionaries continued earlier forms of ministry, while also responding to new demands. Before the United States entered the war, European refugees, particularly Jews in Germany and eastern Europe, were a contentious topic among the American public. Regrettably, when it comes to America's record on aiding Jewish refugees prior to the war as much of Europe succumbed to fascist regimes, the United States chose not to be a haven for the oppressed. Denying entry to a boatload of refugees on the *St. Louis* in 1939 and failure to pass the Wagner-Rogers bill that would have facilitated the resettlement of several thousand Jewish children attest to America's intransigent disposition.[34]

The growing refugee crisis did, however, draw more attention after America entered the war, though by that time many persecuted Jews and other minorities were left without options. Often American agencies provided relief overseas, but occasionally they aided refugees coming to America. As the war continued, the refugee crisis became more acute for some Protestants.[35] A Southern Baptist women's periodical noticed in 1942, "Our land is filled with refugees. Since the war began there has poured into our country a stream of humanity that makes America a potential 'Land of Destiny'. From the persecutions of Europe have come men and women of science, of finance, of arts and letters. For a period they are our mission opportunity."[36] Denominations occasionally sponsored work, seen in the organization of the Episcopal Committee for European Refugees.[37] Czech Presbyterians within the PCUSA aided their own who had fled Europe through the Jan Hus Presbyterian Church and Neighborhood House in New York City, and New York's Second Presbyterian Church offered some assistance to Jewish refugees in America.[38] Work frequently was channeled through the American Christian Committee for Refugees. Initially referred to as the American Committee for Christian Refugees, it changed its name in 1944 to reflect the committee's efforts "in caring for refugees without discrimination as to race or creed."[39]

The refugee crisis stemming from the European front was not the only ministry opportunity during the war. Shortly after the United States declared war on Japan, Roosevelt issued Executive Order 9066, displacing an entire population of Japanese Americans living on the West Coast. As historian Anne M. Blankenship has demonstrated, Protestant work among relocated Japanese Americans reflected the general temper of their approach to immigration: measured concern that often followed the government's lead, while still advocating for equality and relief for those affected. Mainline Protestant Christians aimed to alleviate the hardships Japanese faced rather than challenge internment itself.[40]

While many Protestants simply accepted the government's decision to intern Japanese, several examples survive of attempts to challenge this policy, often led by former overseas missionaries.[41] According to a Northern Baptist Christian Friendliness pamphlet, "Many letters were written to the United States Department of Justice concerning the release of true Americans."[42] At the outset of Japanese internment, at least one Protestant organization even advocated for "selective evacuation."[43] According to a denominational spokesperson later in 1948, "The Presbyterian Church, U.S.A., has officially been on record by action since 1942 that rights and justice be given to Japanese-Americans and all those upon whom enforced segregation was placed by our government early in the war."[44] Some Presbyterians even aided Japanese who were being evacuated by storing their possessions and accepting power of attorney to watch over Japanese property.[45] Prominent mainline figures such as Harry Emerson Fosdick and Reinhold Niebuhr became increasingly vocal as the camps continued.[46] One Presbyterian noted that he was "a member of the California Church Council, which is taking steps to rally the churches to oppose unjust anti-Japanese legislation, and also appears at the judicial hearings in behalf of the Japanese." The same person later wrote, "Our most sacred Christian and democratic principles are truly at stake in the policy of the evacuation and resettlement of the people of Japanese ancestry in America."[47] While writing in 1942 to a Japanese minister, a Methodist lamented, "We have read of your experiences with deep chagrin over the fact that such things happen to American citizens and we devoutly pray for the day when democracy may be so clear and so strong in our country that things like this will never happen again."[48] Congregationalists also offered a meager critique in 1942. During their General Council, Congregational leadership acknowledged that "national security justified the evacuation of Japanese residing in vital military areas on the West Coast"; nevertheless, the same Congregational body denounced "the fact that all persons with any Japanese blood, citizens as well as aliens, were as a group subjected to evacuation without hearings or other means of determining loyalty."[49] Outside of these denominational responses, some leaders from the Young Men's Christian Association (YMCA) provided a more concerted critique of Japanese internment, as historian Sarah M. Griffith has demonstrated.[50]

The FCC and HMC organized most forms of Protestant relief at Japanese internment camps. Ecumenical efforts included the Western Protestant Church Commission for Japanese Service that cooperated with the government's War Relocation Board in facilitating work in assembly centers where Japanese were located before being sent to permanent camps. It was later renamed the Protestant Commission for Japanese Service. In 1942, another Protestant organization was formed, the Committee on Resettlement of Japanese Americans, with the intent to facilitate settling Japanese Americans outside the camps. Denominations continued to sponsor work as well. As of 1943, Presbyterians fielded "thirteen ordained Presbyterian ministers, two theological students, and six women workers," and it provided $20,000 the previous year for work in the camps. The Episcopal Church also turned its attention to the camps where it witnessed not only material needs, but also an "evangelistic opportunity."[51]

During the war, Japanese internment camps tested the extent to which Protestants were willing to acknowledge cultural and religious pluralism. The Protestant Commission for Japanese Service began translating a hymnal into Japanese, and during Christmas it provided for the needs of children in the camps, "Christian and Buddhist alike."[52] The Committee on Japanese Resettlement, another Protestant relief organization, even accused the Protestant Commission of conceding too much to Japanese culture.[53] Religious services in the assembly centers and camps also compelled Protestant ecumenism. Weekly religious services were organized along Protestant, Catholic, and Buddhist lines, and the Protestant denominations were required to offer "union" services together. Episcopalians, however, were concerned over this format since it might lead to the "loss of identity and the heritage which our fellow churchmen greatly value." The union services also tested the boundaries of midcentury Protestantism, as Seventh Day Adventists were not allowed to participate and Jehovah Witnesses' publications were restricted.[54]

Religious services in the assembly centers and camps, however, provided opportunities not just for Protestant ecumenism, but also for a broader form of religious pluralism as Protestant, Catholic, and Buddhist services were offered. According to the report of one Protestant missionary, Buddhism should be permitted, since it posed no serious threat to Protestant work. The same report, however, could not say the same for Shintoism, which it tied to militant nationalism. After Japanese internment ended in 1945, the HMC helped organize a meeting of the National Conference on Japanese Americans in New York, where "[a] mong those attending were representatives of Protestant, Roman Catholic, Jewish and Buddhist Churches."[55] Despite their concerns, Protestants had to come to terms with this form of religious pluralism outside of the Judeo-Christian framework they were more accustomed to.

As resettlement ensued and Japanese internees were forced to return to an American society reluctant to accept them, mainline Protestants remained actively involved. The Committee on Resettlement of Japanese Americans and a few denominations already had experience aiding Japanese resettlement, as Japanese Americans were allowed to resettle farther east outside of the camps shortly after they were evicted from the West Coast if they had sponsors. Many Japanese students left for institutions of higher education during the internment years.[56] For those church members eager to help Japanese transition out of the camps, the Committee on Resettlement, representing the FCC, HMC, and Foreign Missions Conference of North America, printed a booklet in November

1944 titled "How Can We Help Japanese American Evacuees?: Suggestions for Church Women," and another in January 1945 titled "Relocating the Dislocated."[57] The Southern California Council of Protestant Churches and Church Federation of Los Angeles called on Californians to "take a positive stand for a true demonstration of Christian and democratic principles" as they welcomed returning Japanese Americans. Presbyterians and American Friends even started a hotel to help returning Japanese.[58] Between 1946 and 1948, Congregationalists spent more than $75,000 for missions work among Japanese Americans as a part of the denomination's "Postwar Emergency Program," one element of which was to help Japanese Congregationalists "re-establish themselves in their old homes or new communities to which they have moved, following relocation."[59] When the government considered compensating Japanese in 1948, the PCUSA wrote Senator John S. Cooper requesting such action, which would be a "minimum by way of reparation that our government can make to these people."[60] And, reflecting interest in Japanese Americans after the internment years, Texas Southern Baptists continued to sponsor an annual Nisei Assembly, a summer camp offered to Nisei and "persons of any Japanese generation."[61]

Midcentury Social Sensibilities

A century earlier, the 1844 riots in Philadelphia targeting immigrant Catholics led many religious leaders to denounce militant nativism. Violent attacks on ethnic communities were more than they could stomach.[62] A similar response is evident following World War II as many American Protestants were even less inclined to support forms of nativism that appeared racist or politically extreme, whether perpetrated by Nazis in Europe or the Klan at home. Along the way, white Protestants developed certain social sensibilities and an increasing openness to cultural diversity.

At the same time that Congress was passing restrictive legislation during the 1920s, some Protestants were promoting greater awareness of racial and ethnic inequality. This was demonstrated as early as 1922, when the FCC began hosting Race Relations Sunday every year to encourage racial inclusiveness among US churches, a practice that continued into the 1940s. Outside of the FCC, many denominations also turned their attention to race relations during this time. The Methodist Church hosted a Conference on the Status of Minority Groups in a Christian Democracy in 1942.[63] A Northern Baptist pamphlet played off of the themes of health in "Christianity's Formula as Sure as Vitamins" to promote a religious remedy to social and racial ills. Another Northern Baptist pamphlet, "Will You Help," encouraged building relationships with minorities in one's community, instructing its readers on the first page, "Look for an opportunity to start another acquaintance with someone of another language or race."[64] Even some voices within the Southern Baptist fold began to challenge the entrenched racism of the South. A 1942 *Royal Service* issue included the following call to prayer: "Pray that He may deliver us from racial prejudice, that would draw a circle and shut them out, and that His spirit may help us draw a love-circle and take them in." It continued, "The five million strangers within our gates, the majority unchurched and unsaved, are our peculiar responsibility. They are in 'our wave-length'—neighbors to whom we can tell the Good News with ease and understanding." The SBC went on to pass a Charter of Principles in Race Relations in 1947.[65]

Protestant reaction to the Zoot Suit Riots in 1943 is also telling. For a couple of days that summer, sailors stationed in Los Angeles began lashing out against Latino men on the streets, known for wearing zoot suits, which were popular at the time among minority groups, who were not serving in the military. These attacks carried out by white servicemen soon spilled over into both Mexican and African American communities. *Christian Century* covered the series of mob attacks in Los Angeles that summer. The publication criticized the mainstream press for downplaying the issue of race; the *Century* referred to the confrontation according to what it was, a series of "race riots." The *Century* tried to empathize with the trials of minorities and believed the press should be comparing both Japanese internment and the Zoot Suit Riots to developments in fascist Italy and Nazi Germany. "No voice was raised to point out that what the native fascists of California had started with the exile of 112,000 Japanese-Americans, they and their agents were now continuing with at least twice as many Mexican and Negro Americans." The article then noted the international ramifications of such racism. "No other aspect of our national life has proved so vulnerable to Axis propaganda."[66] A month later, *Christian*

Century challenged those who were complaining about Mexican officials troubled over the treatment of Mexican Americans. The editorial claimed that critics were "utterly blind to the fact that no nation can any longer oppress or endanger the racial minorities within its borders without creating an international crisis and adding to the danger of war. Hitler should have taught them that."[67]

Speech was another component of evolving Protestant social sensibilities. A Christian Friendliness pamphlet delineated "ten tips to tactful talkers." The pamphlet proscribed such terms as "Darky," "Wop," "Dago," "Pickaninny," "Chink," "Jap," "Coon," "Nigger," "Bohunk," "Greaser," and "Kike," names the pamphlet found "unpardonable." It also warned against phrases that reflected "an unconscious belief in white supremacy or anti-Semitism," such as "Indian giver," "Nigger in a woodpile," "White man's time," "Chinaman's chance," and "Jew me down." The document went on to denounce stereotypes, such as "Jews are mercenary" or "Catholics are bigots." It also discouraged separating people into groups; rather, the pamphlet counseled its readers to refer to others as "Americans" and "fellow citizens." The pamphlet, however, also admonished fellow Baptists who were quick to apologize for minorities; instead, it noted, "What is needed is equality of opportunity—not immunity from responsibility."[68]

In her book *Getting Acquainted with Jewish Neighbors* published in 1945, Mildred Moody Eakin, who helped oversee religious education within the MEC, instructed Sunday schoolteachers on how to encourage children to accept Jewish Americans. Readers were taught the similarities between Judaism and Christianity, Jewish distinctives and holidays, famous Jewish Americans, and even a song in Hebrew. Within the text is a tacit acknowledgment of cultural pluralism whereby Jewish Americans were considered an important part of society. Among several goals of the study was the aim to help children "learn to expect that 'different' people will prove to be interesting and probably likable, that to be suspicious of them just because they are different is always foolish and may do much harm." Eakin also encouraged church schoolteachers to help students "learn what an important part Jews have played and are playing in the building of America."[69] For many mainline Protestants, combating prejudice in the postwar period was a task that rested on the shoulders of Sunday school teachers and Christian parents.

Home missions during the war continued to give Protestant women opportunities to minister to immigrant women and families, providing subtle forms of empowerment in denominational work at the same time as the iconic "Rosie the Riveter" inspired women to join the American workforce. One Northern Baptist pamphlet for women announced, "The Christian Friendliness missionary must have the ability and confidence to meet emergencies as they arise." The publication explained, "She must be informed concerning current laws, news and population changes. She must be able to recruit and train volunteers. She must be a counselor and a public speaker. She must live her message."[70] Such work allowed mainline Protestant women a level of autonomy in the face of denominational patriarchal structures, while also holding in tension cosmopolitan ideals and distinct gender and cultural norms.

Many Protestant women active in home missions continued their work among immigrant communities during the war, and once the war was over, Protestant women turned their attention to war brides of both white and ethnic servicemen. A Northern Baptist pamphlet lamented the challenges that awaited the ethnic soldiers whose wives came from overseas: "Japanese-Americans and Chinese-Americans returning to their homeland from service in World War II bring with them their wives from Japan and China; only to find discrimination in a so-called Christian nation."[71] Another Christian Friendliness leaflet encouraged readers to "[f]ind out about service men and women of different races returning to your community. . . . Call on Gold Star Mothers in minority group families. . . . Help foreign wives of American G.I.'s in their adjustment to life in this country."[72] Women involved in home mission work aimed to meet the particular needs of immigrant women caught up in the exigencies of World War II, and in the process appealed to a "spiritual bond of our common motherhood."[73]

During the war and immediately following, society at large stressed the role that families and childrearing played in stable societies. *Parents' Magazine* in 1947 described one nursery program in New Haven, Connecticut, as an "Incubator of Democracy." The nursery, aided by the National Conference of Christians and Jews, strove to bring together middle-class Protestant, Catholic, and Jewish children, black and white, in an effort to instill the virtues of tolerance in the next generation. The article demonstrates the convergence of postwar religious pluralism, racial concerns, and childrearing at the beginning of the baby boom.[74] Within this climate, Protestant ministry to immigrants often stressed the role of families.[75] Some Protestant missionaries recognized the service of ethnic Americans in the war and the price their families paid. In light of the contingencies created by the war, a Christian Friendliness report encouraged women to assist immigrant families who either lost men in the war or welcomed back injured servicemen. "Mothers need help where they have become heads of families and have gone to work."[76] Such an emphasis on family helped define forms of ministry during this period and later encouraged Protestants who kept up with immigration policy to advocate on behalf of family reunification.

Race relations, inclusive language, the role of women, and the importance of family all helped define Protestant social sensibilities during and after the war. One final value stressed during this period was a limited form of religious pluralism. In December 1948, Benson Y. Landis, an active leader in the FCC, was riding on a train when he spotted Msgr. Luigi Ligutti a couple of seats away, a moment he ascribed to a "kind providence." The Protestant Landis and Catholic Ligutti discussed several topics on that trip; Landis later confessed that his wife "was never able to get a word in edgewise." During their impromptu conversation, Ligutti mentioned his hope to produce a statement by representatives "within the three faiths" concerning immigration policy. Ligutti then referenced the work of another Catholic figure, William J. Gibbons, S. J., who was open to meeting with FCC officials on the matter.[77] This chance encounter highlights another key ideal often at the nexus of Protestant home missions and immigration, a Judeo-Christian religious pluralism that remained in vogue following the war.

The assurance of a "Tri-Faith" America, as historian Kevin Schultz has noted, was reinforced often through the work of the National Committee for Christians and Jews. It is no coincidence that the organization recognized every year this tri-faith religious pluralism in what was referred to as Brotherhood Week, incorporating a word already ubiquitous among Protestant social reformers.[78] A striking example of this form of religious pluralism was demonstrated during World War II. In 1943, Catholic, Jewish, Protestant, and Eastern Orthodox representatives signed a Declaration on World Peace that outlined seven principles touching on rights and morals. The Protestant signers acknowledged in a separate statement that they shared with other religious leaders an understanding that "moral and religious convictions should guide the relations of nations." They concluded their statement, however, with a Protestant admonition: "Beyond these proposals we hold that the ultimate foundations of peace require spiritual regeneration as emphasized in the Christian Gospel." Many ecumenical and denominational figures eventually signed the statement, including FCC President and Episcopal Bishop Henry St. George Tucker, Methodist G. Bromley Oxnam, John Foster Dulles, and Ruth Stafford Peale, the wife of Norman Vincent Peale.[79] Such relationships among the three faiths often fostered concerted efforts to address immigration reform and refugee needs in the coming years, but as the above statement made by Protestants suggests, they held this ideal in tension with their own distinct religious convictions.

Exclusion on Its Way Out

The war may have spurred various social sensibilities, but it also encouraged mainline Protestants to pay careful attention to legislation affecting immigrants. Rather than calling for a complete overhaul of immigration policy, Protestants often strove, through piecemeal attempts, to open America's doors to previously excluded groups. In so doing they joined a host of other reformers and diplomats working at this time to open up immigration to people from Asia.[80] They first set their sights on overturning Chinese exclusion that had been in place since 1882. In their efforts to pressure Congress to end exclusion, Protestants demonstrated their loyalty to the war cause as they recommended admitting only wartime allies. They also communicated their tacit approval of the national origins system by acknowledging only miniscule quotas for Chinese immigrants if exclusion were overturned. Some Protestants stressed the importance of family values by advocating naturalization for Chinese men, which would allow wives back in China to reunite with their husbands in the United States.[81] Along the way, mainline Protestants aimed to be "politically practicable," rather than make unrealistic demands. General Secretary of the Church Peace Union Henry A. Atkinson acknowledged, "I think the time has come for us to base our appeal definitely upon the proposal that China be put immediately on the quota system, instead of making a general appeal for a liberalization of the law."[82] Many Protestant dignitaries wanted such liberalization but understood that political change in America required patience and calculation.

Many of the Protestant leaders discussed here subscribed to the political liberalism of their day. In his history of liberalism as a political ideology, Edmund Fawcett identifies specific periods of history in which liberalism developed and was practiced differently. He states that between 1880 and 1945, it morphed into a form of liberal democracy, and then between 1945 and 1989, its practitioners defended it in the face of fascism and communism. He writes, "Liberalism as I take it here was a search for an ethically acceptable order of human progress among civic equals without recourse to undue power."[83] In many respects, mainline Protestant denominations during this time touted a similar form of liberal democracy in response to reactionary anti-immigrant voices and the threats that fascist and communist ideology posed.[84]

By the end of 1942, many Protestants like Atkinson approached the political sphere with caution, reflecting careful attention to the political climate. Others, however, were ready to take immediate action. The Church Federation of Los Angeles announced its intent to "create and stir up sentiment against the oriental exclusion laws of the United States." By the spring of 1943, FCC leaders met with INS officials and began crafting a plan to challenge Asian exclusion. This also involved forming alliances with such groups as the Catholic Welfare Conference and Chinese United Associations. With congressional hearings approaching, the FCC then voted on a statement in May 1943 that leaders sent out to potential supporters for their signatures. The statement denounced "discrimination on account of race" in Asian exclusion, claiming that "such racial discrimination does violence to the Christian view of one humanity under God, is contrary to the democratic principles upon which this country was founded, and to proved scientific facts." It called upon Congress "to allow natives of all friendly countries, otherwise admissible, to enter this country under the existing quota system and become citizens on the same terms as immigrants from non-Oriental countries."[85] FCC officials mailed the statement to 55,000 ministers, eliciting support from numerous individuals and church councils. The declaration soon received press coverage in the *New York Times* and *New York Herald Tribune*.[86] In correspondence with an FCC official, the Executive Secretary of the Committee for Church and Community Cooperation in Los Angeles County even anticipated, probably prematurely, that "[m]illions of church people would like to see the change made."[87]

That summer, mainline Protestant leaders worked on numerous fronts. FCC representatives spoke before a congressional committee on May 26, 1943, following the American Legion whose testimony at the hearing ran counter to the FCC's positions.[88] As momentum continued in Congress into the summer of 1943, Protestants also contacted their representatives. The Wisconsin Council of Churches wrote Samuel Dickstein, chair of the House Immigration Committee, that such exclusion was tied to recent US conflicts with China and Japan and that the "removal of this racial slur would go a long way toward convincing the peoples of the world of the honesty of our war aims." In another letter sent to other members of Congress that summer, the Wisconsin Council drew upon the ideal of brotherhood and acknowledged that it "believes that all men are members of one great family under God, and that all racial discrimination is contrary to the Divine will, as well as to the democratic principles upon which our country was founded."[89] U. G. Murphy from Seattle wrote Roswell Barnes in the FCC that he was concerned about the role the United States would have in promoting peace after the war if Asian exclusion was not addressed. He went on to express both missional and patriotic concern. "Unless the Church of Christ in America very promptly and clearly cuts itself loose from our present national attitude toward Orientals, the Cause of Christ in all of Asia will get a violent set back." Murphy then assured Barnes, "I am praying for you men, up on the front line, and am hoping that we, as followers of Christ, as well as Americans, shall be able to present our case so clearly to our fellow citizens that something will be done to rectify some of the harm done by our totally unchristian and un-American attitude toward Orientals and all persons of color."[90] That summer FCC officials even put pressure on the president of the American Federation of Labor, William Green, who was less inclined to support the legislation. He responded by suggesting the FCC respect the AFL's "same right to present the point of view of labor regarding Immigration Legislation" that the FCC had in promoting its position.[91]

Minnesota Representative Walter H. Judd, a former Congregationalist missionary to China, proved to be the leading congressional ally the

FCC had in this fight to end Chinese exclusion. His concern over Asian restriction found willing support among mainline Protestant figures, but Judd's earlier work in China as a medical missionary made him a brother in arms. Though a freshman congressman, Judd put his former experiences in China to good use and took the lead in winning support for ending Chinese exclusion.[92] Judd's close ties to mainline Protestants and his affinity to many of their midcentury ideals later came to a head in 1949 when he spoke at an interracial rally in Chicago sponsored by Christian Friendliness workers of the NBC. He gave a speech titled "How to Build Unity," and according to a Christian Friendliness report, Judd urged "at every point that the Christian way is *the only way.*" The report noted that there were Muslim and Jewish attendees at the rally who expressed interest in Christianity and that the event included presentations by displaced persons, foreign students, and war brides.[93] FCC officials relied heavily on their ties to this likeminded statesman in the years to come.

As the summer of 1943 progressed, the FCC kept the churches abreast of legislative prospects during the next session of Congress that fall. "This allows," proclaimed the FCC, "our Christian forces two months in which to carry on an education work in the interest of letting members of Congress know how strongly Christian sentiment supports the principle that our immigration policies should no longer retain the stigma of racial discrimination." On the precipice of legislative action, church councils and denominations continued to send their support to the FCC. The Council of Church Women of Rochester and Monroe County (New York) resolved to support ending Chinese exclusion, and noted its "hope that there will be further revision of the immigration laws to permit the admission on a quota basis and the naturalization of *all* Orientals." The Episcopal Church passed a resolution in October 1943 also backing principles established earlier by the FCC on Asian exclusion. A Methodist even expounded in a missive that October that "Christian morality and political strategy seem at this moment to coincide." Walter Van Kirk, Executive Secretary of the FCC's Department of International Justice and Goodwill and the foremost leader in the FCC on matters of immigration reform, wrote in October 1943 that despite the "inadequate" nature of the current bill, he hoped it was a first step in immigration and naturalization reform.[94]

As Congress reconvened that fall, many observers hoped Chinese exclusion was destined to end. Congressman Judd kept the FCC informed throughout the proceedings, and in October, Van Kirk sent out another FCC petition, which eventually solicited nearly 1,000 signatures, including that of such mainline dignitaries as Georgia Harkness, Reinhold Niebuhr, Harry Fosdick, and G. Bromley Oxnam. At this time Van Kirk concluded, "It will be impossible after the war to establish a world community based on justice and brotherhood unless we take steps now to remove from our statutes discrimination against the Chinese on account of color." Van Kirk observed the contradictory nature of exclusion when the United States also considered the "Chinese as military allies." Upon receiving the petition, Indiana Senator Raymond E. Willis commented, "The names are impressive, and your suggestion cannot but be heeded, couched as it is. It looks at this time as though the requested outcome of the bill mentioned would be favorable." Writing to Luman Shafer, who was serving on the FCC's Commission to Study the Bases of a Just and Durable Peace in November 1943, Representative Judd acknowledged that a Senate vote was likely, but suggested "we ought not to rest on our oars."[95] The following month, after the bill passed through the Senate, President Franklin D. Roosevelt signed it into law, officially ending Chinese exclusion.

The following year Protestants did not "rest on" their "oars." They instead began promoting a bill to end Indian exclusion, a measure sponsored by Senator Emmanuel Celler and Representative Clare Boothe Luce. In this new legislative battle, the FCC cooperated closely with the India League of America.[96] Van Kirk went before Congress again, a task he would carry out repeatedly over the next several years, and presented a statement that had the backing of many denominational figures. Van Kirk appealed to America's "declared purpose to establish amongst the nations a new world order of justice and of human brotherhood," while also noting that the meager quota that Indians would receive meant that "the action here proposed could be taken without any risk whatever to our economic, political, and cultural patterns of living." Following his comments, he faced stiff questioning from politicians at the hearing, and his answers elucidate several positions of one of the FCC's most prominent spokesmen. First, Van Kirk acknowledged that quota numbers were not as significant as removing racial barriers. When asked about the prospect of Japanese immigration, Van Kirk affirmed that only

Asian nations not at war with America should be allowed immigration. While he largely dodged the question of an eventual Japanese quota, he did hint that Japanese should be treated equally. To this point, the chairman of the hearing curtly noted, "So far as I am concerned, I would not want to see a quota for Japan for the next thousand years." Van Kirk then commented, "That is not under discussion." Apparently oblivious to Van Kirk, the chairman, Samuel Dickstein, then added, "That goes for the Germans, too. I think something should be done about cutting the German quota." The questioning then turned to decreasing overall quota numbers, and though acknowledging that the primary issue was ending racial exclusion, Van Kirk argued that he was not in a position to speak on the matter but that the "Federal Council does not ask that our immigration restrictions against peoples of other countries be relaxed." Van Kirk's responses largely reflect the historic position of white Protestants that immigration restriction and quotas were necessary, as long as they were not racially discriminatory.[97] Indian nationals would have to wait another two years, however, before Congress rescinded their exclusion.

As the war came to a halt in 1945, white Protestants continued their drive for immigration reform in the legislative arena, largely in response to members of Congress who aimed to take advantage of a postwar climate that had historically aided restrictionists, as seen in the passage of the 1921 and 1924 laws following World War I. In July 1945, Texas Representative Ed Gossett sponsored a bill proposing to cut current quotas in half over the next ten years. While Protestant leaders generally supported limited restriction through set quotas, drastically reducing total immigration went too far. Once the bill made it to the House Committee on Immigration and Naturalization by February 1946, Protestants voiced their opposition. The American Christian Committee for Refugees communicated its concerns to Committee Chairman John Lesinski. Oxnam, now president of the FCC, also telegrammed Lesinski, noting that the FCC's Executive Committee "recommends that no downward alteration of existing quotas in immigration laws be undertaken at this time." Van Kirk and the Methodist Woman's Division of Christian Service also opposed such measures.[98] Mainline Protestant leaders were unwilling to lose ground to nativist forces following World War II.

Though Gossett's bill never passed, mainline leaders believed more work remained as long as Japanese immigrants were excluded from entering the country and denied naturalization. In the years that followed, mainline leaders worked to overturn Japanese exclusion now that the United States was no longer at war with Japan. In keeping with their prior fruitful relationship, Van Kirk reached out to Judd in 1946 to discuss the "propriety of the churches taking action now on the matter of repealing our exclusion legislation with respect to the Japanese."[99] While the FCC relied on its ties to Judd, other groups at this time considered the FCC an ally, including the Japanese American Citizens League. FCC leaders were also in touch with the Committee for Equality in Naturalization. The FCC moved forward in 1947, passing a resolution calling on the government to "complete Congressional action in removing the principle of discrimination in our immigration and naturalization laws respecting Orientals."[100] At the same time, the Protestant Council of the City of New York published an editorial in the *New York Times* calling for an end to Asian exclusion, especially in light of human rights and America's role in the world, and the Methodist General Conference passed a resolution in May 1948 supporting Japanese and Korean immigration.[101] Most Americans, however, were not ready to open the nation to Japanese immigrants. Ruth Isabel Seabury of the American Board of Commissioners for Foreign Mission noted in a letter to Van Kirk that some people she talked to feared "that hordes of Orientals will be coming to the country as a result."[102]

As historians Mary L. Dudziak, Cindy I-Fen Cheng, and Gene Zubovich have argued, this impetus for human rights among more progressive diplomats and politicians, which also spurred immigration reform and the decision to end Asian exclusion, was largely a product of the sociopolitical context of the 1940s and '50s. American statesmen and ministers alike recognized the importance during this time of contrasting American freedom and democracy with either fascist or communist totalitarianism. This in turn forced many white Americans to admit to the myriad racial injustices in their own nation. Mainline Protestant leaders were no exception. Key mainline Protestant leaders channeled their time and resources toward ending racial segregation, while also supporting international human rights embodied in the 1948 UN Declaration of Human Rights. These themes all converged for certain mainline leaders, especially Thelma Stevens, who rallied Methodist women to combat racial prejudice in America at this time by sponsoring civil rights legislation and immigration reform.[103]

As Congress took up legislation during the spring of 1948 that proposed reopening immigration to Japan and other Asian nations, Judd wrote Van Kirk, "Knowing the active interest of yourself and the Federal Council of Churches in the elimination of racial barriers in our immigration and naturalization laws I would like the testimony of your orgnization [*sic*] at the hearings."[104] Van Kirk was unable to go this time, and Judd chose instead to read a statement Van Kirk wrote for the congressional hearing that April. The Japanese American Citizens League later wrote Van Kirk thanking him for his "excellent statement."[105] A couple of months later, as the bill was then in the Senate, Van Kirk went before a Senate subcommittee to advocate for further immigration reform for Asians.[106] Before the committee members in July 1948, Van Kirk appealed to both national and spiritual interests. "This is an action dictated by the ethical precepts of the Christian religion and by the concern of the American people that the principle of democracy and fair play shall become operative throughout the world." Van Kirk then counseled the Senators at the hearing, "I can assure the members of this Committee that the action here recommended has the unqualified approval of the great majority of the Protestant churches of the United States."[107]

Six days later, Alson J. Smith, a representative of the Methodist Federation for Social Action, also spoke before the same Senate Judiciary Subcommittee on the matter of immigration reform. His statement wove together multiple themes reflecting both the progress and inertia within Protestant positions on race, immigration, and pluralism since the early twentieth century. He assured his interlocutors that he valued the nation's heritage, even acknowledging the "Anglo-Saxon nature of our laws, customs, and traditions." Smith noted, however, that "we believe that it is more important to preserve the spirit of Anglo-Saxon fair-play and justice . . . than it is to preserve the Anglo-Saxon racial strain." He then challenged the national origins policy from 1924. Smith recognized that such quotas favored northern Europeans and concluded that the system "seems to us not only unChristian in that it sets up judgments which are in violation of both the letter and the spirit of the New Testament, but also unAnglo-Saxon in that it violates the very spirit of the Magna Carta." Smith then drew from recent history: "Furthermore, the 'National origin' provision makes us subscribe as a nation to a doctrine of racial difference the best-known exponent of which was the late Adolph Hitler and which we know to be biologically ridiculous as well as ethically outrageous." Smith asked, "Have we, in two world wars, spent our treasure and the blood of our sons to make the world safe for a democracy which we ourselves refuse to practice?" Smith then turned to Asian exclusion. He reminded the committee of the ways that Japan during World War II used such racism to tarnish America's image. But in keeping with many other Protestant leaders, Smith acknowledged that he was not advocating "unrestricted immigration." He pointed to labor concerns and assimilation challenges, even admitting that "as a Protestant church group we are interested in maintaining the predominantly Protestant character of the country." But Smith believed this was best left to the marketplace of American religion, rather than immigration restriction.[108]

A flurry of letters by local church councils was sent to Congress following the FCC's appeal in 1948 to end Japanese exclusion. A spokesperson for the Church Federation of Indianapolis suggested immigration reform for Asians was "in keeping with our Judeo-Christian and democratic political and ethical principles."[109] The Council of Churches in Quincy, Massachusetts, and the Erie (Pennsylvania) Council of Churches chimed in on the issue, and farther south, the San Antonio Council, Missouri Council, and Oklahoma City Council of Churches also sent their support for overturning Asian restriction.[110] While supporting the cause of Asian immigrants, the Council of Churches of Buffalo and Erie County also took the opportunity to call for legislation to aid displaced persons following World War II.[111] The postwar refugee crisis could not be ignored, and many mainline Protestants called for action, a topic covered in the next chapter.

By 1949, a bill sponsored by Judd that aimed to end Japanese exclusion made it before the Senate. Despite efforts like those of the Methodist Church, which called upon its members to write their senators to support the legislation, it was clear to many observers that the bill would face strong resistance. Nevertheless, Judd and Van Kirk stayed in touch that spring. Van Kirk traveled to Washington, DC, and met with several other senators, but soon discovered Senator Pat McCarran's strong resistance to the bill would be insurmountable. For another round of Senate hearings that July, Van Kirk resubmitted the FCC's 1947 statement and outlined several points that comprised the FCC's position on Asian exclusion. The statement succinctly demonstrated elements of mainline Protestant concern over immigration policy that had been in place since the 1920s. Van Kirk first acknowledged that the "Christian gospel which has played such a vital part in the evolution of our nation exhalts [*sic*] the dignity and worth of man regardless of race or color." He noted that the fate of missions was closely tied to political decisions concerning race in America. Van Kirk then turned to international relations and the nation's ties to the United Nations, asserting, "The churches believe that the removal of the stigma of racial discrimination from our immigration and naturalization laws will vastly strengthen the moral position of our nation before the world." Finally, Van Kirk justified the FCC's position on the basis of American diplomacy in the region and East Asia's stability.[112] Despite the work of Judd and Van Kirk, the bill did not make it out of the Senate. Japanese immigration would have to remain a concern of mainline Protestants for a few more years.

Conclusion

In 1946, President Truman demonstrated publicly the liberal ties he had forged with mainline Protestant leadership. He spoke before the FCC biennial session held in Columbus, Ohio, that year and was introduced by one of mainline Protestantism's leading progressive ministers, Bishop Oxnam. In his speech, Truman brought together the themes that had defined much of Protestant work among immigrants. Truman acknowledged the social gospel heritage of his audience when using such expressions as "social justice" and "Brotherhood of Man." Truman stressed the close ties between religion and democracy and acknowledged the grave challenges these two ideals faced following World War II. And with references to "dignity," "decency," "righteousness," and "liberty," Truman alluded to the American Way of Life that home missionaries worked to preserve as they ministered to immigrants. Truman even acknowledged the Judeo-Christian pluralism that many Protestants had accepted by midcentury. "The Protestant Church, the Catholic Church, and the Jewish Synagogue—bound together in the American unity of brotherhood—must provide the shock forces to accomplish this moral and spiritual awakening." And, though never specifically

Figure 3.1. The inaugural session of the National Council of Churches in 1950, where the theme "This Nation Under God" stressed the importance of religion and national identity during the early Cold War. Miller-Ertler Studios, courtesy of the Presbyterian Historical Society, Philadelphia, PA.

mentioning immigration, he still recognized America's diverse heritage: "We have this America not because we are of a particular faith, not because our ancestors sailed from a particular foreign port."[113] Truman's speech before mainline Protestants in 1946 affirmed much of their work in the realm of immigration and ethnic communities over the preceding 20 years.

Truman's speech also came at a time when the United States and the rest of the world found themselves stumbling into the Cold War. Indeed, the day before arriving at the FCC meeting, Truman had been in Fulton, Missouri, where former British Prime Minister and wartime ally Winston Churchill gave his "iron curtain" speech. As the Cold War set in, Americans continued to grapple with national identity. For most Protestants, America was bound to serve a providential purpose as a supposedly Christian nation while atheistic communism took root in

Russia and China. Mainline Protestants embraced this calling in 1950 when they restructured their ecumenical ties and renamed the FCC. Now taking the title "National Council of Churches" (NCC), the organization's attendees at its inaugural session met under a banner proclaiming "This Nation Under God" and used the theme "building of a Christian America in a Christian world." The opening statement of the convention acknowledged the National Council's mission: "By word and deed and in the name of Christ who gave his life for all mankind it affirms the brotherhood of men and seeks by every rightful means to arrest those forces of division which rend the nation along the lines of race and class and stay its growth toward unity." In the coming years, immigration would test Protestant commitments to improving race relations and promoting national accord. Mainline Protestants considered how they treated the foreigner, whether immigrant or refugee, in a context intimately tied to the nation's new role as a superpower becoming entrenched in a Cold War.[114] Through refugee resettlement and continued home missions, American Christians found they had tangible ways of demonstrating appreciation for diverse cultures, while also working to bolster the Protestant character of the nation. This pluralistic bargain, however, proved difficult to sustain.

4

Strangers in Mayberry

The Church of Christ has provided a way of salvation not
only through a faith and fellowship adequate even for the
wandering refugee; it has been as well the friendly Christian
hand reaching across the sea to welcome the refugee to a
new home of opportunity and hope in America.
—Roland Elliot, "Article on Refugees"

The Radio and Film Commission of the Methodist Church produced a
30-minute episode in 1955 called *The Tourist*. In this short film, a church
decides to sponsor a displaced person (DP) from war-torn Europe. The
episode's location resembles the stereotypical American community
largely popularized by the Andy Griffith Show; even Howard McNear,
who performed the role of the local Methodist minister, was the same
actor who starred as Mayberry's fidgety barber. As the plot unfolds, a
local mechanic initially withholds his support from his church's decision
to resettle a refugee. The curmudgeonly mechanic resorts to hackneyed
arguments against foreigners and suggests DPs will simply take jobs they
did not earn and that it is "our money that is being displaced." For the
mechanic, giving work to a refugee is a crude form of "Lend Lease."
The Methodist minister, however, advocates on behalf of refugee resettlement and stresses that this is an opportunity to practice Christian
brotherhood as a nation with a "Christian background." The mechanic
eventually warms up to the idea of the local church sponsoring a DP
after a traveling European correspondent reporting on a recent session of the United Nations is stranded in the town for a couple of days.
Through personal interaction with a foreigner, the mechanic changes
his perspective.[1] This film reflects the confluence of many themes
within American culture and midcentury Protestantism, including continuing social gospel sentiments, a developing religious media culture,
and the postwar refugee crisis. By the 1950s, Americans were no longer

Figure 4.1. A scene from the Methodist short film *The Tourist* promoting refugee resettlement. Courtesy of the General Commission on Archives and History of the United Methodist Church, Madison, NJ.

witnessing multitudes of new immigrants coming to their towns, but due to refugee resettlement and the vitality of ethnic communities that were products of earlier immigration, mainline Protestant attention to the foreign-born continued into postwar America as white Christians worked to define the mission of a Protestant America and the merits and drawbacks of pluralism.

Following World War II, the white Protestant establishment reaffirmed its commitment to the far-reaching mission of the United States in light of foreign and domestic conditions. During the 1950s especially, American Protestants continued to stress home missions to immigrant and ethnic groups. These programs reflected progressive social gospel ideals, notions of what it meant to be American, and a continued evangelistic mission. Alongside their home mission work among ethnic groups, many mainline Protestant groups sponsored refugees during the years immediately following World War II as large numbers of Europeans were displaced and as the Cold War ensued. Together, Protestant responses to immigrants and refugees demonstrate efforts to sustain a level of pluralism while maintaining a Christian nation with global, providential responsibilities.

Christian Nation through Home Missions

By midcentury, Protestant denominations continued to seek out immigrants in order to share the gospel message and provide social services to those in need. Earlier sentiments that formed the basis of home missions to immigrants continued within most mainline programs. Through extensive settlement house programs and ministries appealing to specific national or language groups, many white Protestant churches, especially in urban centers, came into contact with ethnic minorities and worked to practice the social gospel tenant of the brotherhood of man.[2] Most mainline denominations, contrary to fundamentalist claims, also continued to cultivate evangelistic efforts as a part of their mission to reach the immigrant, and in so doing, help ensure America remained a Christian nation. A 1952 article in *Christian Century* titled "Evangelizing a Procession" demonstrates the persistence of these ideals. In defining home missions, the author, longtime home mission leader Hermann Morse, acknowledged, "Its over-all purpose—to extend the redemptive ministry of the gospel to all people throughout our land so as to make America truly Christian—relates it in some significant way to every aspect of contemporary life."[3]

In addition to older European immigrant communities, Protestant home missionaries paid considerable attention to other groups, particularly Asian immigrants and Spanish speakers. Similar work was done among Asian populations, work given further precedence when the US government recognized Chinese immigration once more in 1943 and Japanese immigration in 1952. Upon establishing communism in China in 1949, Mao Zedong only added further impetus to some Chinese to immigrate to America.[4] Moreover, following a concerted effort to minister to relocated Japanese during the war, Protestant denominations continued their work among Japanese communities and proudly noted what they believed to be their progressive stance taken during the wartime furor.[5]

Despite deportations during the 1930s, Mexican immigration increased during the 1940s, due in part to the Bracero Program that encouraged Mexican laborers to come work in America during the labor shortages World War II created. The NCC maintained a Committee on Spanish American Work, and all major Protestant denominations sponsored robust missions work in the Southwest among the Latino population, either through denominational programs or regional associations and conferences. Missions work often came in the form of radio programs, religious educational institutes, programs for children, settlement house work, and college scholarships. In the case of Southern Baptists, they categorized missions work among Mexican Americans and other ethnic groups along the lines of "language," rather than race.[6] As of 1960, the SBC, Methodist Church, and United Presbyterian Church in the United States of America (UPCUSA) were each contributing more than $600,000 annually to missions work among Spanish-speaking people.[7] Home missionaries of Latino background were often employed by Protestant denominations; when considering a female worker for work in Port Arthur, Texas, in 1951, Methodist planners noted, "As to the qualifications of a worker, we believe that a worker of the same background of the people she works is very essential. As many of there [sic] people speak only Spanish, a worker not speaking both English and Spanish would be handicapped."[8] Congregationalists also continued to sponsor work in New Mexico, though not without certain difficulties. When they considered integrating the Mexican and Anglo congregations in Gallup, one report acknowledged that lingering "racial tension," class differences, and transportation difficulties stood in the way. Nevertheless, Congregational leaders were hopeful concerning their work in New Mexico, since the Mexican community there was learning English, which was in keeping with the progression of immigrant communities and Protestant missions elsewhere.[9]

Despite their affinity for missions to Mexican immigrants at this time, mainline Protestants continued to overlook the more immediate challenges the Mexican American community faced. In 1954, the Eisenhower administration sponsored "Operation Wetback," an intensive deportation initiative led by Immigration and Naturalization Service (INS). While the formal drive to deport Mexican immigrants was not officially initiated until 1954, local and federal law enforcement had already begun aggressively targeting Mexican immigrants during the early 1950s, largely under the guidance of former military officer Joseph Swing. Between 1953 and 1955, at least 800,000 Mexican immigrants were forcibly sent back south of the border.[10] Much like during the 1930s when repatriation efforts were under way, mainline Protestants were largely oblivious to governmental efforts to force Mexican immigrants back across the border. While mainline Protestants actively sought legislative solutions to Asian restriction, they often deferred to their missional duties and did not enter the political fray when it came to government policy concerning Mexican immigrants. A home missions conference conducted by the NCC in January 1954 met to discuss missions to Spanish speakers and acknowledged that "both 'wetbacks' and legitimate migratory workers—at least 2 million people in all— need the help of the church and the government working together."[11] Such help, however, did not speak to the crisis Mexican Americans were facing while the INS systematically deported thousands of immigrants back to Mexico during Operation Wetback.

An ambivalence among mainline Protestants toward the status of Mexican immigrants became apparent by 1960 when Congress considered whether to continue the still extant Bracero Program. The NCC's official position was for the government to end the program, as it attracted migrants who competed with domestic workers and did not always guarantee just working conditions for braceros. In calling for the government to conclude the Bracero Program, an NCC statement at the time even recognized the "necessity of providing adequate enforcement of the immigration laws on the Mexican border to prevent resurgence of the vast influx of so-called 'wet-backs' of a few years ago."[12] This conservative position by a seemingly progressive organization exposed the NCC to criticism from more conservative pockets of American Protestantism. Later in 1964 and 1965, when the Bracero Program did expire, the southern *Presbyterian Journal* took this opportunity to criticize the apparent irony of a liberal NCC wanting to terminate a program that admitted Mexican workers (laborers some of the southern readers of the *Presbyterian Journal* certainly employed and relied upon).[13] While mainline Protestants continued to sponsor robust home mission programs in urban centers across the nation that met the needs of many European and Asian immigrant communities and would help resettle

European refugees displaced following World War II, the Protestant response to the legal challenges Mexican Americans faced in the southwest was tepid at best.

As mainline Protestants during the 1950s followed earlier precedents of overlooking the plight of Mexican immigrants, they continued to sustain a theological and missional tradition that encouraged more progressive positions elsewhere. Midcentury Protestant home missions drew heavily from the earlier social gospel movement. Multiple mid-century historians, such as Henry May, Paul Carter, and Robert Moats Miller, recognized in their own time that social gospel principles from the late nineteenth and early twentieth centuries endured.[14] Theological propositions that underpinned the movement, particularly the brotherhood of man and fatherhood of God, were regularly cited into the 1950s, and Protestant groups continued to minister to immigrants in ways established at the turn of the century during the peak of the social gospel movement. The New York Episcopal Diocese funded denominational work on Ellis Island into the 1950s; an Episcopal Woman's Auxiliary report covering ministry conducted on Ellis Island in 1949 noted that the "year has been crowded with many G. I. brides and Displaced Persons in addition to the usual quota of stranded people."[15] On the other side of the country, Methodists sponsored the same worker, Katharine R. Maurer, from 1912 to 1951, who ministered to the needs of immigrants coming to the San Francisco Bay area through Angel Island.[16]

The continuity of earlier social gospel programs is also demonstrated through the continued settlement house work that several Protestant denominations maintained. A compelling example is the legacy of Maryal Knox, a member of the Madison Avenue Presbyterian Church. For 50 years, Knox worked among Italian, Puerto Rican, African American, and "gypsy" families in East Harlem through settlement work, aiming to "show different groups how to get along." She helped run a neighborhood club for children, provided entertainment for mothers, and advocated for public housing projects in the area. For the children, sewing and art lessons were provided, and the club even took children on outings to Madison Square Garden to watch the circus and a "wild-west show." As a result of later postwar developments, Knox also welcomed displaced persons into her community. Having worked 50 years in her neighborhood, Knox's career began during the early years of the social gospel movement and continued into the midcentury.[17]

But Presbyterians were not the exception when it came to operating settlement houses later in the century. Into the 1950s, the Episcopal Church and Methodists continued to sponsor settlement houses and community centers. In their settlement house work, Methodist women defined the gravity of the need: "Too often our Christian leaders locally are ignorant of existing conditions in our cities which defy Christian principles of the brotherhood of man and respect of the rights and dignity of each individual regardless of race or economic condition." Even Southern Baptists practiced a similar form of work called Good Will Centers, which were meant to address the spiritual, physical, educational, and recreational needs of the local community. Southern Baptists acknowledged that these centers followed in the vein of prior settlement efforts, such as London's Toynbee Hall and Chicago's Hull House, though they made the qualification that their Good Will Centers were "[s]ocial settlements with an evangelistic approach."[18]

Women of the American Baptist Convention (formerly NBC) through their Department of Christian Friendliness also promoted a home mission program directed toward immigrants that was both socially progressive and evangelistic. In a leaflet titled "Objectives in Christian Social Relations" for 1954 and 1955, among many recommendations, it encouraged American Baptists to write their congressional representatives on matters of immigration and refugee policy, "[s]eek to win at least one person of another racial or national ground to Jesus Christ," "[t]each English," "[a]ssist in study of citizenship requirements," and help with the "[i]nterpretation of each other's culture and customs."[19] The same program continued: Christian Friendliness leaders depended largely on local women to implement denominational programs, noting that

> it is as individuals that we show personal concern for that newcomer, helping the refugee mother learn the intricacies of shopping at the supermarket, welcoming the Negro moving in the house next door, hiring the Puerto Rican who applies for a job, looking upon each individual not as being of different color or culture, but as a child of God and therefore our brother or sister in Christ.[20]

For such ends, Christian Friendliness leaders depended largely on local church women to implement denominational programs that inculcated such religious and cultural ideals.

Immigrant ministries by midcentury often entailed cosmopolitan ideals and a budding respect for cultural pluralism. A pamphlet describing Christian Friendliness work in Massachusetts following World War II offers a glimpse. As American Baptist women met with and assisted local immigrants, including Poles, Armenians, Filipinos, Italians, and Russians, they made attempts to accommodate foreign cultures. Reflecting on a visit to a Russian family, a Christian Friendliness worker surmised, "Every nationality has made its imprint on American life and all of them have made some valuable contributions." In the same leaflet on missions work in Massachusetts, it was reported that one church service hosted 20 nationalities who joined in worship, and the service even included singing multiple national anthems.[21] American Baptist women also sponsored what they called "Camp Friendly," a program that brought disadvantaged children from New York and Connecticut to homes in the countryside. The hallmark of the program was the diversity it inspired. During one summer, program organizers reported that they sponsored three Arabians, eleven Chinese, five Germans, three Japanese, twelve African Americans, two Norwegians, nineteen Puerto Ricans and Latinos, and ten whites.[22] By midcentury, a diffusion of social gospel ideals and evangelistic aspirations largely defined home missions to immigrant and ethnic communities.

In their attempts to spread the gospel message among the various nationalities represented in America, Protestant home missionaries tacitly accepted forms of cultural pluralism while working to build a Christian community that would transcend language and racial barriers. Reflecting on their work with Latinos, a Presbyterian report recognized that the denomination needed to set aside hopes for Americanization and instead "adjust our program of approach and service to the culture and mores of the people."[23] One Southern Baptist even acknowledged that "there is a spiritual oneness that can be deeper and more significant than language, race, or culture."[24] While describing Methodist community center work, one report proclaimed that "cultural identities are fine, but to discriminate on account of color, nationality, or religion is false."[25] A NCC book on missions to Spanish-speaking populations published in 1959 echoed similar sentiments. The text cited multiple contemporary social scientists and historians, such as Gunnar Myrdal and Oscar Handlin, and implored, on the basis of Christian missions, "majority" white, Protestant Americans to no longer marginalize "minority" groups on account of race, religion, language, class, and education, including Spanish-speaking groups in the Southwest. In an essay titled "Cultural Democracy" included as an appendix, Anne O. Lively criticized earlier Americanization efforts premised on the melting-pot theory. Instead, she called for cultural democracy, acknowledged in a footnote as cultural pluralism. While such a theory welcomed cultural differences and was suspicious of an assimilation agenda, it still acknowledged, "Cultural diversity—if adequately understood and practiced—does not negate the central unity that each society must have to function as a whole."[26] But what that "central unity" was remained unclear.

Sensitivity to cultural pluralism remained evident in the area of language. Protestant home missionaries often incorporated foreign languages into their mission work, just as missionaries overseas accommodated local cultures linguistically. Presbyterians aired a radio program for Spanish speakers in New York City called "Cantares de Mi Tierra," and Texas Baptists did something similar. Donato Ruiz, a minister in central Texas, noted the potential use of the airwaves: "Radio has been the best means to overcome obstacles no other instrument could. . . . The master and secret key to open the doors of every home and family in all the San Angelo area is surely the use of radio."[27] One SBC report reprimanded Baptists who allowed language to be a barrier. "We deal with these people in all the other realms of life in spite of the handicaps of differences of language and customs. It is unbelievable that we should continue to put these forward as excuses for neglect in the realm of religion when two million souls are involved."[28] An NCC study even advocated a bilingual approach: "Among Anglos, cultural reciprocity is limited without bilingual exchange and the old pattern of cultural influence (i.e., a one-directional flow toward Anglo ways) rather than cultural interflow continues to predominate."[29] In the end, evangelization and ministry often trumped any aversion to using Spanish rather than English. When English was stressed, it was usually for more pragmatic purposes, such as equipping immigrants to attain jobs; nevertheless, underlying this position was still a latent understanding that English was a staple of being American.[30]

Anglo and Mexican American Protestant collaboration was on full display in 1960, when the Mexican Baptist Convention of Texas joined the Baptist General Convention of Texas (BGCT). The Mexican Convention, independent since 1910, voted to join the BGCT in 1960, with the stipulation that a three-year trial period be implemented. The messengers sent to the Mexican Baptist Convention by their respective churches voted 70 to 17 to join the BGCT. Once united, the Mexican Convention retained a fair amount of autonomy as it continued to meet annually as a department under the BGCT.[31] Martha Ellis, director of the Woman's Missionary Union Language Missions of the BGCT, declared in 1961 that there was "now one Texas Baptist Convention and one Woman's Missionary Union of Texas composed of English speaking and Spanish speaking organizations."[32] While such a union almost certainly entailed some accommodation of Anglo Baptist ways for Mexican Baptists in Texas and Anglo paternalistic oversight, the merger also remarkably allowed a certain amount of agency for Mexican Americans. Later, Ricardo Peña, president of the Mexican Baptist body between 1980 and 1981, commented, "Whatever anyone may say, the truth is that we have enjoyed freedom in planning and developing our programs, supported by ample budgets which before merger we lacked."[33]

Home mission programs also interpreted race in a fluid manner. The 1959 NCC study of missions to Spanish speakers consulted the work of current social theorists who acknowledged the social construction of racial prejudice and that racial categories changed over time.[34] In many cases Protestant home missionaries conflated race, ethnicity, and nationality.[35] A meeting of the NCC's Committee on Spanish American Work demonstrated this. Referring to a recent study of churches and race relations, Paul Warnshuis "indicated he was concerned because the proposed research program seemed to be thinking exclusively in terms of Negroes, whereas there are the very same problems involving cultural groups. The hope was expressed that if such a project were carried out it might be on a broader basis, to include racial, cultural and ethnic groups."[36] Such a loose interpretation of race is also evident in a Southern Baptist pamphlet describing mission center work in New Orleans. Titled "Is It Jus'

For Whites?," the pamphlet recounted the ruminations of a missionary who led work in the area. The missionary described various scenarios where a lack of ministry to the local African American community stood in stark contrast to the work being done for "eighteen nationalities, ranging from very white to almost black, yet none were Negro."[37]

Out of this very broad and inconsistent treatment of race was a progressive bent. As the civil rights movement advanced, denominational leaders began to push for integration and justice for ethnic and national groups, alongside African Americans, as a way to combat America's racial sins. A midcentury Methodist program establishing work projects for young adults along the Rio Grande noted, "Among the campers were Latin Americans, Anglo-Americans, and Negroes." Such an endeavor was reported as an interracial success. Some Southern Baptists tied to home missions, as historian Alan Scot Willis has demonstrated, also advanced the argument that racial divisions were social constructs; instead, all people were united in a common need for salvation in Christ. But even in their attempt to combat racism, Willis demonstrates that Southern Baptists largely overlooked the cultural paternalism inherent in their mission programs.[38] Mainline Protestant concern over racial prejudice also reinforced increasing acceptance of Catholics and Jews. Racial injustice came in many forms and was closely related to religious bigotry. In her 1952 booklet of worship programs for Protestant women that promoted the theme of "Righteousness Exalts a Nation," Georgia Harkness listed multiple examples from history and several ideals that help define "What is America?" For one of her answers to that question, Harkness referenced a 1939 concert in Washington, DC, that now serves as a milestone in the civil rights movement. America, according to Harkness, "is Marian Anderson, a great Negro Protestant artist, singing the Roman Catholic aria 'Ave Maria' in praise of Jesus' Jewish mother beside the Lincoln Memorial in the nation's capitol."[39]

Protestant home missionaries promoted a moderate form of cultural pluralism in their work among immigrant communities and consequently separated themselves from the hard-lined Americanization program that had defined earlier efforts. This did not mean, however, that immigrant ministries were divorced from national causes. As the Cold War heightened American fears during the 1950s of a godless Soviet Russia, many Americans believed it was important to maintain America as a Christian nation. The phrase "one nation under God" was inserted into the Pledge of Allegiance in 1954, and "In God We Trust" was made the national motto in 1956. Some Protestants reached the conclusion that the nation's destiny was closely tied to evangelization and domestic ministry. For white Protestants, the stakes were high; immigrants and ethnic Americans must be given the gospel.

A 1952 article describing Presbyterian work reinforced this perspective in its title, "Because We Are . . . 'A City Set on a Hill': National Missions Seeks to Make America a Light to the World," a clear nod to the nation's supposed religious destiny inherited from the Puritans. The article sounded a clarion call for Presbyterians to save America through home missions. For the writer of this article, America's ethnic diversity reflected "thousands upon thousands from every corner of our land, speaking many dialects, unable to understand each other, puzzled, baffled, and often outraged by their neighbors, being brought together in brotherhood as children of one loving Father."[40] For many Protestants, home mission programs were the key to maintaining a Christian nation; once people converted to Protestant Christianity, the nation would affirm its religious identity.

Protestants' desire to make America a stronghold for Christianity encouraged them in part to consider the correlation between evangelism and religious nationalism. White Christians took up the task of evangelization and hoped that redeemed souls, regardless of ethnicity, would make America Christian. A 1949 Southern Baptist report on work among Latinos concluded, "If we are ever to have a Christian America from the political standpoint, in the Southwest at least, it is imperative that the Spanish-speaking voting populace be evangelized."[41] In his foreword to a report on the prospects of ministry among braceros, Dallas P. Lee, head of the BGCT's Language Missions Department, commented, "God has brought a mission field to Christian America."[42] Even ethnic Protestants sometimes affirmed this logic. A 1950 Methodist report for the California Oriental Provisional Conference noted, "The Methodist Church is in a strategic position to serve these Oriental people in the United States and preach Christ to them that our racial communities may not be pagan groups in the midst of Christian America."[43] Ministering to minority groups was contributing to America's progress, in the minds of many Protestants.

By the 1950s, American society was beginning to expand upon the notion of the United States being a Christian nation, coming to the conclusion that America was instead a Judeo-Christian country in which Protestants, Catholics, and Jews were learning to live peaceably together. The most famous interpretation of this phenomenon was sociologist Will Herberg's groundbreaking book *Protestant, Catholic, Jew* published in 1955, in which he claimed that by midcentury, to be American was to identify as either a Protestant, Catholic, or Jew. Herberg argued that these three faiths represented a "triple melting pot" (a term he credited to Ruby Jo Kennedy) whereby third-generation immigrants hoped to retain a semblance of their ethnic religious heritage while also accepting the "American Way of Life" and democratic principles these three faiths espoused. For Herberg, even as ethnic groups tried to maintain their religious roots, they were only assimilating further within the confines of American culture. Accordingly, Protestants found it necessary to extend democracy and tolerance to Jewish and Catholic immigrants.[44] By all appearances, the 1960 election of John F. Kennedy suggested this was true, and during his campaign, Kennedy reassured Protestants that his Catholic faith posed no threat to America religious freedom. Historian Kevin Schultz traces these interpretations of a "Tri-Faith" America during the twentieth century and suggests Jewish and Catholic interests, with the help of liberal Protestant luminaries, worked to usher in a form of pluralism that granted equal treatment to all three religions in American society.[45]

Despite these gains in pluralism among Protestants, Catholics, and Jews, mainline Protestants at the denominational level still worked to maintain a Christian nation with a more Protestant coloring. Herberg argued this amounted to a "syncretistic culture-religion in which the historical Christian faith and the cult of the American Way have been merged into a new kind of American religiosity, which has been taken over by the non-Protestant groups to the degree that they have become American."[46] While progressive leaders within the NCC worked comfortably with their Catholic and Jewish counterparts, at the lower reaches of the church, religious pluralism was not as celebrated. Most notably, anti-Catholicism persisted within home mission programs directed toward immigrants. A 1962 report sponsored by Texas Baptists assessing ministry opportunities among Mexican bracero workers suggested, "God has given Evangelicals an opportunity to strike at the very heart of Roman Catholic power in Mexico! It has been almost impossible for missionaries to penetrate this citadel, but now its men in great numbers have come to our very doors." In a sense, Baptists believed they were fighting a veritable war with Catholicism. The report also echoed timeless Protestant interpretations of Roman Catholic faith. The study claimed that braceros's "faith and reliance is in the forms, ceremonies, rites and idols of a Cristo-pagan Roman Catholicism." In addition, "The Roman Catholic Church in Mexico and the United States has launched a campaign to bring politicians and legislature, and the United States government to their aid."[47] The report on bracero ministries, though coming two years after Kennedy's election, reveals Southern Baptists still held on to deep reservations concerning Catholicism. Speaking before the SBC in 1961, E. S. James, the editor of the *Baptist Standard*, even suggested that Catholicism threatened the separation of church and state through "controlled immigration and uncontrolled multiplication."[48] Concern for building structures also reflected Baptist competition with Catholics. One request for a hospital in San Antonio compared Catholic and Baptist structures in the city. "There is no Baptist institution in San Antonio except a recently-organized Mexican Orphanage which is caring for fewer than 25 children. Catholics have two orphanages, one seminary, one university, two colleges for women, and 51 kindergartens, grammar and high schools; and the largest hospital in the city."[49] While Baptists ultimately labored for the spiritual transformation of souls, even the condition of buildings did not go unnoticed in their efforts to best Catholics.

Concerns over Catholicism's religious and political influence, however, were not limited to more conservative groups like Southern Baptists. Besides public intellectuals who still occasionally criticized the Catholic Church, some mainline Protestants were also wary.[50] An article in *Presbyterian Life* in 1952 criticized Catholicism's legacy in New Mexico and suggested that Protestants were helping improve the region. The following month, the periodical published the response of a concerned priest from Wisconsin, before printing a rebuttal to the priest's comments a month and a half later.[51] Moreover, the 1950s witnessed significant Puerto Rican migration to the US mainland, and a Presbyterian report questioned the influence of Roman Catholicism among

Puerto Ricans.[52] Congregationalists active in home missions drew from earlier themes of assimilation and reticence toward Roman Catholicism, recognizing that the "place of the Protestant church is to care for those who drift away from the Roman church which results from their 'americanization.'"[53] For some Protestants, old habits died hard, and religious pluralism was not a certainty among many white Protestants, despite the advances of Judeo-Christian ideals at midcentury.

As Protestants worked to maintain a religious identity for the nation, they also were aware of America's global position following World War II. Often Protestants stressed the symbiotic relationship between home and foreign missions. In 1953 the Episcopal Diocese of California noted its ability to train foreign missionaries before they are sent to China, Japan, and the Philippines because of the local Asian population and opportunities at the University of California and regional missionary centers.[54] Sometimes Protestants hoped that Mexican immigrants, particularly bracero migrants, would take the seeds of their faith and plant them back in Mexico if ever they returned.[55] Many Protestants were convinced that racism and prejudice were hurting America's global image and that their treatment of minorities would hinder or help their work overseas. American Protestants also believed they were contributing to America's role in the Cold War. When describing the need for further Methodist work among migrant Mexican families often without food, one home mission superintendent noted, "Yet there are some who are thinking that agitation for relief of the condition is communism. Actually this is the type of situation where communism has a chance to get its roots down. When our Mexican neighbors find the spirit of Christ in our hearts, as we labor to alleviate their suffering, then communism will have no appeal."[56] The crusade against communism for many Protestants was won on both foreign and domestic battlegrounds.

The World Council of Churches demonstrated this confluence of domestic and global initiatives in 1954 as it met on the campus of Northwestern University in Evanston, Illinois. Speaking before those in attendance, President Dwight D. Eisenhower touched on numerous themes pertaining to America's position in the world, noting that the "conference, representing forty-eight nations and 163 groups, spiritually brings the world to the center of the North American Continent." Stressing the international import of the gathering, Eisenhower recited

John Wesley's famous quip, "The world is my parish." Eisenhower also explicated America's global responsibilities following the devastation of World War II and the challenges of the Cold War: "To preserve the individual freedoms we prize so highly, we must not only protect ourselves as a nation, but we must make certain that others with like devotion to liberty may also survive and prosper."[57]

Eisenhower also alluded to America's immigrant and pluralist heritage. He assured the crowd, "Moreover, we are a nation of many people out of many lands. . . . With our diversity, if you could look at us from afar, we would be theoretically impossible. But we do exist, and in reasonable harmony." Later in his speech Eisenhower recognized the growing phenomenon of religious pluralism in America: "A score of religious faiths, large and small, are represented in the membership of our present Congress."[58] A month earlier the *Saturday Evening Post* featured an article on the approaching meeting and briefly addressed the Council's relationship to religious pluralism. The *Post* suggested the postwar refugee crisis would be an important topic at the meeting in Evanston, and it optimistically concluded, "Whether the refugees were Protestant, Catholic, Jewish, Moslem or Buddhist, white, black or bronze, enemy or friend, made no difference."[59] For many observers, mainline Protestants had achieved a level of liberal ecumenism that was extended to other faiths, an orientation that resonated with the current Cold War context, international cooperation, and humanitarian relief.

Refugees

Protestant work conducted domestically among immigrants often reflected more global concerns. This was made manifest following World War II and during the Cold War when people displaced by warfare and revolution looked to come to America. With increasing support for the United Nations and human rights, alongside racial concerns reinforced by the horrors of Nazi Germany and the burgeoning civil rights movement, mainline Protestants during the 1950s were eager to welcome refugees, otherwise known as DPs, with humanitarian aid and opportunities to resettle elsewhere.

Church World Service (CWS), an organizational branch of the NCC, coordinated most mainline Protestant work, helping refugees through humanitarian relief overseas and assisting some refugees, mostly Europeans, to resettle in America. Between 1945 and 1960, CWS sponsored 112,703 refugees and facilitated their resettlement in the United States.[60] It garnered the support of many mainline denominations and even received assistance from the Assemblies of God and the Relief Committee of the SBC. In their appeal for support, CWS tapped into the Protestant historical consciousness, referring to displaced persons as "Delayed Pilgrims." CWS called on US Protestants to "wake up to the fact that *Christian conscience and self interest* alike urge immediate action. The DPs are our own blood-brothers in Christ. They need us. But we need them, too. Their skills, their devotion to democracy, won through hardship and suffering, their labor and their Christian leadership, are all assets we can use."[61]

The US government passed refugee legislation in 1948 and 1953, which allowed for the resettlement of 415,000 and 205,000 refugees respectively, and measures to aid Hungarian refugees starting in 1956.[62] Many Protestant groups closely watched what occurred in the halls of Congress and issued statements supporting measures to resettle refugees in America. Starting in 1946 the FCC indicated at its biennial meeting that it would back efforts by the Truman administration to resettle refugees, and the American Christian Committee for Refugees also turned its attention that same year to German refugees who identified as Protestant or were of no particular faith and were looking to resettle in America.[63] In 1952, the NCC articulated the context for needed immigration and refugee relief. "The plight of the world's uprooted peoples creates for the United States, as for other liberty-loving nations, a moral as well as an economic and political problem of vast proportions." The statement went on to outline the causes for the recent refugee crisis: "Among these peoples are those displaced by war, and its aftermath; the refugees made homeless by reason of Nazi, Fascist, and Communist tyranny and more recently, by military hostilities in Korea, the Middle East, and elsewhere; . . . and the escapees who every day break though the Iron Curtain in search of freedom."[64]

In addition to the NCC, other national and local Protestant groups committed themselves to refugee resettlement following World War II. Many Protestant denominations backed the Displaced Persons Act passed in 1948, which was designed to resettle 205,000 DPs in the United States by 1950, though overlooking aspects of the law that placed Jewish and Catholic refugees at a disadvantage.[65] The Methodist General Conference supported this legislation and "[called] upon our churches in local communities to welcome displaced persons and to aid in their adjustment to life in the United States."[66] The PCUSA pledged to resettle 3,000 refugees under the 1948 Displaced Persons Act, and its more southern counterpart, the Presbyterian Church in the United States, also backed the government's decision to move DPs to America as long as they were "carefully screened."[67] The New York Episcopal Diocese resolved, after some debate, to support refugee relief for the "flight of hundreds of thousands of freedom-loving people from Communist oppression."[68] Even the SBC, though outside the ecumenical National Council, passed a resolution in 1947 supporting government policy to admit refugees, noting the "persecution or fear of persecution by reason of their race, religion, or political beliefs, and desire above all else to start a new life in a nation where there is freedom of speech, freedom of worship, and freedom of movement."[69]

The Protestant Council of Church Women in New York City established the Protestant Hospitality Center near a dock where refugees entered. As of 1949, one report noted that recent refugees being ministered to had arrived speaking German, Latvian, Estonian, Polish, Ukrainian, and Russian. These refugees had fled unspeakable horrors in Europe during the war, and they left a lasting impression on Protestant aid workers. One Estonian woman shared her experiences as a forced laborer under Nazi rule who helped saw lumber in German forests. The disparity between Americans and recent refugees to New York City struck Protestant workers. After a seemingly innocent bus trip down Fifth Avenue, volunteers noted, "The most vivid of the [refugees'] many new impressions were the abundance of chocolates on display in candy stores, the supply of soap to be seen in the 5¢ and 10¢ store windows, and the numbers of dogs on leashes wearing sweaters, a thing almost unbelievable to one young Latvian lass who had been lamenting the loss of her only well-worn sweater!"[70]

Protestant commitment to refugee relief was put to the test by the end of 1952, however, with the termination of the Displaced Persons Act nearing. Protestant leaders soon began to appeal for further refugee resettlement.[71] As Director of Immigration Services for CWS, Roland Elliot at the start of 1953 commented on the urgency of the moment and the opportunity to rectify past restriction, which he believed was "dangerously akin to the theories of a superior race." Elliot cautioned, "The Church's voice—or its silence—may well be determinative in deciding the destiny of the refugees, and of America."[72]

Thereafter, Protestants were at the forefront of an effort in 1953 to call for further refugee resettlement. The NCC repeatedly sent memos to its constituents keeping them abreast of policy developments. Besides writing to the president and members of Congress, attempts were also made to meet with such policymakers. In March 1953, delegates representing the Jewish National Community Relations Council, Catholic Welfare Conference, and NCC scheduled time with Senator Robert A. Taft, and National Council leaders—alongside representatives of the National Lutheran Council—even met with President Dwight Eisenhower at the beginning of May.[73] By that time, Eisenhower was already pushing for further refugee relief. The General Secretary of the NCC telegrammed Eisenhower the NCC's support, concluding, "Your action in this matter is in accord with the American tradition of concern for the oppressed and will be welcomed by many of our churches for humanitarian reasons."[74]

In the weeks that followed, as Congress considered refugee policy, Walter Van Kirk, a NCC departmental executive director, spoke before the Senate Sub-Committee on Immigration concerning refugee relief. He declared, "By admitting its fair share of these homeless and destitute persons the United States would stand before the world as the deliverer of the oppressed and the defender of those who, at the risk of their lives, have sought release from the bondage of Communist oppression." Van Kirk reminded the Sub-Committee, "Accordingly, by helping the refugees we help ourselves. By defending the right of the refugees to life and liberty we earn for ourselves the respect of the freedom loving nations of the earth."[75] By the end of 1953, Protestant leaders got their wish in the form of the Refugee Relief Act of 1953. Through the work of Congressman Walter Judd, the act even made allowances for Asian refugees.[76] In a statement in September 1953 reflecting on this legislative victory, the NCC declared, "Therefore, we express our gratitude to God, for this new occasion to demonstrate the reality of Christian brotherhood in the world."[77]

New refugee crises soon developed after Congress passed the Refugee Relief Act of 1953, only heightening the need for refugee resettlement in the United States. The 1956 Hungarian revolution against Soviet intrusion produced more refugees displaced by political upheaval, and mainline Protestants responded by supporting Eisenhower's decision to provide special relief and by calling for more sponsors. CWS joined various other relief agencies in fostering resettlement, with Executive Director R. Norris Wilson serving on Eisenhower's President's Committee for Hungarian Refugee Relief.[78] In December 1956, following Eisenhower's decision to admit several thousand Hungarian refugees into the United States, the National Council applauded his efforts, and took the opportunity to declare that additional legislation was needed. The statement noted the benefits of further refugee assistance: "performance of Christian service," "national interest," and "better international relations."[79] Though they applauded government efforts to resettle displaced Hungarian refugees in 1956 and 1957, the NCC criticized the parole system the government used to admit many people fleeing Hungary, a policy they believed put Hungarian refugees at a disadvantage once in America since it was a temporary status that did not guarantee permanent residency.[80]

Then in 1959, another refugee crisis occurred, this time in the Western Hemisphere, as Fidel Castro's communist revolution triumphed in Cuba. With just over a decade of experience in refugee work, CWS and most of the major Protestant denominations provided assistance, along with the NCC's Department of Home Missions and Department of Social Welfare. Just between 1961 and 1962, CWS helped resettle more than 8,000 Cuban refugees. To transport refugees into the interior of the United States, CWS sponsored a series of charter flights known as "Flights in Freedom." In Miami, Protestant denominations even organized a Protestant Latin American Emergency Committee, a group that included not only relief centers of mainline denominations, but also those of Southern Baptists, Assemblies of God, Plymouth Brethren, and Seventh Day Adventists. According to one estimate, 5,000–7,000 Cuban refugees were receiving aid in any given month within the Protestant centers. Reflecting its concern for both spiritual and material needs, the UPCUSA assisted Cuban refugees in Miami through the work of the First Spanish Church and the United Presbyterian Center.[81] In 1963,

Southern Baptists allocated $50,000 for Latin American refugee resettlement, and the denomination helped relocate 270 Cubans in 1964.[82]

Protestant denominations orchestrated a veritable media blitz to promote the cause of refugee resettlement. *Christian Century* ran numerous articles, and denominations and agencies produced pamphlets and memoranda en masse.[83] One CWS pamphlet appealed to its Protestant constituents: "A hundred thousand of these people look to our Protestant and Eastern Orthodox Churches in America as their only hope. Roman Catholics, Jews, care for their own. But *our people* may come only when we say, '*here is an assurance*.'" The pamphlet continued, "Today they are Refugees—uprooted—homeless—despairing. Tomorrow they may be your friends, your neighbors, bringing new life and resources to America—even as our ancestors did before us."[84] Another pamphlet, aptly titled *The Fence*, criticized the McCarran-Walter Act and pointed out shortcomings in US refugee policy. Promoted by multiple Protestant, Jewish, and even labor organizations, *The Fence* sold 85,000 copies by 1959.[85] In a pamphlet published in 1950, the Christian Friendliness program announced its agenda. For displaced persons, the pamphlet noted that American Baptist workers must provide "assistance with English and citizenship requirements, aid in social adjustments, guidance in spiritual matters and church relationships, and sympathetic understanding when the New Americans encounter problems." The pamphlet continued, "Successful resettlement is a long range process which has full integration into American life as its ultimate objective," and it furthermore directed workers to help refugees without visas. Evangelical aspirations were also included with these more social objectives. Christian Friendliness leadership reminded fellow Baptists, "Our churches must be prepared not only to win converts from these groups, but also to hold them for the Kingdom's enterprise."[86] Much like their work with immigrants, Protestants during the 1950s aimed to include spiritual ministry alongside humanitarian aid.

In addition to creating pamphlets, denominations also produced book-length studies and other forms of media. American Baptists published a book in 1962 on their refugee efforts around the world, including resettlement work in the United States.[87] The Methodist Church devoted a radio segment to "What Can I Do to Help Cuban Refugees?" on its Night Call show. During the program, the announcer interviewed

Figure 4.2. Poster encouraging Baptist churchgoers to sponsor refugees under the Refugee Relief Act of 1953. Courtesy of the American Baptist Historical Society, Atlanta, GA.

the CWS worker in Miami, who then fielded questions from listeners who called into the station.[88] The United Council of Church Women even produced a drama for local churches titled *This Citadel of Faith*.[89] Finally, to help equip sponsors to consider the social significance of their work, in 1960 CWS printed a manual on the "integration" of refugees. In its treatment of integration, as opposed to assimilation, the book embraced a form of cultural pluralism whereby the "newcomer needs to learn the validity and value of American ways without giving up his own identity." The book concluded, "It is with the realization of the Brotherhood of Man that differences are accepted; and with the realization of the Fatherhood of God that they are creatively resolved."[90] Through their refugee work, US Protestants were formulating a subtle interpretation of pluralism that drew from earlier social gospel ideals. Protestants eager to help refugees welcomed immigrant cultures while remaining confident that the nation's Protestant identity remained intact.

The sponsorship of DPs even became a theme for film. Methodists produced the short film *The Tourist* (mentioned previously), and Presbyterians invested in a full-length project. In the movie *More for Peace* released in 1952 and backed by the PCUSA and several other denominations, a soldier named Bill Grayson, played by Peter Graves (most famous for his later roles in the *Mission Impossible* television series and movie *Airplane*), returns to his Midwestern hometown after serving in the Korean War. Upon his arrival, he notices the community has sponsored a DP family. With limited employment opportunities, the DP family pursues a job that Bill had hoped to procure. Eventually, Bill assists a local carpenter in crafting a cross from wood taken from Hiroshima after the atomic bomb. The carpenter explains his desire to "take a part of a tree killed by man's hatred and make it into a living symbol of God's love." While helping with the project, Bill comes to recognize his prejudice and then tries to help the DP family, eventually allowing the DP family to have the job he earlier desired. Overall, the film emphasized the themes of global military conflict and individual Christian responsibility and aimed to highlight the "role of the church on the community level." The PCUSA intended for the film to be shown in Presbyterian churches and saw this as an opportunity to cooperate with Hollywood.[91]

Multiple accounts survive of positive resettlement experiences in local communities beyond the fictional ones just described, often

STRANGERS IN MAYBERRY | 143

through the sponsorship of individual church congregations. A report from Fairmount Presbyterian Church in Cleveland Heights, Ohio, described its work in resettling 60 DPs coming from Ukraine, Bulgaria, Poland, Germany, Czechoslovakia, Latvia, and Hungary. The glowing report stressed the work ethic of the refugees and their ability to attain housing and employment, and gradually other modern conveniences. The report concluded, "To see the friendships develop between the New and the Old Americans, to see the feeling of goodwill and understanding evolve from this project, is to see Democracy at its best and Christianity at its most meaningful."[92] The First Presbyterian Church of Berkeley, California, sponsored at least 11 families during the 1950s, and concluded, "We consider this an important way to express our Christian and humanitarian concern for all freedom-seeking people." The Berkeley church also supported the government admitting more refugees.[93] Langdale Methodist Church in Alabama sponsored a family in 1960, and apparently this caused a local sensation; television, newspaper, and radio journalists joined the church members as the family arrived. Church members bought the husband a suit and the wife dresses, and a schoolteacher taught English to the family in the evenings. The church reported, "The whole community has responded most graciously to them. . . . Our problem right now is how to keep our people from smothering them with too much attention."[94] A 1960 *New York Times* article featured the success of a Methodist church in Cranford, New Jersey, that aided the resettlement of 29 refugees during the 1950s.[95] The president of Kansas State Teachers College, John E. King, who also served on the Presbyterian Board of National Missions, helped enroll 25 Cubans in his school.[96] And refugee resettlement was not limited to the continental United States; St. Mark's Episcopal Church in Hawaii sponsored a Cuban lawyer.[97] American Baptists even appointed former Latvian refugees Tabea Korjus and Adolph Klaupiks to assist resettlement work for the denomination.[98]

In Newton, Massachusetts, the Central Congregational Church sponsored multiple postwar refugee families. In the case of the Latvian Dreimanis family, the church posted a $1,000 bond since Teodors Dreimanis, the family's father who had formerly been a civil engineer, had his leg amputated while serving in the military and would have been considered a "likely public charge." Central Congregational members also sponsored two other families, which included locating housing and furnishing appliances and furniture for the families. The church helped secure jobs for two of the refugee men with the New England Power Service Company. Nearly three decades later, church members reconnected with these former refugees still living in the United States, while the church was considering sponsoring refugees of another overseas crisis, the Vietnam War. Looking back on the assistance his family received, Dreimanis communicated his "most sincere thanks to every member" of the church in helping them settle in a "new world of freedom." As one historian who attended the church noted in 1975, "Thus there is precedent and experience from the past which may be relevant for the present—and future."[99]

Mainline Protestant leaders, however, did encounter some concerns among their constituencies when it came to refugee resettlement. A listener from Denver called into the Methodist radio show asking about the utility of accepting Cuban refugees in 1965, and another caller was adamant that communist refugees would not be tolerated, since Americans were in the middle of "fighting for the security of our country."[100] In 1953, the Episcopal Diocese of New York voted to pass a resolution calling for immigration reform and refugee resettlement, but not before "much discussion, pro and con."[101] One Methodist minister from Pennsylvania wrote Gaither P. Warfield, General Secretary of the Methodist Committee for Overseas Relief, asking about qualifications for people who wished to seek refuge in America. He pointed out that his church sponsored a family he believed was already economically self-sufficient back in West Germany. Warfield responded by noting that some refugees' needs, rather than being primarily economic, were psychological. He assured the minister that the denomination was not "in the immigration business," but rather facilitated the resettlement of refugees who had not "integrated" within their former society. Warfield recounted a refugee family he knew who was financially secure in West Germany but who could not find peace living so close to Soviet power.[102]

Denominational leaders also had to contend with the racial and economic concerns of 1950s America. Methodist leaders considered the climate of race relations in various regions of the United States during the early years of the civil rights movement. When it came to resettling

Dutch Indonesian refugees, often considered racially mixed, Methodist workers believed such work should be done in the Southwest and Northwest because of "climate and certain racial limitations" elsewhere in the country.[103] The Congregational First Church of Newton sought in 1960 to sponsor a family of mixed Dutch and Indonesian heritage, but demonstrated concern over whether they would be able to find lodging "in a neighborhood friendly to a family of mixed race . . . where little brown children will be very welcome."[104] Evident in *The Tourist* and *More for Peace*, Protestants also had to respond to economic concerns and Congressional demands that refugees have job assurances. Protestant leaders understood the economic and cultural concerns of policymakers but were also working from a vantage point that infused spiritual, humanitarian ideals. One NCC memo in 1954 concluded that instead of advocating for further changes to the Refugee Relief Act, Protestants could instead "use the very difficulties of this program as a challenge to prove that we are more interested in helping people than simply in filling jobs."[105]

In the decade and a half following World War II, Protestants in America were forced to come to terms with pluralism as they worked with refugees. Their work highlighted the aspirations and limitations of Protestant interpretations of pluralism. National Council leadership often worked alongside their counterparts in the Jewish National Community Relations Council and Catholic Welfare Conference. Some Protestant leaders were even concerned about the sectarian divisions in refugee relief.[106] During the Cuban refugee crisis, after CWS fulfilled most Protestant Cuban needs, it lent a helping hand to Catholic Relief Services. CWS leadership guaranteed that its Protestant assistance would respect refugees' Catholic faith.[107] In a Cuban Refugee Center newsletter, produced under the auspices of the federal government, an anecdote demonstrates the popular hope for tri-faith cooperation: "A protestant family is helping a Cuban family of the Catholic faith buy a house. Members of a Methodist church are furnishing it. A man of the Hebrew faith, handling the sale, joined the spirit of cooperation by buying the refugees a lawn mower."[108]

While some mainline Protestant figures intended to promote refugee relief programs that were nonsectarian, other Protestants were more conscious of religious differences in resettlement work. Occasionally comparisons were made with Jewish and Catholic agencies in order to spur Protestants to sponsor more refugees. The New York Episcopal Diocese recognized in 1949, "The Roman Catholic and Jewish groups are making valiant and effective efforts for their people. So far the non-Roman churches have been slow to accept their responsibility, in spite of the fact that 20% of all the Displaced Persons are non-Roman Christians—many of them Eastern Orthodox, who look naturally to the Episcopal Church for aid."[109] In 1952 some Protestants criticized Congressional legislation, known as the Celler bill, that aimed to link refugee relief to the needs of overpopulated regions, especially in Italy; Protestant leaders considered this proposal a Catholic initiative. As one article in the *Christian Century* surmised, "Without doubt, Roman Catholics see in it an opportunity to increase their religious and political power in the United States."[110]

While Protestant interpretations of Catholic and Jewish refugee relief were varied at best, Protestant groups still sponsored refugees of multiple faiths. CWS denied that "the religious affiliation of refugees was a criterion used to foster or prevent resettlement assistance." During the four-year tenure of the Refugee Relief Act of 1953, the statistics of the Episcopal, Methodist, Congregational, and Disciples denominations show that they resettled 382 Muslims, 19 Buddhists, a Sikh, along with 1,222 Roman Catholics and 13 Jews. Overall, these numbers pale in comparison to the 7,476 Protestant refugees these denominations sponsored, but it also suggests that small measures of religious pluralism did not concern Protestants.[111] *Christian Century* even noted an instance where Buddhist refugees in New Jersey donated money to CWS to assist refugees in Tibet, supposedly out of gratitude for the assistance they had previously received from Protestants.[112]

This apparent comfort with religious pluralism can be explained in part by the more universal, humanitarian ethic of Protestant relief efforts during the twentieth century. The tidal wave of support among mainline Protestant leaders for the United Nations, human rights, and international brotherhood encouraged this openness to pluralism. One Methodist booklet observed, "Many American boys and girls have had wonderful firsthand experiences in thinking in terms of world citizenship as they have had the chance to know the displaced persons who have come to their towns."[113] The perception that America stood as a safe "haven" amidst global turmoil only encouraged these international perspectives. One NCC leader remarked that "the tradition of America as the haven of the oppressed is a matter of deep concern to American Protestantism."[114] A 1957 NCC resolution even concluded by recognizing "our nation's character and its sense of world responsibility."[115] This confluence of internationalism and pluralism among liberal Protestants earlier in the century, traced by historian David Mislin, helped establish an amenable context for refugee resettlement.[116]

But it also reflects a particular interpretation of pluralism. Protestant efforts to work among refugees and immigrants during the twentieth century anticipated cultural pluralism, but not widespread religious pluralism. By the 1950s, mainline Protestant leaders generally praised the diverse cultural heritage of America. Historian Robert L. Fleegler traces the development of the concept he calls "contributionism" in American culture during the twentieth century. For Fleeger, contributionism reflected the increasingly popular interpretation that America's national identity was largely tied to past immigrants, especially European immigration from the late nineteenth and early twentieth centuries.[117] Such thinking is evident in a CWS piece: "Distinctive contributions would primarily stem from the preservation of the newcomer's identity. Such preservation of identity, elastically applied, builds up a creative tension between the old and the new, which makes the newcomer's contribution all the more significant."[118] This attention to cultural pluralism and the contributions of immigrants, however, led to a more ambivalent concern for religious pluralism.

This ambivalence is evident in a Methodist pamphlet on refugee work. The booklet stressed the importance of cultural pluralism, stating that the "American concept of integration is not that of assimilation—remoulding the newcomer in everything from clothes to ideology." Yet later the pamphlet noted that some refugees, "without changing their original religion or church affiliations, are attending Methodist services. . . . Orthodox, Moslem, Roman Catholics, and people without religion—many hundreds of them have been given an opportunity to see how we worship and live."[119] While refugees outside of Protestantism were welcome, it is implicit that their attendance at Methodist services was a denominational success. This ambivalence is further illustrated in a Presbyterian periodical published in 1957 on "social progress." The program acknowledged America's "melting pot" tradition, with the aside that "[t]his cultural pluralism is not without its problems." The text then briefly assented to a limited view of religious pluralism by pointing out the prominence of Protestants, Catholics, and Jews. It then suggested, "Yet one of our greatest assets is this very cultural and religious diversity. As the United States continues to consolidate its national life, one of the basic issues will be the proper relation of the whole to its parts and the parts to the whole."[120] Maintaining the "whole" while welcoming diversity would continue to puzzle Protestants for years to come, especially as more immigrants entered America practicing religions other than Protestantism, Catholicism, and Judaism.

The apogee of postwar refugee concern came between July 1959 and June 1960 during what the UN recognized as World Refugee Year. The event, and its American organizer the US Committee for Refugees, received abundant support from mainline Protestant groups. The NCC and denominations used the occasion to call for legislation that would admit more refugees and reform immigration policy. The work of Francis B. Sayre, Jr. is telling. As Dean of the National Cathedral and grandson of Woodrow Wilson, he served from a platform of white Protestant stature, and as chairman of the board of directors for the US Committee for Refugees, Sayre was active in the work of World Refugee Year, even penning "A Litany for Refugees." By 1960, Protestants were convinced that the United States stood for freedom in a world threatened by communism, and as cultural gatekeepers, they had become more accommodating to immigrants and refugees bringing their cultural differences. With their support for World Refugee Year and diligence to refugee resettlement during the 1950s, it comes as no surprise that mainline Protestants would actively respond to further refugee needs as the twentieth century continued.[121]

Conclusion

During the decade and a half following World War II, native, white Protestants representing the religious establishment in American culture grappled with an increasingly diverse nation. This is evident in their home mission programs fostering understanding and comity between white Protestants and immigrant communities, while also maintaining a Protestant Christian vision for the nation's future. Protestant agencies demonstrated a similar outlook in their efforts to resettle refugees. The American Way of Life, for many Protestants, remained a strong indicator of what separated the United States from a world caught up in revolution, disorder, and terror. Often unwittingly, Protestants expected foreigners to assimilate to a national culture, while also promoting cultural pluralism and diversity.[122] Meanwhile, many Protestants were certain that the Judeo-Christian identity of the nation would remain intact.

While a few liberal Protestants by this time were moving away from such a designation, most of the rank and file still held out hope for a Protestant nation.[123] The Judeo-Christian orientation of the United States was non-negotiable for most Americans during the immediate years following World War II. By 1949, Soviet Russia had its own atomic bomb and China had fallen to communism. As the Cold War gained momentum during the late 1940s, many Americans began to believe that the very survival of western, Christian civilization was at stake. "Godless" communism had extended its reach throughout eastern Europe and into East Asia. For most Americans, the nation had no choice but to continue in its mission to nurture a Christian democracy that would win the day. And for many mainline Protestants, a strong home missions agenda was key to maintaining a Christian nation, while refugee resettlement was a means to counter communist advances in war-torn Europe.

One of the more lasting results of postwar Protestant home missions and refugee relief is the impetus they provided to reforming US immigration policy. Mainline Protestant criticism of the 1952 McCarran-Walter Act, believed to perpetuate a discriminatory immigration policy, was closely tied to concerns for refugees and the welfare of immigrants. A 1957 NCC statement declared that "the manifold problem of ministering to refugees is so integrally related to our basic Immigration Law."[124] Concerns for immigration reform would be met later in 1965 when Congress finally replaced the discriminatory system of quotas based on national origins that had been in place since 1924. An unintended consequence was that religious pluralism increased at a rapid pace in the years following 1965 and became a more established ideal within society, while the social prominence of mainline Protestants soon began to erode.

5

Paving the Way for Pluralism

The Statue of Liberty, standing at one of our important gate-
ways, symbolizes what immigration to America has meant to
the families of many of us and to the moral, spiritual, economic
and cultural growth of this nation, under God.
—Bishop Gerald H. Kennedy, "Statement Presented to the Committee on Platform and Resolutions of the Democratic Party"

By 1960 mainline Protestant leaders, and their constituents to a limited extent, demonstrated a growing tolerance for ethnic diversity and
concern for immigration reform. This increasingly benevolent attitude
toward the "foreigner" was largely the product of earlier home mission
work premised upon a combination of social gospel and cosmopolitan
ideals, evangelistic goals, and cultural superiority. As the twentieth century progressed, World War II, the civil rights movement, the Second
Red Scare, and other midcentury developments reinforced growing
Protestant support for pluralism in response to fascism, communism,
racism, and bigotry at large. The civil rights movement in particular
gave liberal Protestants who had been advocating immigration reform
for many years the extra push needed to get legislation passed. In short,
a gradual diffusion of earlier social gospel sentiments among church
members and increasing openness to ethnic, racial, and religious equality led mainline Protestants unwittingly to help cultivate conditions for
the acceleration of pluralism by the 1960s. At the same time, these Protestants held firmly to the notion of an American way of life. In no other
area was this more apparent than in their drive for legislative reform.

Legislating Pluralism

As the Cold War emerged during the late 1940s, home missions and
racial tolerance quickly became tools Protestants used to set apart

American democracy from foreign communism. This concern for foreign affairs, united with social gospel aspirations and missions work, led to a robust political activism and commentary. As mainline Protestants traversed the road of liberalism, they began to contemplate further the discrimination inherent in the quotas enforced in the 1924 immigration legislation. Since that time the US immigration policy was one of restriction based upon discriminatory quotas assigned to various nations, with the exception of Asian immigrants, who were excluded entirely. Many Protestant denominations affiliated with the NCC gradually recognized that the 1924 laws racially discriminated against not only Asians, but also southern and eastern Europeans and people from other regions of the world. For most Protestant denominational and ecumenical leaders, legislative reform was the answer.

Protestants had to be careful, however, when entering the legislative fray. Not only did liberal Protestant leaders have to account for their more conservative constituents who were less willing to promote a progressive political agenda, but they also had to acknowledge the American tradition of the separation of church and state. While their actions often contradicted this notion of separation between the two spheres, mainline Protestants were convinced they could address political issues that they believed had broad significance, just as long as they avoided lobbying specific legislation. By 1957, mainline Protestants acknowledged that churches could employ government funds to assist social work, as long as the funds were "not used for religious ministrations." Further, "they should take steps to prevent the promulgation of a particular faith or doctrine at public expense. Spiritual care for all must be made available and special arrangements for persons of other faiths should be made." As for government regulation of church social work: "The setting of such standards does not violate the principle of church-state separation as long as the standards apply equitably to all agencies," a principle that echoed the Supreme Court's position of neutrality in matters involving religion and First Amendment jurisprudence.[1] In many respects, maintaining this logic of the separation of church and state reinforced pluralism because aiming for impartiality in social work fostered a respect for diversity.

Other Protestants made a more humanitarian argument for legislative reform, claiming that they were not succumbing to partisan politics and legislative meddling when they were simply trying to help people in need. For Margaret Bender, a leader in the Methodist Women's Division, immigration was not a political issue, but rather a social problem affecting the well-being of individuals. Bender responded in 1961 to an angry church member in Louisiana who was concerned that the Methodist women's program was too political. Bender responded, employing a different interpretation of "political." She wrote, "To me, political matters are those in which political parties take sides. The need for the reform of the present immigration laws does not fall in this class. It has appeared on both party platforms in almost the same terms for the last two political elections. . . . It seems to me that this becomes more of [a] human matter than a political one."[2] For Bender, and others, they were only being political if they entered partisan debates over specific legislation.

Reflecting the principle of impartiality and growing acceptance of pluralism, Protestant leaders often joined other organizations outside the framework of Protestantism to promote immigration reform. As with refugee work, they often worked alongside Catholics and Jews through various cooperative endeavors.[3] Protestants also cooperated with nonreligious groups. For instance, Detroit Protestant, Jewish, and Catholic entities worked alongside civic organizations to sign a joint letter to their congressional representatives addressing immigration policy.[4] In Buffalo, a Committee for Immigration Legislation Policies was organized by the Buffalo Council of Churches, International Institute, National Catholic Welfare Conference, Jewish Community Service, Board of Community Relations, Labor Committee to Combat Intolerance, Anti-Defamation League, and Buffalo Council of Social Agencies.[5] NCC leaders even participated in the American Immigration and Citizenship Conference and spoke at the National Conference of Social Work in 1953 and 1954 on immigration matters.[6]

Moreover, many individual Protestants signed their names to various statements promoting immigration reform, safely bypassing any church-state concerns. The Committee for Equality in Naturalization was one such example. In 1951 it advocated reform that would overturn Asian exclusion and provide citizenship to Japanese. The roster for the Committee as of 1951 included not only a plethora of civic leaders, diplomats, college presidents, and civil rights leaders such as A. Philip Randolph and Eleanor Roosevelt, but also Christian public figures such as Harry

Emerson Fosdick, Reinhold Niebuhr, and others affiliated with various regional and national Protestant groups, along with Jewish and Catholic leaders.[7] In 1952 the *New York Times* published a statement criticizing immigration legislation that was signed by individuals affiliated with the Young Women's Christian Association, American Jewish Committee, Massachusetts Congregational Conference, Negro Labor Committee, labor and ethnic groups, American Veterans Committee, Cleveland Baptist Association, National Association for the Advancement of Colored People, and the Hebrew Immigrant Aid Society. Notable midcentury scholars such as Oscar Handlin, Arthur Schlesinger, Sr., and the theorist of cultural pluralism, Horace Kallen, also signed the document.[8] Some Protestants even ventured into more hostile waters. A. D. Willis boldly requested information from the NCC before he served on the Resolutions Committee at the National Society of the Sons of the American Revolution Convention in 1953. Referring to recently passed legislation that continued a restrictive immigration policy, he tersely noted, "Undoubtedly, the McCarran-Walter Act will be 'resoluted' upon—or maybe 'pronounced' is a better word."[9] He did not have high hopes that the SAR would critique the law as many NCC leaders were doing.

To reinforce their protest, Protestants repeatedly wrote legislators and courted various statesmen. By the early 1950s, Congress began working to revise US immigration policy, and at the center of this policymaking was a congressman from Pennsylvania named Francis E. Walter. Walter had served as representative of his state since 1933, and eventually established strong cold warrior credentials while serving on the House Un-American Activities Committee (HUAC). Though he was a moderate, if not conservative, voice in Congress at this time, Walter was still willing to listen to liberal, mainline Protestants. Over the next decade, Protestants developed an ambivalent relationship with Walter; they appreciated Walter's attention to immigration policy but were concerned about his restrictionist proclivities.

Confronting the McCarran-Walter Act

A window of opportunity was opened in 1951 and 1952 as Congress began to reconsider US immigration law, and Protestants saw this as their chance to promote a more progressive immigration policy and thus remedy earlier restriction. Amidst the flurry of legislative proposals, two rival camps formed within Congress. Senator Pat McCarran of Nevada and Congressman Walter proposed legislation that, while reintroducing Asian immigration, would maintain the national origins basis of immigration quotas and implement safeguards for deterring and deporting communists who entered the country. Immigrants with an Asian family heritage, even if born outside of an Asian nation, were forced to fall within an Asian national quota, thus making race a continued factor in restricting Asian immigration. Senators Herbert H. Lehman and Hubert Humphrey and Representative Emmanuel Celler, however, promoted a more liberal bill that would base the quota system on the 1950 US population, rather than 1920, and would identify Asian immigrants on the basis of where they were born.[10]

Beginning in 1951, while they were also busy working for refugee relief, Protestants recognized the legislative stirrings and believed an opportunity was at hand to advocate for immigration reform. Mainline Protestants began courting Walter and initially felt that his proposals would help alleviate previously burdensome immigration laws and overturn Asian exclusion.[11] One NCC information leaflet published in February 1952 even noted that Walter's recent position "appears to be preferred by the advocates of a more liberal immigration policy."[12] Soon thereafter, however, Protestants began to reconsider the bill Walter was co-sponsoring and recognized the more liberal option that Lehman, Humphrey, and Celler were working toward. NCC official Walter Van Kirk sent telegraphs to several members of Congress in March 1952, declaring that the "adoption of restrictive measures embodied in pending omnibus immigration bill would gravely imperil moral stature of United States and adversely affect America's leadership among free nations." Van Kirk suggested instead that the "quota system should be made more flexible for reasons of self-interest and for furtherance of international goodwill."[13] That same month Van Kirk even scheduled a lunch with Lehman, indicating his decision to support the work of Lehman, rather than the bill McCarran and Walter sponsored.[14]

As mainline Protestant leadership began to criticize the McCarran-Walter bill, they also began throwing their support behind the proposals of Senator Lehman. The Women's Division of Christian Service of the Methodist Church advocated Lehman's bill during the early spring

of 1952, concluding that it was "an effort to remove sex and racial discrimination, and to improve the quota system without doing a major job
on revision of immigration laws."[15] After corresponding with Lehman,
J. Henry Carpenter, Executive Secretary of the Protestant Council in
Brooklyn, reported to Van Kirk, "This is one bill which I feel we can
back in every way possible. It eliminates the Oriental Exclusion Act and
any other provisions in the immigration act, that would keep people out
on the basis of race, color, creed or national origin." Caught up in his
excitement over the bill, Carpenter conceded, "It is one of those almost
too good items to really go through, but still I am sure we should back
it in every way."[16] The coming months would prove that such a proposal
was in fact "too good" to be true.

While the legislative particulars were being drawn up that spring, the
NCC began to work on its own position on immigration and refugees.
The final statement was approved through the National Council's General Assembly in March 1952. The policy statement made three recommendations to Congress. First, the NCC called for Congress to "make
the quota system more flexible." Second, the statement requested that
"all discriminatory provisions based upon considerations of color, race,
or sex would be removed." Finally, the NCC asked Congress to reexam-
ine US visa and deportation policies, which many people at the time
interpreted as abuses of power as they were used to combat supposed
communist subversives.[17]

In the 1952 statement, the National Council appealed to the principles
of mercy, justice, and national morality in calling for legal reform, while
also acknowledging Cold War concerns and internationalist perspectives. Cold War rhetoric is subtle, but present throughout. The resolution referred to the United States and "other liberty-loving nations,"
and speaking to the refugee crisis, it noted those "who every day break
through the Iron Curtain in search of freedom." Addressing the US government in what were then the early years of the Cold War, the document declared that "enlightened immigration and naturalization laws
would add immeasurably to the moral stature of the United States." In
keeping with its ecumenical foundations and attention to internationalism and universal brotherhood, the report also affirmed America's
global role. The NCC applauded US involvement in UN initiatives and
declared, "The National Council of Churches rejoices in the knowledge

that the United States, as a member of the family of nations, is a party to these humanitarian endeavors." The report unapologetically supported both US global leadership and participation in the United Nations during the turbulent postwar period.

NCC leaders quickly mailed out copies to fellow combatants, including the Jewish leader Jules Cohen with the National Community Relations Advisory Council, the Anti-Defamation League of B'nai B'rith, and members of Congress, including Walter and Lehman.[18] Lehman commented that he "read the statement with interest and was very favorably impressed with it." Lehman assured Van Kirk that such sentiments were in line with his proposed Humphrey-Lehman bill. Lehman then identified their "common objectives" of "humanization of our present immigration laws" and refugee relief that would assist "our own welfare" and the "advancement of the struggle against Communist imperialism."[19] Arthur Greenleigh, of the United Service for New Americans, wrote that "it is one of the finest statements on general principles which I have yet seen. It is an excellent frame of reference in the common struggle for immigration legislation in keeping with our American tradition."[20] Owen E. Pence, of the World Alliance of YMCAs, wrote Van Kirk that "the positions taken by your General Board are sound."[21] Representative Charles R. Howell of New Jersey acknowledged that the statement's positions "represent substantially my own feelings about the immigration revision legislation" and that Van Kirk could "count on my strong efforts to help adopt a liberal bill."[22] Congressman Walter simply assured Van Kirk that through a resolution he was currently promoting, the NCC's concerns over refugees were being addressed, though he sidestepped the larger topic of immigration policy.[23]

While the NCC produced its statement, other Protestants continued to decry the McCarran-Walter bill Congress was considering. Samuel McCrea Cavert, as General Secretary of the NCC, criticized McCarran's half of the legislation, Senate Bill 2550, and wrote members of Congress declaring that the National Council was "officially committed to the principle that immigration and naturalization laws in keeping with our democratic tradition and our concern for human rights should provide for . . . fair hearings and appeals respecting the issuance of visas and deportation proceedings."[24] William F. Hasting, director of the Congregational Christian Service Committee, Inc., wrote the *Christian Cen-*

tury demanding it reconsider its soft position on the bill as of May 1952. Hasting believed a *Christian Century* article he had read suggested "half a loaf seems better than no bread." But Hasting then asked, "What if the bread be adulterated or poisoned?" Hasting instead promoted the Humphrey-Lehman bill.[25]

Despite the staunch protest of numerous liberal Protestants and other public figures, Congress eventually passed what became known as the McCarren-Walter Act in the summer of 1952. To the dismay of advocates for reform, the act basically ensured national origins would continue to define quota restriction, and it also instituted a platform that favored immigrants on the basis of labor skills. Overall, it only nominally acknowledged liberal concerns. It did end Asian exclusion with the help of Congressman Walter Judd, who had earlier worked to overturn Chinese exclusion. As a result, this brought to an end the policy of basing naturalization on race that dated back to the nation's founding era; nevertheless, it gave only token quotas to Japan, China, and other parts of the Asian Pacific. The act also wedded African American concerns with the issue of immigration in that it limited West Indian immigration through its own quota separate from the quota established for Britain.[26]

The passage of the McCarran-Walter Act did not silence the protest of Protestants, especially in the Protestant press. The popular mainline serial *Christian Century* chimed in on the debate. Its perspective was initially more ambivalent, praising the end of an immigration policy excluding Asian immigrants, but disagreeing with the national origins quota system that remained intact.[27] The next year, however, the *Christian Century* increased its criticism of the law.[28] The progressive Methodist periodical *motive* simply referred to the law as "a bipartisan bit of racial bigotry."[29]

After Congress passed the McCarran-Walter Act, but before President Harry Truman decided whether to veto or sign the bill, Protestants continued to work diligently in the political arena. Roland Elliott of CWS wrote people asking them to encourage Truman to veto, and Van Kirk also wired President Truman describing the NCC's hope that he would veto.[30] Senator Lehman sent Van Kirk a letter in June, likely a form letter to the senator's supporters, acknowledging, "I know we could not have made as good a fight as we did without the support and enthusiasm shown by the National Council of Churches of Christ in USA." Lehman confirmed that he would back Truman if he vetoed the bill.[31] Another letter from a member of Congress assured Van Kirk he voted against McCarran-Walter and that he would "continue my efforts to eliminate any semblance of racial or religious discrimination from our laws."[32]

As promised, Truman vetoed the bill. In his veto message, Truman lambasted the discrimination that the 1924 quota established and that the McCarran-Walter Act continued. In his message before Congress, Truman appealed to the social gospel rhetoric still in vogue by the mid-century among his Protestant constituents. "It repudiates our basic religious concepts, our belief in the brotherhood of man, and in the words of St. Paul that 'there is neither Jew nor Greek, there is neither bond nor free * * * for ye are all one in Christ Jesus.'" The social gospel ideal of the brotherhood of man had clearly made its way to the White House by 1952 and infused the debate over immigration. For Truman, there was no excuse for the McCarran-Walter Act to continue to restrict immigrants on the basis of race and ethnicity. "It is incredible to me that, in this year of 1952, we should again be enacting into law such a slur on the patriotism, the capacity and the decency of a large part of our citizenry."[33] Like other contemporary critics, Truman did not believe challenging the law contradicted a commitment to the nation; rather, such positions reinforced each other.

After Congress overturned his veto in the summer of 1952, Truman organized a Commission on Immigration and Naturalization to investigate public reception of the law, on which served, among others, the Jewish Philip B. Perlman, Catholic Monsignor John O'Grady, Lutheran Thaddeus F. Gullixson, and Clarence E. Picket with the American Friends Service Committee. As the committee listened to the testimony of civic and religious figures in 11 cities during the fall of 1952, Protestant, Catholic, and Jewish representatives voiced their criticisms of the McCarran-Walter Act. Van Kirk wrote to various Protestant leaders to prepare them should they be asked to testify before the committee, and he referred them to the NCC's statement from March.[34] Congregational minister Myron W. Fowell wrote to Van Kirk: "We fought this legislation hard over a long period of time through our state Social Action Committee and through the Legislative Committee of the Massachusetts Council of Churches of which I am chairman. I plan to go to the hearing tomorrow and register the sentiments of these two committees along with a resolution passed by the delegates of our last Annual Meeting."[35]

Other Protestants rallied to the cause and spoke before the commission, including NCC official Earl F. Adams, Washington National Cathedral Dean Francis B. Sayre, Jr., Presbyterians Edward D. Auchard and Harold H. Henderson, Methodist Charles B. Boss, Jr., and Southern Baptist Joseph M. Dawson, representing the Baptist World Alliance.[36] Van Kirk himself went before the commission, declaring, "The Immigration and Naturalization Law of 1952, as approved by Congress, is at some points not compatible with the spirit and intent of the principles set forth by the National Council of Churches, principles which are dictated alike by consideration of Christian justice and love of country." Van Kirk made it clear that the National Council was not calling for unfettered immigration, but simply a quota system "without discriminations predicated upon national origin or racial heritage."[37]

Following the commission's hearings, it published a report titled *Whom We Shall Welcome*. In the introduction the authors of the report acknowledged the broad basis of support for such an endeavor: "It is noteworthy that all the major religious faiths of America urged the President to appoint a commission for this general purpose." They went on to note the recent pronouncements of the NCC, CWS, and PEC. Later in the introduction, the report drew heavily upon America's immigrant heritage, essentially Robert L. Fleegler's "contributionism," and clearly favored cultural pluralism, in line with many mainline Protestant figures. "The Commission believes that an outstanding characteristic of the United States is its great cultural diversity within an overriding national unity." The report also recognized that the Judeo-Christian consensus was opposed to the law. The report noted that "leading Protestant, Catholic, and Jewish organizations criticized the act of 1952 for similar reasons; and that, in some places, a single representative was authorized to speak for many lay and religious organizations of different denominations."[38] Van Kirk later commented on the commission's report, assuring critics of McCarran-Walter that "[s]trong support will be forthcoming from the Christian leaders of many denominations."[39] Protestants may have lost a legislative battle, but they were far from giving up on the war for immigration reform.

In the years that followed, numerous Protestant figures and agencies continued to speak out against McCarran-Walter.[40] Before 1952 was over, a group of Minnesota Protestants suggested amending the legislation to assist more displaced persons, basing quotas on the 1950 population instead of 1920 (a nod to the previously proposed Humphrey-Lehman bill), extending unmet quotas to additional groups, no longer attributing quotas according to "color, race, or sex," and reforming visa and deportation practices.[41] In 1953, the American Baptist Convention (ABC) and Methodist Church both passed resolutions demanding changes to the McCarran-Walter Act, and that same year the indomitable Methodist Bishop G. Bromley Oxnam went on record announcing that the law included "bad philosophy, archaic provisions and un-American procedures."[42] The Episcopal Diocese of Michigan passed a resolution in February 1953 "requesting the Congress . . . to replace immediately the McCarran-Walter Act with another piece of legislation which would be more in accord with our American spirit."[43] And the New York Episcopal Diocese voted against McCarran in 1953, declaring it "perpetuates a quota system based upon the now out-moded census of 1920 and upon racial theories that are scientifically unsound and contrary to the clear implications of the Christian doctrine of man."[44] The PCUSA Foreign Mission Board, reflecting the close relationship between home and foreign missions, also went on record in March 1953 calling for revision.[45]

Just like his Democratic predecessor, the Republican Dwight Eisenhower upon being elected in 1952 did not let the issue die, instead mentioning it in his State of the Union address in February 1953. Eisenhower remarked that "we are—one and all—immigrants or the sons and daughters of immigrants," and he admitted that "[e]xisting legislation contains injustices. It does, in fact, discriminate." Despite Eisenhower's overtures, Protestants gradually began to realize by spring of 1953 that Congress was not going to budge. Because nothing could be done to revise McCarran-Walter, Protestants instead focused on refugee relief through emergency legislation in 1953.[46] The Jewish social reformer Jules Cohen believed Protestants were choosing "to capitulate much too early in the game" when it came to immigration policy.[47] But by the fall, Protestants had conceded to political pragmatism. PCUSA official Clifford J. Earle noted in a letter the decision by Congress to set aside revision of the McCarran-Walter Act in order to pass refugee legislation.

He counseled his colleague, William N. Wysham, on pursuing immigration reform, "Your only possible action, of course, would be a letter to the White House, and the Washington Office suggests that this would be a waste of influence which might better be held until the next session of Congress when it is possible that something may break."[48] Earle and other Protestants decided to bide their time.

The Consequences of Protest

Mainline Protestant concerns over the McCarran-Walter Act coincided with a tense moment in US cultural and political history. Americans' earlier fears of nonwhite racial groups immigrating to the United States waned in the face of potential communist subversion. Historian David H. Bennett notes that, following a prolonged war fighting fascist powers only to witness the rise of communism, the threats the American public perceived by midcentury came "from the head and not the blood."[49] Such hysteria over the communist threat evolved into another full-fledged Red Scare in which one's views on the McCarran-Walter Act served as a litmus test for their commitment to counter communist infiltration. "It should be unnecessary to comment on Mr. McCarran's implication that opponents of the act must be Communists or Communist sympathizers," asserted the *New York Times*. "Opponents of the McCarran Act include men and women of every religion, of every national strain, including his own, of every political party, of every occupation and every walk of life."[50] Despite the views of the *Times*, opposition to the new immigration law continued to elicit accusations of communist sympathy. But the Second Red Scare was not the only source of resistance liberal Protestants faced while advocating immigration reform. The positions they took occasionally undermined their relationship with fellow believers. There was a price to pay for protest during the 1950s, and Protestant critics of the McCarran-Walter Act soon encountered it.

One pocket of dissent came from within Protestant denominations. In 1961, CWS commissioned a study by Benson Y. Landis titled *Protestant Experience with United States Immigration*, outlining the history of immigration, ethnic churches, and white, mainline efforts to assist immigrants and refugees over the last 50 years. Benson recognized what he called a "paradox." Benson noted, "There are clear and definite national policies—but constituencies appear indifferent, or uninformed. Indeed, probably large portions of constituencies may not be in agreement with national pronouncements—on immigration or other great issues."[51] Indeed, in 1960 the First Baptist Church of Wichita, Kansas, even worked to separate the ABC from the NCC on account of multiple grievances directed toward the more liberal policies of the NCC, including immigration reform.[52] By the 1960s, liberal Protestants at the helm of denominations, seminaries, and ecumenical groups found themselves increasingly distant from their moderate and conservative counterparts on public policy, national identity, and the contours of American culture.[53]

Disgruntled church members were not shy in voicing their concerns when immigration policy was on the line. Ivan H. Peterman from Pennsylvania wrote the PCUSA's Board of Christian Education, criticizing its support for the *Fence*, a pamphlet that critiqued the McCarran-Walter Act and appealed for refugee resettlement. Peterman, self-identified as a "long-time Presbyterian," inquired concerning the denomination's support for the pamphlet "without any consultation of the church membership." Apparently a constituent of Congressman Walter, Peterman articulated his concern that the pamphlet, and broader criticism of the law, were simply hurting America. "'The Fence' is merely part of an under cover [*sic*] drive, which Representative Walter would be able to explain, to complete a latter-day influx by people with widely divergent viewpoints to those of the earlier immigrants who made America what it is today." Peterman then warned, "We have discussed this pamphlet in our mens' [*sic*] class [at church]; there was no sympathy or favor for it, including the pastor. If that information guides you in future, perhaps this letter is not in vain."[54] Emily Keenan of Illinois wrote the Methodist Women's Division of Christian Service in 1957 concerning a recent Methodist pamphlet and its criticism of McCarran-Walter. Keenan countered several points made in the leaflet and surmised the publication was "emotional but not logical" in its promotion of liberal immigration reform. Keenan concluded, "In my opinion, it is dangerous grounds for the Methodist Church to broadcast literature against the Laws of the United States." Replying to the letter, Thelma Stevens, executive secretary of the Women's Division, affirmed her continued criticism of the law and noted that the McCarran-Walter Act was a "great handicap to the democratic processes" and threat to America's global image.[55] Finally, while discussing immigration policy at the 1961 meeting of the NCC's General Board, one delegate even announced, "I'm perfectly willing to leave some things to Congress without churchmen horning in on every decision."[56] Fundamental to such debates were divergent visions of what defined American culture and perennial debate over the role of the church in society.

Mainline leaders, however, could also stir vociferous supporters among the denominational faithful. Maurice Gross wrote a bishop of the Methodist Church in 1961 concerning his frustration over the recent suggestion made by the General Secretary of Laymen's Work that those who challenged the McCarran-Walter Act were following communist "propaganda." Gross bluntly charged, "He sounds very little like a follower of John Wesley and much more like a follower of John Birch." He continued, "It shames me for my Church to see leadership of its lay program at the national level in such naive and reactionary hands."[57] Among the Protestant rank and file could be found a variety of views on immigration restriction.

Not all confrontation, however, remained within the personal correspondence of the parties involved. Eventually, more liberal Protestants had to account for their positions before the American public. California journalist Franklin Hichborn published an exchange he had with an unnamed pastor "of one of the largest Protestant churches of our country." The minister had criticized the McCarran-Walter Act and challenged Hichborn's earlier claim that the refugee program was being abused by the "unassimilable of immigrants." In his published response, Hichborn touched on communist fears and referenced the "well-financed minority seek[ing] to 'liberalize'" the McCarran-Walter Act, a minority Hichborn claimed was based in New York. He lamented that the pastor he wrote to took part in such endeavors and was "misinformed, or the victim of propaganda, or both." Hitchborn then arrived at the heart of his concerns: the threat critics posed to America's Christian heritage. He suggested America was becoming more secular, resorting to an argument that would become common parlance among culture warriors several decades later. Resorting to anti-Semitic language, he believed America had accepted the "Talmudization of Christianity," a "curious hybrid which would have enraged John Wesley and scandalized our forebears." Hichborn recognized, but clearly did not support, the position some Protestant ministers had taken on immigration and pluralism in America.[58]

Even Senator McCarran spoke out against Protestants who disapproved of his law. Early in January 1953, in response to the report of Truman's Commission on Immigration and Naturalization, McCarran decried Protestant support of such an initiative. Likely in response to the arguments some Protestants were making, McCarran boldly declared that "the rock of truth is that the Act does not contain one iota of racial or religious discrimination."[59] Then in March and April 1953, *Christian Century* and McCarran directly challenged each other. In a March editorial, *Christian Century* voiced its concerns about the prospects for delegates entering the United States to attend the World Council of Churches meeting the following year and used it as an opportunity to encourage protest of the McCarran-Walter Act and the difficulties it created for people of other nationalities in coming to America. The periodical provocatively stated, "As now worded, this law raises an iron curtain of restrictions on even temporary entry which will make it difficult if not impossible for a world ecumenical conference to meet here."[60] The following month, Senator McCarran responded in a rebuttal published in the *Century*. McCarran simply noted that according to US immigration policy, "no one is inadmissible to the United States as a visitor unless his presence in this country would endanger the public safety." McCarran then explained that the publication was either wrong in its earlier claim that such a law would restrict the travel of World Council members, or that *Christian Century* was suggesting those attending were actually subversives. McCarran then asserted,

> I submit that in all fairness, my letter should be published in The Christian Century as a rebuttal to the editorial which is highly prejudicial of an act which was endorsed by the immigration and naturalization service, the visa division, the department of state, the department of justice, the Central Intelligence Agency, and by over 100 patriotic, civic and religious organizations as fair and sound legislation which was urgently needed for the best interests of the United States of America.

Following McCarran's response, *Christian Century* editors included a parenthetical disclaimer that McCarran still did not answer their original concern that WCC representatives from communist coun-tries or regions with a fascist past would be able to attend the Evanston, Illinois, meeting of World Council delegates.[61]

Mainline Protestants also felt the wrath of fundamentalist and evan-gelical Protestants on their right, including fundamentalists Carl Mc-Intire and Billy Hargis, who identified mainline Protestant criticism of immigration legislation as a communist ploy. Hargis claimed that the NCC "propagandized Congress for passage of amendments which would open wide the gates of our first line of defense," drawing upon the popular trope among restrictionists that immigration reform was essentially opening the borders.[62] Midcentury evangelicals also ques-tioned the NCC's positions on immigration. Organized in 1942 under the National Association of Evangelicals (NAE), conservative Protes-tants began to leave mainline denominations at this time because of per-ceived liberal theological and cultural positions. As they organized, they began to engage the public square, so that by the 1960s they developed various organizations and grassroots movements, with funding from the oil magnate J. Howard Pew, that projected a conservative sociopoliti-cal agenda. Such mobilization was already occurring during the 1950s over immigration and what they perceived to be the liberal inclinations of mainline Protestants. Many evangelicals felt that mainliners simply neglected the gospel message of Christianity when taking on political policy matters.[63]

In a phone conservation between two mainline NCC officials, they expressed fears in 1957 that the "National Assoc. of Evangelicals is un-leashing a campaign" to oppose immigration reform "and the NCC for supporting it." They then went on to discuss their concern that the NAE was "(a)ccusing NCC of conspiring with Jews and Roman Catholics to let down the bars."[64] That same year the NAE passed a resolution op-posing any immigration reform on the grounds that the national ori-gins system was adequate. The NAE statement established its concerns over calls for reform, "purportedly on the grounds of humanitarian-ism," a less than subtle jab at liberal Protestants' agendas at the time. The NAE also made it clear that liberalizing immigration policy would only compromise American freedoms and the "future of America by assimilating into the population large numbers of people who have little historic attachment to, or understanding of, the American Christian heritage."[65] The NAE's Secretary of Public Affairs, Clyde W. Taylor, also communicated concern that the proposed legislation would open more opportunities for immigrants outside of northern and western Europe, suggesting that such groups are "Roman Catholic and decidedly of minority cultural emphasis" rather than immigrants that have historically contributed to America's "main cultural emphasis."[66] Much of their critiques resonated with the more conservative elements within mainline Protestantism, which helps explain the political trajectory of evangelicals following World War II. As historian Gaston observes, much of the Judeo-Christian language that was in vogue among midcentury moderates transferred to more conservative evangelical groups during the latter half of the twentieth century with the rise of the Religious Right.[67]

In their crusade against the McCarran-Walter Act, mainline Protestants provided their more conservative critics the opportunity to use the Cold War climate against them. Mainline Protestant leaders who disparaged the McCarran-Walter Act eventually brought unwanted attention from the government during Senator Joseph McCarthy's anticommunist crusade. As early as 1948, the Committee on Un-American Activities published a booklet titled *100 Things You Should Know About Communism and Religion*, in which it identified the YMCA, YWCA, and Methodist Epworth League as potential "Communist target(s)" and proclaimed that the Methodist Federation for Social Action was a "tool of the Communist Party."[68] The Methodist Federation later drew the ire of McCarthyites, in part because of its criticism of the McCarran-Walter Act and support for the American Committee for Protection of Foreign Born.[69]

In the case of Methodist Bishop Garfield Bromley Oxnam, his record of progressive social ideals eventually caught the attention of the House Un-American Activities Committee.[70] Oxnam voluntarily appeared before the committee to defend his legacy and make clear that he did not support communism, a decision that resulted in a ten-hour hearing rife with strong personalities, rhetorical wit, and strident sparring At this time Congressman Walter, who had co-authored the immigration act the previous year, was on the committee. He appeared to take Oxnam's prior criticism of his law personally and grilled Oxnam on the matter. Walter's interrogation was so persistent that other committee members could barely get a word in edgewise once the two went at it. Walter ques-

Figure 5.1. Methodist Bishop G. Bromley Oxnam (right) being sworn in before the House Un-American Activities Committee in 1953, where he had to account for his criticism of the McCarran-Walter Act. George Skadding / The LIFE Picture Collection via Getty Images.

tioned Oxnam, "Could you have taken the position, if you were properly quoted, that you were opposed to the immigration policy of the United States because you were not concerned with the number of Communists coming into this country?" Oxnam responded to this by reaffirming his disregard for the Communist Party and declaring, "I'm fundamentally opposed to the whole Communist movement and would do everything within my power to keep them out." Oxnam then turned the tables on Walter, bringing up the fact that President Truman had even vetoed the act. Oxnam shot back, "Well, you wouldn't call him interested in letting Communists in, would you?" The two men continued to argue, before another committee member finally was able to intervene and steer the questioning to other topics. Five years later, there was still bad blood between Oxnam and Walter. Oxnam surmised in a speech that if Walter was tasked with writing the inscription used on the Statue of Liberty, rather than the famous words of Emma Lazarus, Walter would have written: "Keep them, the tempest tos't from me. / Turn the key, and lock the unfriendly door."[71]

Arriving at the Hart-Celler Act of 1965

Despite the challenges of the Second Red Scare, Protestant leaders continued to work toward immigration reform and revision of the McCarran-Walter Act. In so doing, they highlighted the international ramifications of the law and the racial discrimination embedded in the immigration quotas. In 1954 Charles H. Seaver published the booklet *As We Do Unto Others* for the NCC's Department of International Justice and Goodwill. The pamphlet reflected a growing recognition that the 1924 law limited others beyond just Asian immigrants. "It is based on the assumption that Americans of British or Irish or German birth or ancestry are better citizens than Americans of Italian, Greek, or Polish birth or ancestry."[72] This increasing concern for racial injustice was certainly a product of the much larger drive for civil rights at that time.

Progressive immigration views capitalized on the burgeoning civil rights movement during the 1950s and the historically fluid understanding of race among white Protestants during the first half of the twentieth century.[73] Oftentimes, when confronting racial discrimination, mainline Protestants were addressing not only African American civil rights protest, but also the plight of Latinos and Asians. As one NCC official noted, "Certainly, in this period when the Churches' concerns have been made manifest in the area of civil rights, the Churches should not fail to seek the removal of the racist characteristics of the present immigration law."[74] Protestant social workers had come to identify the racial foundation of an immigration policy based on national origins. A NCC statement in June 1952 titled "The Churches and Segregation" called upon churches to "renounce the pattern of segregation based on race, color or national origin as unnecessary and undesirable and a violation of the Gospel of love and human brotherhood."[75] In 1959, the Episcopal Church formed the Episcopal Society for Cultural and Racial Unity in an effort to encourage "greater implementation of the inclusive nature of the Church and the elimination of all barriers in the Church based upon race, class, or national origin."[76] Such sentiment was also evident in a statement by the Methodist Church's Council of Bishops in 1963 that called on pastors to accept visitors "without regard to race, color, or national origin." It concluded with an appeal "to deepen by word and deed the brotherhood of man and make this a reality instead of a hope."[77]

A fluid interpretation of race by Protestants encouraged more concerted attention to immigration. This is evident in the position some Southern Baptist women took in 1950 that conflated race, ethnicity, and nationality. In a piece titled "How Christian Is America?" the writer outlined a program for Southern Baptist women and selected several social issues, including the status of minorities. "One of the most difficult problems is the treatment of minority groups. This includes Negroes, Jews, Mexicans, Indians, Japanese, Chinese, Puerto Ricans and other foreign born living among us." The author then confessed, "If we face the issue, we realize that the problem is ours—with us—not the minority group. Our attitude towards people who are different creates the problem. We do not want to share equally with them the fruits of freedom which are ours in America." Referencing the 1947 Southern Baptist Charter on Race Relations, the author noted, "Written primarily to help us in our relations with Negroes, it will apply just as well to people of other groups."[78] Most Protestant home missionaries conflated race, ethnicity, and nationality in a way that drew attention to immigration during the civil rights movement.

Nevertheless, tying nationality to racial identity also perpetuated distinct racial categorizations, which were never treated equally. At a time when many European immigrant groups were transitioning to "whiteness," the American public, as historian Robert Fleegler notes, considered Asian and Mexican immigrants as racially "other" and did not celebrate these groups as a part of America's immigrant heritage.[79] These racial discrepancies help explain in part why mainline Protestants, and most other Americans, grew more critical by midcentury of the unfair treatment of "white" immigrant groups from southern and eastern Europe within the quota system and sponsored a resettlement program that went to great lengths to aid primarily European refugees, whose economic appeal and class status also made them desirable.[80] In the meantime, Operation Wetback went largely unopposed and Asian immigrants were given meager quotas.

Inspired by the concurrent civil rights movement, Protestants entered the latter half of the 1950s determined to seek change in immigration policy. In 1956, continuing Cold War developments such as the Suez Canal crisis and revolutions in Hungary and Czechoslovakia kept refugees and immigration in the public eye. Eisenhower's State of the Union for that year called for immigration reform and a quota system based on the 1950 census, while also acknowledging America's immigrant history.[81] The following year, Senator John F. Kennedy began working for further immigration reform in Congress. Protestants soon entered the fray.[82]

In January 1957, the Methodist Board of Missions passed a resolution melding the continuing refugee crisis with the need for immigration reform and pointing out that the Board was "concerned about the worldwide effect of restrictions contained in the present law, which seems to have racial implications."[83] Kenneth Maxwell, executive director of the NCC's Department of International Affairs, wrote in 1957 to Senate Majority Leader Lyndon B. Johnson, advocating "an improved non-discriminatory immigration and naturalization policy." Maxwell noted, "We are concerned because of moral and human values and also because we believe these issues are important in our international relations."[84] The United Church Women also passed a resolution that year addressing immigration and refugees, and one of their spokeswomen appealed to Johnson for refugee relief.[85]

Protestants also maneuvered politically beyond just letter writing by continuing to testify before Senate subcommittees. In October 1955, the NCC encouraged people to provide testimony in line with the NCC's March 1952 statement.[86] Eugene Carson Blake, as president of the NCC, prepared a statement for the Senate Judiciary Subcommittee on Immigration in 1955. Blake reaffirmed the NCC's principle not to "address itself to lengthy detailed consideration of the specifics of the legislation," but rather to promote "principles which it believes are dictated by considerations of Christian justice and love of country." Blake affirmed that the NCC was not calling for "unlimited immigration" and recognized the importance of safeguards against subversives, but he wanted the law not to consider "national origin or racial heritage." Blake also appealed to international cooperation. He believed his proposals "would be in accord with the spirit of the United Nations Charter, to which our country is a party, and with the Universal Declaration of Human Rights to which we are a signatory," and would reflect "comradeship with the freedom loving peoples of the earth." Clearly, Blake had imbibed the international impulse of his era as he spoke for immigration reform.[87]

Aside from testifying before congressional subcommittees, mainline Protestant leaders demonstrated their political savvy in other ways. In 1957, representatives of the NCC, National Lutheran Council, and Common Council for American Unity were able to secure time to meet with Representative Walter, Speaker of the House Sam Rayburn, Lyndon B. Johnson's assistant George Reedy, Joseph M. Swing with the Immigration and Naturalization Service, Senator Arthur Watkins, and White House staffer Max Raab.[88] NCC leaders were also aware of shifting political alliances. In a phone call between Kenneth Maxwell and Charles M. Smith, they considered the current legislative climate and believed Walter was "a man under pressures." They then speculated about the opportunity other representatives, more favorable to immigration reform, had: "[Walter's] anxiety may be the leverage by which some action may be possible."[89] Bishop Gerald H. Kennedy even gave an impassioned speech at the Democratic convention in Los Angeles during the summer of 1960 before its Committee on Platform and Resolutions, where he reaffirmed the NCC's traditional position on immigration reform. He concluded with an appeal for an immigration law that would be "commensurate with our national ideals and international long term interests."[90]

Protestants put their political networking skills to use in April 1961 when the National Council organized the Consultation on Immigration Policy in the United States. Religious leaders representing most mainline Protestant denominations met with key policymakers in Washington, DC for two days in April to discuss immigration reform. The conference program included speeches given by many mainline Protestant divines, women and men, along with such political figures as New York Senator Kenneth B. Keating, Under Secretary of State Chester Bowles, United Nations High Commissioner for Refugees Felix Schnyder, and California Representative D. S. Saund. As we saw earlier, President John F. Kennedy even sent a message of support. In addition to these speakers, the conference also included a panel of respondents, including Former Administrator of the Bureau of Consular and Secretary Affairs John W. Hanes, Jr., New York Representative John V. Lindsay, and none other than Congressman Walter himself, who evidently had not entirely burned his bridges with all mainline Protestants following his interrogation of Bishop Oxnam eight years prior.[91]

In many respects, one could argue that this conference represented one of the final demonstrations of mainline Protestant influence in America in its ability to marshal such prominent political and religious figures. It was definitely a high-water mark for Protestant efforts to usher in immigration reform. The Christian and internationalist tenor of the consultation was reinforced in its "Summary of Concerns," approved by the attendees. The first two sentences read: "Under God, men and nations are responsible to each other and for the welfare of all mankind. The implications of God's sovereign claim upon all men have been proclaimed by the advent and example of His Son, Jesus Christ, in human society." In the summary statement, those in attendance also agreed that the 1924 quota law was a disgrace on account of its racial preferences and that equal justice for the naturalized and native-born was necessary. Overall, the consultation's platform was a call for immigration reform that balanced both "national interest" and "moral values," twin foci of much of Protestant social work in America.[92]

Within a year of the consultation, the NCC produced another policy statement on immigration reform. Once the NCC approved the statement, copies were sent to President Kennedy, Attorney General Robert Kennedy, Secretary of State Dean Rusk, the Commissioner for Immigration, and leading members of Congress.[93] Even Francis Walter received a copy in the mail, though he made it clear he was not fully in agreement with the statement.[94] The document directly confronted the quota laws and provided several policy suggestions, including basing immigration quotas on the 1960 census. The 1962 NCC statement also reinforced both the moral and national emphases stressed during the Consultation the year before. It asserted, "In a world of dynamic change, our nation's immigration policy must be shaped by the requirements of moral principles and human values, as well as considerations of national welfare." It recognized the need for "(a)dmission of persons with occupational skills generally employable in the United States" and "persons whose coming will tend to stimulate rather than jeopardize economic health and growth in the United States."[95]

In keeping with the ubiquitous notion of the brotherhood of man found within mainline Protestant social positions, the statement assumed a strikingly global focus. It acknowledged America's leading global position and also noted that repressive sociopolitical circumstances in different parts of the world contributed to increasing migration. The NCC report declared its hope that the "immigration policy and practices of our Government will move further toward . . . the fulfillment of the responsibilities of the international position of the United States in its crucial role in helping to develop world community." Rather than just fixing immigration laws in the United States, the NCC recognized that when framing immigration policy, the Congress must take into account the rest of the world.[96]

In a political climate increasingly more receptive to immigration reform, John F. Kennedy hoped to revamp immigration policy. He became publicly linked to the immigration issue after the positions he took during the late 1950s while serving in the Senate and in a pamphlet, *A Nation of Immigrants*, he wrote for the Anti-Defamation League on immigration. Segments of this booklet were printed in the *New York Times* in August 1963, when at the same time, he called for immigration reform as president.[97] Indicative of Kennedy's support for the 1961 Consultation, his public image linked to immigration reform resonated with many mainline Protestant figures. In 1963 they backed an open letter to Kennedy that declared, "We are greatly encouraged and wish to express our appreciation for the outstanding leadership you are giving in this major field of human rights." It was signed by various groups and societies representing American Baptists, CWS, the Methodist Committee for Overseas Relief, National Board of the YWCA, PEC, UPCUSA, along with various civic and labor organizations.[98] Following Kennedy's assassination, Lyndon Johnson and others would see to it that Kennedy's proposals were not discontinued.[99]

By 1964, the political climate had shifted since the McCarran-Walter Act passed 12 years earlier, and immigration reform that would rectify the national origins quota system was back on the table. In May 1963, Walter, the principal opponent to major revision to the national origins system, died. McCarran had passed nine years earlier. Without their opposition, the pendulum swung toward immigration reform.[100] In his State of the Union address in January 1964, Lyndon Johnson, after commenting on his vision for racial equality, addressed immigration. "We must also lift by legislation the bars of discrimination against those who seek entry into our country, particularly those with much needed skills and those joining their families. In establishing preferences, a nation that was built by the immigrants of all lands can ask those who now seek admission: What can you do for our country? But we should not be asking: In what country were you born?" He then outlined his foreign policy, whose basis echoed a pluralist ideal. Johnson aspired for a "world made safe for diversity, in which all men, goods and ideas can freely move across every border and every boundary."[101] Five days later, the Johnson administration hosted a conference on the topic of immigration reform and invited various politicians and social reformers. Those in attendance included leaders of several religious advocacy groups, including Church World Service.[102]

Continuing its work on immigration reform, in 1964 the NCC prepared another statement for the Subcommittee on Immigration and Nationality of the House Judiciary Committee, in which it confirmed Protestant support for Emmanuel Celler's work in Congress where he advocated HR 7700, the bill Kennedy had promoted the year prior that aimed to eliminate the national origins system.[103] That same year the Methodist Church published yet another pamphlet deconstructing the McCarran-Walter Act. It frequently cited the Truman commission's report *Whom We Shall Welcome* and the 1961 Consultation. Using a series of tabs, it took the reader through the challenges facing immigration policies, critiquing the McCarran-Walter Act but also recognizing immigration still needed some federal regulation, just providing it was not discriminatory.[104]

Despite President Johnson's acknowledgment of immigration reform in 1964, Congress did not begin to address it in earnest until 1965, with the aid of Congressmen Philip Hart and Emanuel Celler, who carried the mantle of Kennedy's earlier bill.[105] Early that year, sensing the shifting political climate, the NCC passed a final resolution on immigration reform. At the February 1965 meeting of the NCC held in Portland, Oregon, the body voted on a resolution backing President Johnson's recent appeals for revising US immigration policy. The ecumenical meeting and the passage of the resolution reflected two themes closely tied to the evolving Protestant position on immigration over the last 40 years: the leadership women provided and the prominence of racial concerns. Thelma Stevens of the Methodist Women's Division presented the resolution to the gathering, and the opening address by Martin Niemoller stood as a stark reminder of the Nazi oppression and racial theories that many postwar Americans worked to distance themselves from. The actual resolution criticized the "inequitable racial and national barriers" previous legislation enacted and called for an end to quotas based upon national origin, while also echoing many of the reforms outlined in the NCC's statement from 1962.[106]

Later that spring and into early summer, mainline Protestants contributed to the gaining momentum of immigration reform. The Congregationalists' Council for Christian Social Action resolved in February 1965 that "[a]s the Civil Rights Act of 1964 attempts to eliminate from our society practices based on racial discrimination, there is need for revision of the Immigration and Nationality Act of 1952 to eliminate the ethnic and cultural bias of the national origins quota provisions of the act."[107] Then in March, Robert D. Bulkley, as Secretary of the Office of Church and Society of the PCUSA, wrote to Presbyterians active in local programs. Commenting on the "unfair and unfortunate discrimination against people in eastern and Southern Europe, Asia, and Africa," Bulkley declared that "it is also just another not too subtle way of saying to the peoples of the world that we judge some of them to be of inferior stock and therefore hardly suitable to admission to our land."[108] Bulkley's comment represented how far some Protestants had come since 1924 in their understanding of racial discrimination in immigration quotas. Protestants also turned their attention to the airwaves. In May 1965, the ABC Radio Network aired a program on "The Churches and United States Immigration Policy" that included talks by NCC, CWS, and American Friends Service Committee representatives.[109] Mainline Protestant leaders used all means at their disposal in this final push to overturn immigration restriction, including speaking directly to Congress itself.

Congregationalists, now under the denominational umbrella of the United Church of Christ (UCC) after 1957, also pressed their members to support immigration reform. The Council for Christian Social Action devoted its entire May 1965 edition of *Social Action* to the immigration debate. With a provocative image of the Statue of Liberty behind barbed wire gracing its front cover, the publication compiled several essays relating to the legislation being considered and the responsibility of American churches. The opening editorial made it clear that the civil rights movement had raised the stakes for equality and justice in the United States. The editorial compared the vicious irony from earlier that spring, when the civil rights marchers in Montgomery encountered a Confederate flag at the state capitol, to the "treason to our American way of life to allow an immigration policy that admits persons on the basis of race and national origin instead of on the basis of open opportunity to share in the life and promise of our land." The edition included essays by Senator Philip A. Hart, John W. Schauer, the director of the Immigration and Refugee Program of CWS, and James Sheldon of the UCC's Council for Social Action, along with a copy of the NCC's February 1965 statement.[110]

Just as earlier mainline Protestant protests of the McCarran-Walter Act had stirred up opposition, their promotion of the 1965 reform also drew criticism. The *Wall Street Journal* went after the NCC on the front page of its March 5, 1965, edition. The editors referred to the NCC as "lobbyists" and hinted at the irony that mainline leaders promoted various political reforms, including for immigration and migrant labor, in a nation where church and state were supposedly held separate. The *Wall Street Journal* suggested mainline Protestant Christians were instead confusing their spiritual responsibilities, noting, "Church 'missions' flock to Washington." According to Walter Moeller, a representative from Ohio, the NCC was "like any other pressure group." The piece then concluded, "The rising criticism begins to worry the churchmen. The National Council of Churches studies how far it can go as a non-profit religious organization before it must register as a lobbyist."[111]

Meanwhile, over the course of spring and summer of 1965, Congress debated and conducted hearings to consider the proposed immigration reform. Denominational and ecumenical groups filed multiple statements responding to the proposed legislation. Representatives of the ABC, United Church of Christ, UPCUSA, CWS, the Episcopal Diocese of Los Angeles, and the Women's Fellowship of Christ's Church, Vermont, all either submitted or read statements to the Senate Subcommittee on Immigration and Naturalization favoring an end to quotas. During the committee hearings, Illinois Senator Paul H. Douglas, while promoting immigration reform, brought up his earlier experience working with Jane Addams, who he referred to as a friend and the "only authentic saint I have ever known." For Douglas, the legacy Addams left behind in her social work at Hull House confirmed that immigrants could make the adjustment to American society and even enrich the nation's culture. The social gospel legacy clearly reached into the 1960s.[112]

Testimony by Ruby Curd of the League of Christian Women from Virginia, however, demonstrated that not all Protestants were of the same mind when it came to the proposed immigration legislation. Curd criticized advocates for immigration reform who when making their argument referenced "The New Colossus," the poem by Emma Lazarus inscribed on the Statue of Liberty. "We believe that it is possible," Curd surmised, "that some of our lawmakers and public officials may have been consciously or unconsciously influenced by a bit of sentimental poetry added to a public statue back in 1908." Instead, the League of Christian Women recommended a temporary moratorium on immigration, rather than liberalizing immigration policy.[113]

The progressive mainline Protestant establishment clearly did not speak for all, or even most, Protestants in America. In fact, a survey conducted at the time revealed that the majority of Protestants opposed any increase in immigration.[114] Protestant evangelicals made their opposition clear at this point. Leaders within the conservative, largely southern, Presbyterian Church of the United States, even though tied to the NCC, frequently criticized the NCC for its "radical" positions, including immigration reform during the 1960s.[115] Commenting in a December 1964 edition of *Christianity Today* on the topic of Christian social positions, seminary professor Harold B. Kuhn criticized an earlier article in *Christian Century* that advocated immigration reform and challenged the racism of current policy. Kuhn contested that tossing out the McCarran-Walter Act and national quotas would be detrimental to the United States, for "some nationalities are so conditioned by culture that they meet our national needs better than others. To modify the immigration procedures along lines demanded by some would mean, virtually, the importation of southern Europe's Appalachia to our shores."[116] The National Association of Evangelicals (NAE) even continued its support of the quota system while Congress considered reform in 1965. Drawing from historic nativism embedded in anti-Catholicism, the NAE argued that immigrants holding to a closer relationship between church and state threatened religious freedom in the United States. Moreover, the NAE stated that the government policy in place since 1924 of basing immigrant quotas on national origins only helped "protect our society against infiltration by influences subversive of the American way of life."[117] Not only were Protestant evangelicals beginning to coopt the language of a "Judeo-Christian" nation at this point, but they also continued to promote the notion of an American way of life at a time when it was becoming more passé among liberal political, social, and religious leaders.[118]

After robust debate, Congress still voted in favor of immigration reform that September. A couple of days later, President Johnson signed the Immigration and Nationality Act of 1965, often referred to as the Hart-Celler Act, ending four decades of immigration restriction based on race and national origins. In a speech before the Statue of Liberty, Johnson conceded "that for over four decades the immigration policy of the United States has been twisted and has been distorted by the harsh injustice of the national origins quota system." Johnson went on to echo the pluralist, internationalist vision that many of his mainline Protestant supporters believed: "Our beautiful America was built by a nation of strangers. From a hundred different places or more they have poured forth into an empty land, joining and blending in one mighty and irresistible tide. The land flourished because it was fed from so many sources—because it was nourished by so many cultures and traditions and peoples."[119] As Johnson demonstrated, many Americans had come to embrace their immigrant heritage and, to a certain extent, the nation's cultural diversity.

The demographic changes that the reform would usher in over the next several decades were not evident in 1965, to politicians and Protestants alike. At the beginning of his speech, Johnson acknowledged, "This bill that we will sign today is not a revolutionary bill." At the time members of Congress believed they were passing only moderate immigration reform and used this line of reasoning to win support from the American people. In fact, Johnson's administration coaxed conservative support for the bill with the assurance that prioritizing family reunification would only bolster the numbers of largely "white" immigrants already in America. The law itself would not be implemented until 1968, and immediately following the bill's passage, many contemporaries were

Figure 5.2. President Lyndon B. Johnson signing the Immigration and Nationality Act of 1965, ending the discriminatory national quota system. New York City stands in the background, the site of decades of Protestant home missionary work among immigrant communities. Corbis Historical via Getty Images.

oblivious to the changes in immigration to come, due in part to greater public attention to the continuing civil rights movement and the belief that the legislation introduced only incremental reform.[120]

In a similar vein, the 1965 reform went largely unnoticed in the Christian press after the law passed. *Christian Century* did not provide comment in 1965, and in 1966 the publication only gave brief mention to the law in the context of increased Japanese immigration. Overall, this speaks to the lacuna in the perspective of many Americans concerning the coming changes, while also confirming that many mainline Protestants were satisfied that the legislation would not significantly increase immigration numbers. Support for the 1965 law also reflected lingering concerns over Mexican immigration in that the law placed Mexican and other Latin American immigrant under a hemispheric quota, thus establishing numbers for the first time. Nevertheless, some mainline Protestants were beginning to realize the exploitative nature of the Bracero Program and supported its conclusion in 1964.[121]

Crucially, Protestants were largely unaware of the significance this legislation had for religious pluralism. As the law allowed greater opportunity for non-European immigrants, the bill would indeed introduce "revolutionary" cultural and social changes in the coming years. Immigration increased by 4.4 million between 1960 and 1980, and while Europeans and Canadians were the majority of immigrants during the 1950s, during the 1970s, Mexico, the Philippines, Korea, Cuba, and India provided the most immigrants to the United States.[122]

Conclusion

In his 1964 book, *The Protestant Establishment*, University of Pennsylvania sociologist E. Digby Baltzell announced that the social hegemony of white, Anglo-Saxon, Protestants was coming to an end. In this dirge, Baltzell wrote that this privileged class was experiencing a "crisis in moral authority" due to its inability to extend power and opportunity to minorities in society. For Baltzell, white, upper-class Protestants had become an exclusive caste that was dying on account of not adapting. The social gospel had challenged its position during the early twentieth century, and World War II helped to undermine the racial consensus upon which it was built. While Baltzell still hoped that Christianity could help stem the tide of racism in America, white Protestant elites would need to adapt to the pluralistic conditions at the time in order to remain credible leaders in American society.[123]

Baltzell's observations proved to be both prescient and misplaced. The Protestant establishment was indeed in decline. While Baltzell was correct that its authority was historically the result of racial and ethnic discrimination, the cultural preeminence of white mainline Protestant Americans was on the verge of dissipating, not because of a lack of toleration, but due to an increasing religious pluralism ushered in by recent immigrants and refugees and the continuance of ethnic communities outside the Protestant fold. Mainline Protestants were largely oblivious to these coming changes. As we have seen, when it came to pluralism, they often supported a form of cultural pluralism, but largely overlooked the coming religious pluralism. When they did discuss religious pluralism, it was often an acknowledgment of America's "Tri-Faith" tradition of Protantism, Catholicism, and Judaism. In a 1957 report promoted by the NCC, one section asked the question: "Would a More Liberal Immigration Policy Encourage More Roman Catholic Immigrants and Change the Relationships Among the Faiths in the United States?" In a rather dry response, the report concluded that increased immigration would "be only a minor factor in interfaith relationships," and that Catholic and Protestant numbers would remain stable. But by interfaith, they were still looking through the lens of pluralist overtures to Catholics and Jews. They did not anticipate the broader religious pluralism to come.[124]

While they did not see it coming, they nevertheless contributed to it. Earlier social gospel sentiments and current events largely shaped mainline Protestant approaches to immigration during this time, and underlying their positions was a developing progressive critique of the racial components of restrictive legislation. Moreover, their continued attention to "national" and "moral" concerns encouraged a robust interest in immigration reform. But in their support for immigration reform lay unintended consequences. The increasing pluralism that the 1965 immigration reform fostered countered mainline Protestant claims on America. By the end of the twentieth century, Buddhist monasteries, Muslim mosques, and Hindu temples joined Protestant chapels, Jewish synagogues, and Catholic cathedrals in characterizing the religious landscape of the United States.[125] Protestant Christians still retained much influence in America, but rather than mainline Protestants leading the way, conservative evangelical groups consolidated political influence through the Religious Right and immigrants themselves brought with them forms of non-western Christian practice largely evangelical and Pentecostal in nature. Often overlooked is that mainline Protestants, through their advocacy for immigration reform and support for cultural pluralism, helped advance these changes.

Conclusion

> Open-mindedness opens closed doors, not all of them, but
> all those which hold culture's universal treasures. Beside the
> open mind there needs to be the open heart, open to all sorts
> and kinds of people, and the lowliest often enter with the
> most precious gifts.
> —Edward A. Steiner, *The Making of a Great Race*

Mainline Protestants were no longer the paragons of American culture
by the end of the twentieth century. Even by 1962, Protestant leaders recognized that their grip on culture was slipping. *Christianity and Crisis*,
a periodical formed earlier during World War II by Reinhold Niebuhr
and others within the mainline tradition, ran two articles in relation to
the question: "Protestantism on the Wane?" Both of the authors, sociologist Will Herberg (a Jewish immigrant from Belarus) and ethicist
Paul Lehmann (the son of an Ukrainian immigrant), conceded that the
Anglo-Protestant tradition was no longer at the helm of US society.[1] The
Immigration and Nationality Act passed three years later only cemented
these trends. Immigration from Latin America and from previously
restricted Asian nations, and in turn a stronger presence of religious
pluralism in the public square, ensured an end to an era in which white
mainline Protestants had served as cultural gatekeepers. Over the prior
40 years, mainline Protestants had done their best to navigate an increasing cultural diversity while still promoting a Protestant orientation for
the nation. Yet this pluralistic bargain proved unsustainable. Instead, in
their efforts to advance immigration reform, they inadvertently helped
usher in a new era of increasing immigration that contributed to their
cultural decline.

As we have seen, much of this struggle was apparent in the work of
mainline Protestant home missionaries, who demonstrated a largely
ambivalent approach to pluralism. Their thinking echoed the work of

philosopher Horace Kallen and his definition of cultural pluralism. The United States was at its best, according to cultural pluralists, when its ethnic communities maintained their own distinctive cultures, while still committing their allegiance to an American Way of Life. Social progressives during the first half of the twentieth century wanted it all—an American melting pot and multifaceted culture alongside a singular, or more "homogenous," national identity.[2] Such aspirations are largely enshrined in the American ideal of *E Pluribus Unum* ("out of many, one"). A Presbyterian publication in 1957 illustrates this ambivalence within mainline Protestant responses to immigration. "Yet one of our greatest assets is this very cultural and religious diversity," acknowledged the writer. "As the United States continues to consolidate its national life, one of the basic issues will be the proper relation of the whole to its parts and the parts to the whole."[3] Consolidation and diversity were held in unresolved tension.

The pluralistic bargain Protestants came to accept helps to clarify this conundrum. Protestants believed a shared Judeo-Christian faith would guarantee common American ideals, as outlined in Will Herberg's monumental midcentury work.[4] Such principles included tolerance and social accord based on acceptance of other cultures. A shared Christian faith encouraged Protestants to give less attention to cultural differences that existed, as they elevated religious identity over culture. This approach became even more important as the Cold War ensued, and a "godless" Russia threatened America. The popular revivalism of Billy Graham and other evangelicals by the 1960s began to stress what mainline Protestants had been arguing for some time—that religion was the foundation for national stability, while cultural differences were ancillary. In the process, mainline Protestants worked to promote a form of pluralism that was more cultural than religious. When they did acknowledge religious pluralism, it was nearly always limited to Protestantism, Catholicism, and Judaism.[5] Many mainline Protestant leaders turned to a more liberal immigration policy that welcomed cultural differences, with the understanding that America's religious identity would remain largely intact. What they did not realize was that they unwittingly helped pave the way for a broader religious pluralism in the future.

In historian William R. Hutchison's pivotal work, *Religious Pluralism in America*, he argued that American history reflects three different stages of pluralism. After the nation's founding and into the early republic, many Americans advocated "pluralism as toleration." But by the end of the nineteenth century, Americans began to consider "pluralism as inclusion." Finally, during the latter half of the twentieth century, Hutchison claimed, most Americans valued "pluralism as participation," though, according to Hutchison, this ideal has yet to be fully realized. It is Hutchison's stage of "pluralism as inclusion" that this book helps illuminate. Protestant positions on immigration and their home mission programs to immigrants and ethnic Americans reflected attempts to "include" immigrants in American life, but, as Hutchison pointed out, inclusive pluralism had many shortcomings, especially in its demands for assimilation and subsequent "forms of subordination."[6]

Not all white mainline Protestants supported an inclusive, cosmopolitan agenda; some instead favored hard-lined assimilation programs or simply wanted to see immigration drastically reduced. A clear gap remained between more liberal denominational leadership and a more conservative laity. A Harris survey conducted around the time that Congress was considering immigration reform in 1965 is telling; according to the poll, 65% of American Protestants did not want to see immigration increased.[7] A Presbyterian confessed in 1957, "In personal terms, we are likely to extol the virtues of our many-faceted cultural heritage, and at the same time make life difficult for the various minorities upon whom much of the pluralism depends."[8] Will Herberg, in his 1962 article in *Christianity and Crisis*, also recognized that white Protestantism was "having to adapt itself to what is, in effect, a minority status in a pluralistic culture that has become post-Protestant, and it is not doing this very well. It is an anxious, downward-heading minority, bristling with an aggressive defensiveness characteristic of such groups."[9] Liberal Protestant leaders often lamented racial and ethnic prejudice in American society, though much of it was coming from their own congregations.

As de facto gatekeepers, mainline Protestants, liberal and conservative alike, often mirrored at varying levels the prejudice and fears of society at large. Denominational leadership, NCC representatives, and CWS spokespeople often made clear that they supported reduced immigration numbers, just so long as government policy did not favor certain national groups over others. It was not until the 1950s that mainline Protestants began to realize that the quota system placed eastern and southern Europeans at a disadvantage, an observation that likely developed alongside the growing understanding that such groups were "white." This form of racial bias explains in part the eagerness with which mainline Protestants supported European refugee resettlement after World War II, while other, nonwhite refugees in other parts of the world were neglected. Even their response to the 1965 immigration reform is telling, since mainline Protestants did not challenge the government's decision to place a cap on Western Hemispheric immigration, which would for the first time officially limit Latin American immigration. This consent to government regulation of Latin American immigration reflected long-standing reservations regarding Mexican immigrants and labor, which helps to explain why the aggressive deportation and repatriation programs led by local and federal government bodies during the 1930s and 1950s went largely unrecognized by mainline Protestants. Much of the mainline Protestant agenda that supported liberal immigration reform was in the end rather moderate, if not conservative. They challenged policies premised on racial discrimination, while still wanting overall immigration numbers restricted.

Irony is also present in the ways that women contributed to mainline Protestant home missions. While the notion of "brotherhood" was ubiquitous among missions work and was meant to be inclusive, it deemphasized the work of Protestant women. This book has largely offered an account of men with access to denominational leadership and publishing opportunities, but while men were at the forefront, women were on the battlefront. Protestant women often were the ones visiting immigrant families and putting progressive ideals into action, while also inculcating American culture in immigrant communities. Many female home missionaries carried earlier social gospel programs into the midcentury. Home missions empowered white female missionaries while still inculcating distinct "American" gender norms among immigrant women and families.

One must also recognize the contributions of immigrants themselves in this narrative. Within mainline Protestant circles, immigrant ministers and staff supplied much needed counsel for home mission programs, while also reinforcing much of the work geared around assimilation that white mainline Protestants promoted. But whether they joined Protestant churches or not, many immigrants retained ethnic cultural practices in the face of strong Americanization programs during the twentieth century. By holding onto their cultural practices and identities, they forced white Americans to accommodate diversity. It is likely that mainline Protestants would have been less interested in cultural pluralism had immigrants not actively maintained their distinctive cultures.

In sum, this book has recounted a history of unintended consequences. Historian Stephen T. Wagner argues that policymakers in 1965 were "looking backwards more than forwards" when they overturned the national origins system.[10] The same can be said for Protestants invested in the debate. Protestants and politicians alike generally did not realize that immigration demographics would drastically change following passage of the Hart-Celler Act. Rising numbers of Asians and Latinos and a broader array of world religions made their way to the United States after 1965. Ten years later, Susan Jacoby wrote in the *New York Times* that immigration had reached its "highest point in half a century."[11] What resulted was far from the "new and compact national consciousness" for which Henry Goddard Leach had hoped in his *Forum* article from 1924. By the end of the twentieth century, most mainline Protestants could not, and would not, refer to America as a Christian nation. This was left to their distant relatives in the Religious Right.

As we have seen, a combination of home missions, Christian convictions, diffusion of earlier social gospel tenets, and the American Way of Life, along with a determination to confront racism and encourage toleration, inspired many ecumenical leaders within the FCC/NCC to promote midcentury immigration reform. Before the ink had dried on the Immigration Act of 1924, liberal minded Protestants began calling for immigration reform. Initially they only challenged Japanese exclusion, which threatened foreign missions and international diplomacy, but by the midcentury they began to realize the discrimination embedded in a system that favored some nations' immigrants over others. Even the most progressive leaders agreed, however, that a quota system was desirable that would limit the rising immigration they had witnessed at the turn of the twentieth century. But they still joined in the effort to lobby against a prejudicial application of the quota system.

While their progressive leanings were certainly not shared by all white American Protestants, liberal Protestant leaders' ideas gradually filtered down to temper the views of local congregations. City and state church councils began to follow ecumenical leaders in calling for immigration reform, and town churches began to sponsor refugees following the Second World War. Archival sources detailing local home mission programs suggest that certain social sensibilities on race and immigration reform were being diffused at the lower reaches of the Protestant church in the United States.

Ironically, while the pluralistic bargain would eventually contribute to mainline Protestantism's cultural decline as religious pluralism increasingly defined the social landscape, increasing immigration during the twentieth century also helped to revitalize American Protestantism. Numerous immigrant and refugee believers contributed to the nation's churches. While still predominantly white as of 2014, 7% of mainline Protestants and 13% of evangelicals identified as either Asian or Latino. By that same year, 14% of mainliners and 16% of evangelicals were either first- or second-generation immigrants.[12] Moreover, many immigrant and refugee theologians who came to America during the twentieth century enriched American Christian thinking. As a part of the pluralistic bargain, Protestants also began to come to terms with their complicity in racist policies and ascribe to forms of justice that drew them to aid the dispossessed. In grappling with pluralism, they realized the prophetic admonition declared in a Presbyterian periodical in 1957: "The danger in a pluralistic society that is prevailingly 'Christian' is that we represent to our fellow citizens not our Lord but our culture, or particular parts of it. In the political realm, we tend to identify democracy with Christianity, and our nation with God." The Presbyterian writer then asserted, "It is not our task to proclaim our culture in the name of the gospel, but to witness to the gospel. This we must do in terms both personal and social."[13] The pluralistic bargain and ensuing religious pluralism loosened mainline Protestants' grip on American society, but in so doing allowed them to reassess and renew the mission of their churches. And this did not signal the ultimate demise of Christianity in the United States. By the turn of the twenty-first century, many immigrants coming were Christians themselves, leading sociologist R. Stephen Warner to conclude that "the new immigrants represent not the de-Christianization of American society but the de-Europeanization of American Christianity."[14]

After 1965, American Protestants encountered multiple opportunities to practice a more welcoming attitude toward immigrants. Some focused their attention on the controversial issue of whether immigrants should have to register with the government.[15] Other mainline Protestants, reversing their earlier tendency to overlook deportation campaigns in the Southwest, began to criticize the practices of the Immigration and Naturalization Service as it targeted undocumented immigrants in places like Los Angeles during the early 1970s.[16] And following the Vietnam War, mainline Protestants assisted in resettling Vietnamese refugees. During the 1980s, several Protestant churches took part in the Sanctuary Movement that aided Latin Americans fleeing political oppression, and some, like the Episcopal Church, provided help to thousands of undocumented immigrants applying for amnesty under the Immigration Reform and Control Act of 1986.[17] And following the terrorist attacks on September 11, 2001, while American nativists began channeling what were earlier in history fears of Catholicism or communism toward Islam, several Protestant groups chose to resist the spate of anti-immigrant sentiments and policies.

In 2010, the American Baptist Churches USA issued a letter calling for immigration reform. The statement recognizes concerns over "national security, appropriate means of border control, and the impact on our economic and social welfare systems," but still concludes that "immigration reform in our country must reflect mercy and justice rooted in God's love." The document also reflects various historical precedents. It notes cooperation with Catholics and Eastern Orthodox Christians and even recognizes the earlier work that American Baptist women conducted within Christian Friendliness programs, what the document refers to as the denomination's "missional DNA." Finally, the signers welcomed the revitalization that immigration brought to American Baptist churches. "God has woven us into a coat of many colors."[18]

As the political parties began sifting through presidential candidates in the fall of 2015, the Stated Clerk of the PCUSA wrote an open letter to then Republican presidential candidate Donald Trump. Pointing to Trump's Presbyterian past, Gradye Parsons noted that the purpose of his letter was "to share with you [Trump] the Presbyterian policies on refugees and immigrants." Parsons declared, "Knowing our Lord was once a refugee, faithful Presbyterians have been writing church policy urging the welcome of refugees and demanding higher annual admissions into the United States since the refugee crisis of World War II." Parsons commented on the denomination's ties to foreign missions and how this fostered concern for refugees. In his letter, Parsons drew from the experience that Presbyterians, and many other mainline denominations, had accumulated in refugee and immigrant work over the latter half of the twentieth century.[19]

Today, it is not just progressive mainline figures who participate in this discussion. As mainline Protestants have lost much of the social and political capital they once had, Protestant evangelicals have filled the void and advocated for moderate immigration proposals, marking a stark shift from their earlier, more restrictive positions. Continuing more traditional forms of home missions while keeping a close eye on immigration policy debates, evangelicals have entered the fray. In the process, many evangelical leaders and organizations have found spiritual solidarity with immigrants and refugees, who arrive already within the evangelical fold. Their numbers continue to add to, and diversify, the evangelical base in the United States.[20]

Evangelicals have inherited many of the debates and talking points that mainline Protestants held at midcentury, while also echoing a similar missional impulse. In 1985, *Christianity Today* featured an article by Don Bjork on "Foreign Missions: Next Door and Down the Street." He drew his readers' attention to increasing immigration from Latin America and Asia, along with the refugee crises that the world still faced toward the end of the Cold War. Evangelicals by the 1980s recognized the changes brought about by the Immigration Act of 1965, and much like earlier mainline home missionaries, they believed an opportunity to share the gospel with people of different nationalities was now "down the street."[21]

Then in 1995, Tim Stafford, a senior writer at *Christianity Today*, wrote a piece responding to the prompt: "Has America's melting pot reached the boiling point?" Stafford answered with a resounding, "no," and provided a comprehensive assessment of the economic and cultural elements of immigration to America during the 1990s. Stafford, like mainline Protestants over the last 70 years, saw immigration as a missions opportunity and believed the Christian church should welcome cultural diversity. Two months later, *Christianity Today* published three

Figure C.1. Feature article in the July 1985 edition of *Christianity Today* suggesting foreign missions had in many ways become home missions with changing immigration patterns. Courtesy of *Christianity Today*.

responses to Stafford's article. Though noting agreement with much of Stafford's piece, a Korean immigrant, Chinkook Lee, felt that the "melting pot" language remained insufficient. Instead, Lee suggested that a "salad bowl" was a better metaphor, in that it recognized the peaceful coexistence of multiple cultures. In another response, Chinese American scholar and minister Timothy Tseng noted that Stafford's article, while helpful, did not sufficiently address the racialized challenges immigrants faced, and, like Lee, Tseng was not comfortable with the "melting pot" reference. Tseng recognized that "by employing an assimilationist approach, he (Stafford) encourages a we/they discourse that subtly assumes 'we' to be white evangelicals and 'they' the 'others' who will dissolve into the American 'melting pot.'" On the other end of the spectrum, the third response, by Leon G. Johnson, was less certain that increasing immigration was a positive development. "Stafford makes quite an assumption," Johnson claimed, "about the ability of Christianity to survive the tides of population migration and cultural upheaval." This late twentieth-century exchange demonstrates the continued fissures within American Protestantism over immigration and cultural diversity. Much like earlier mainline Protestants, voices for cultural pluralism, missions, and a uniform Christian identity continue to contend for the fate of the nation.[22]

In January 2017, various evangelical leaders signed a statement questioning then-President Trump's ban on refugees. They appealed to the Bible, which "teaches us that each person—including each refugee, regardless of their country of origin, religious background, or any other qualifier—is made in the Image of God, with inherent dignity and potential." They also stressed the importance of keeping refugee families together and drew from the Christian missional impulse "to love our neighbors, to make disciples of all nations, and to practice hospitality." They balanced these appeals with the understanding that national security remains important, appealing to the government "to be both compassionate *and* secure."[23] That same month the *Washington Post* published a letter Russell Moore, head of the Southern Baptist Ethics and Religious Liberty Commission, wrote to Trump. In many respects, his letter serves as a testimony to Protestant efforts during the twentieth century to assist immigrants and come to terms with pluralism. Moore highlighted the "church's commitment to welcoming the stranger." He cited Emma Lazarus's words on the Statue of Liberty and acknowledged the nation's failure to aid Jewish refugees during the 1930s. Moore, like other Protestant leaders, called for both "compassion for the sojourner and the security of our citizens," while also noting his concern for the safety of foreign missionaries in the Middle East. Reminiscent of arguments made by many Protestants after World War II, Moore noted the role of the United States as a "model for freedom around the world." In his concluding remarks, Moore identified a concern that lay at the heart of most Protestant responses to immigrants over the last century. He concluded that "assimilation into American life is crucial for both the security of our existing citizens and the well-being of refugee families. Christian churches and other faith communities have proven their unique ability to facilitate such adjustments."[24]

As Moore's statement suggests, certain Protestant responses to immigrants and refugees continue into the twenty-first century. Protestants still grapple with what is the proper relationship between national identity and pluralism, between religion and culture, and evangelicals today often reflect mainline approaches to immigrants and refugees from the last century. If Moore's comments are any indicator, Protestants will over the coming years continue to work through their spiritual and national commitments toward immigration, often with ambivalence. A 2018 Pew survey revealed that 49% of white mainline Protestants and 65% of white evangelicals supported Trump's policy on a border wall along the southern border of the United States, while a majority of both groups agreed that undocumented immigrants who came as children, known as Dreamers, should be given legal status.[25]

This book has shown that, with an ambivalent approach to pluralism, the Protestant gatekeepers of American culture helped to open the doors to increasing immigration from Latin America and Asia that ushered in more evangelical and charismatic forms of Protestantism and a multitude of other religions. In the end, the pluralistic bargain proved untenable. But as Robert McAfee Brown concluded in a 1962 editorial in *Christianity and Crisis*, "Perhaps it is a good thing for the vitality of the Protestant venture that we are no longer in the driver's seat. As long as we pretend that we still are and try to act accordingly, we will maneuver defensively rather than creatively." For Brown this was an opportunity: "Once we accept the fact, we may be able to find new ways to live in a new situation. This will mean accepting the role of tenants in a land we thought we owned, but being 'strangers and pilgrims on earth' is a role we should gladly embrace" instead of opting to "defensively resist."[26] In shedding their cultural supremacy, mainline Protestants gained an opportunity to reassess their mission, roll back more strident forms of xenophobia, contribute to much needed immigration policy reform, and, at a certain level, become "strangers and pilgrims" once more.

ACKNOWLEDGMENTS

This book would not have been possible without the support of count-less individuals and institutions. The guidance and backing received from everyone at NYU Press has been invaluable; thank you for mak-ing this book a reality. Jennifer Hammer helped hone my writing and arguments with exceptional care and acuity, Veronica Knutson offered superb and generous assistance in helping move this book forward, and the copyeditors and production and marketing crew went the extra mile in providing direction and support. It's been a privilege to work with a press that commits itself seriously to its authors and the advancement of scholarship and justice.

Central to this project were the sources drawn from multiple archives. The American Baptist Historical Society Archives, Archives of the Epis-copal Church, Congregational Library and Archives, Presbyterian His-torical Society, Southern Baptist Historical Library and Archives, and the United Methodist Church Archives proved to be indispensable. I especially appreciate the support provided by the United Methodist Church Archives through the Florence Ellen Bell Scholar Award and the Southern Baptist Historical Library and Archives with a Lynn E. May Study Grant. Cindy Johnson of the Woman's Missionary Union Library and Archives also kindly assisted me with pursuing further sources. The reliable and prompt assistance of the Baylor University Libraries and Interlibrary Services made researching and writing this project much more efficient. And I am also indebted to the gracious assistance Fran-ces Lyons, Jan Winfield, Lisa Jacobson, Daniel Pruitt, Lisa Moore at Tu-lane's Amistad Research Center, Sarah Gordon and Daniel Silliman with *Christianity Today*, and Customer Service for Getty Images provided in helping me prepare the images for this book.

My graduate school colleagues and professors inspired my work in manifold ways as this project germinated. Graduate students in Bay-lor's Department of History are a special group, a community of adept scholars and dear friends. I benefited greatly from the editorial insights and help with sources provided by Alina Beary, Nathan Cartagena, João Chaves, Tim Grundmeier, Adina Kelley, Sam Kelley, Patrick Leech, Brendan Payne, Paul Putz, Skylar Ray, and Regina Wenger. I will always be indebted to the History faculty at Baylor University. Beth Allison Barr provided constant support as both professor and Graduate Program Director, and T. Michael Parrish brought to my attention several important sources. While teaching at Baylor, David Bebbington had a formative influence on my development as a historian. In particular, his attention to the "diffusion" of ideas in history inspired much of my interpretation in this book. I also appreciate the invaluable insight that my dissertation committee members, Sarah Gilbreath Ford, Philip Jenkins, James M. SoRelle, and Andrea L. Turpin, provided and the generous assistance they continued to offer as I turned this project into a book. In good Strunk and White fashion, I must recognize at the end of this sequence of professors the faculty member who has contributed the most to my formation as a historian, my advisor Barry G. Hankins. I owe my formation as a scholar and writer to him. Thank you for your vision for the Baylor History Department and the humanity and scholarship you cultivate in your students.

The Eastern Nazarene College community has been a blessing over the last several years as I completed this book. The support, friendship, and counsel of my colleague, Bill McCoy, has been tremendous, and the faculty and staff at the college offered a warm welcome to this Texas expat teaching in Massachusetts. Their devotion to the Christian liberal arts tradition is heartening. Students studying history at ENC inspired my work during the latter stages of this project and continue to make teaching in higher education worthwhile. And I am grateful for the tireless assistance provided by our Director of Library Services, Amy Hwang, and the staff at the Nease Library.

I am also indebted to the host of scholars in the field of American religious history who provided feedback on this project and recommended sources or whose work has helped me grapple with this subject. Countless, unfortunately unnamed, people contributed helpful insights at various conferences. Moreover, I benefited from the support, suggestions, and scholarship of Peggy Bendroth, Heath Carter, Mark Edwards, Chris Evans, Aaron Griffith, Melody Maxwell, David Mislin, Randall

Stephens, Tom Whittaker, and Gene Zubovich, along with the manifold others who have committed themselves to studying immigration and religion during the twentieth century. And of course, without the critical insights of my outside readers, this study would be incomplete. I am grateful for your help in strengthening this book. But of course, as is inevitable with any written history, shortcomings remain, and I take full responsibility for them.

Finally, no scholar's work is separate from the support of friends and family. I am particularly thankful for the encouragement received from the Kelley and Cartagena families while working on this project. Joe and Debora Hoyle provided earnest friendship and hospitality, both before and after my move to Massachusetts. I'm also grateful for the sustaining influences of Mark Ferriero, Amélie Malouin, and my church, Christ the Redeemer Quincy. My brother, sister-in-law, and nephew, Andrew, Stacey, and Emmett; sister, brother-in-law, niece, and nephew, Bethanie, Micah, Eloise, and Nebuchadnezzar; brother and sister-in-law, Daniel and Reagan; and sister, Lydia, all inspired my work. You make life exciting and full of meaning. My parents, Mark and Karla, remain a strong pillar of support in my life, providing steadfast encouragement, love, and wisdom. I am so blessed to have you as parents and friends and value the support you have given me throughout my life. Finally, I am forever indebted to the legacy of my grandparents and their example of faith, hope, and love through their commitment to the church, education, and family.

NOTES

INTRODUCTION

1 Pew Research Center, "Faith on the Hill: The Religious Composition of the 116th Congress," January 3, 2019, *Pew Research Center*, www.pewforum.org.

2 Jones, *The End of White Christian America*.

3 Huntington, *Who Are We*.

4 NCC, *Witness for Immigration*, xi.

5 Cohen and Numbers, "Introduction," in Cohen and Numbers, *Gods in America*, 1, 6–7; Charles Lippy, "From Consensus to Struggle: Pluralism and the Body Politic in Contemporary America," in Cohen and Numbers, *Gods in America*, 298, 300–303; Marsden, *The Twilight of the American Enlightenment*, 97–126; and Hedstrom, *The Rise of Liberal Religion*. See also Lippy, *Pluralism Comes of Age*. Kevin Schultz persuasively demonstrates that a "tri-faith" conglomeration of Protestants, Catholics, and Jews was already in the making prior to 1950. Schultz, *Tri-Faith America*. See also Schultz, "The Blessings of American Pluralism, and Those Who Rail Against It," 269–85. The topics of gender and sexuality in American society during the twentieth century also demonstrate the marginalization of American Protestantism and its internal ruptures. See Griffith, *Moral Combat*.

6 As Maddalena Marinari demonstrates in *Unwanted*, immigrants also organized resistance to the policy of restriction during this period. For recent historical work on immigration and policy during this period, see Marinari, Hsu, and García, *A Nation of Immigrants Reconsidered*; and Yang, *One Mighty and Irresistible Tide*.

7 See for example, Davis, *Immigration, Baptists, and the Protestant Mind in America*; Chang, *Citizens of a Christian Nation*; Phalen, *American Evangelical Protestantism and European Immigrants, 1800–1924*. See also Dinnerstein and Reimers, "Strangers in the Land," 115; Higham, "Ethnicity and American Protestants," 239–59. For a helpful assessment of the historiography of immigration and religious history more generally, see Dolan, "Immigration and American Christianity," 119–47.

8 Concerning historical definitions of pluralism in the United States, see Hutchison, *Religious Pluralism in America*.

9 Hollinger, "Pluralism, Cosmopolitanism, and the Diversification of Diversity," 79–104; Kenny, "The World Day of Prayer," 129–58; Kaufman, *Horace Kallen Confronts America*; Ngai, *Impossible Subjects*, 230–34; Gordon, *Assimilation in American Life*, 141–49; Ratner, "Horace M. Kallen and Cultural Pluralism," 185–

200. For more on Hollinger's treatment of Protestants and cosmopolitanism, see *After Cloven Tongues of Fire* and *Protestants Abroad*.

10 Horace M. Kallen, "Democracy Versus the Melting-Pot," *The Nation*, February 18, 1915, 190–94; February 25, 1915, 217–20; Kallen, *Culture and Democracy in the United States*, 35. Kallen continued to work on this topic later in the century. See Kallen, *Cultural Pluralism and the American Idea*. For treatment of the continued influence of Kallen and the idea of cultural pluralism, see Fleegler, *Ellis Island Nation*; Gleason, "American Identity and Americanization," 43–50; Bon Tempo, *Americans at the Gate*, 23.

11 See Schultz, *Tri-Faith America*; Hutchison, *Religious Pluralism in America*.

12 Gaston, *Imagining Judeo-Christian America*.

13 Cohen and Numbers, "Introduction," in Cohen and Numbers, *Gods in America*, 1; Wild, *Renewal*, 8; Gleason, "American Identity and Americanization," 50; Fleegler, *Ellis Island Nation*; and Higham, *Hanging Together*.

14 John Higham, "Pluralistic Integration as an American Model (1975)," in Higham, *Hanging Together*, 110–33.

15 Jon Butler noted in his presidential address at the 2016 meeting of the Organization of American Historians the importance of institutional religious history and its vitality during the expansion of modernism in early twentieth-century America. Butler, "God, Gotham, and Modernity," 19–33. See also Davis, *The Methodist Unification*, 7.

16 Watson, *Year Book of the Churches, 1921–22*, 250; Graham Reside, "The State of Contemporary Mainline Protestantism," in Hudnut-Beumler and Silk, *The Future of Mainline Protestantism in America*, 18.

17 For historical and scholarly work on mainline Protestantism, see Hutchison, *Between the Times*; Lantzer, *Mainline Christianity*; Coffman, The Christian Century; Hollinger, *After Cloven Tongues of Fire*; Bowman, *The Urban Pulpit*; Bendroth, *The Last Puritans*; Peter J. Thuesen, "The Logic of Mainline Churchliness: Historical Background since the Reformation," in Wuthnow and Evans, *The Quiet Hand of God*, 27–53; Wild, *Renewal*; and Hudnut-Beumler and Silk, *The Future of Mainline Protestantism in America*.

18 US Department of Commerce, Bureau of the Census, *Religious Bodies: 1926, Vol. I, Summary and Detailed Tables*, 15–16; Wuthnow, *The Restructuring of American Religion*, 186.

19 See, for example, Coffman, The Christian Century; Hollinger, *After Cloven Tongues of Fire*, 29, 33.

20 I owe an intellectual debt to David Bebbington for introducing me to the concept of diffusion within religious history. Bebbington, "Evangelicalism and Cultural Diffusion."

21 For a more class-oriented study of immigration, see Bodnar, *The Transplanted*.

22 North American Home Missions Congress, *Reports of Commissions*, 78.

23 Exceptions include Davis, *Immigration, Baptists, and the Protestant Mind in America*; Chang, *Citizens of a Christian Nation*; Wuthnow and Evans, *The Quiet Hand of God*; Reeves-Ellington, Sklar, and Shemo, *Competing Kingdoms*; Yohn, *A Contest of Faiths*; and Banker, *Presbyterian Missions and Cultural Interaction*. See also Hollinger, *Protestants Abroad*, 14–15.

24 "Because We Are . . . 'A City Set on a Hill,'" *Presbyterian Life*, October 18, 1952, 13.

25 In her work on women and Presbyterian missions in the Catholic Southwest during the late nineteenth and early twentieth centuries, Susan M. Yohn addresses a similar dynamic. Yohn, *A Contest of Faiths*, 3.

26 Curtis, *A Consuming Faith*, xiv, 1–2.

27 Carter, *Union Made*; Hedstrom, *The Rise of Liberal Religion*; Evans, *The Social Gospel in American Religion*; Curtis, *A Consuming Faith*; White and Hopkins, *The Social Gospel*; May, *Protestant Churches and Industrial America*; Miller, *American Protestantism and Social Issues, 1919–1939*; Carter, *The Decline and Revival*; Hopkins, *The Rise of the Social Gospel*; Evans, *The Social Gospel Today*; Luker, *The Social Gospel in Black and White*; White, *Liberty and Justice for All*; Edwards and Gifford, *Gender and the Social Gospel*; and Hutchison, "The Americanness of the Social Gospel," 367–81.

28 For histories of immigration policy, see Kraut, "A Century of Scholarship," 140; Zolberg, *A Nation by Design*; Martin, *A Nation of Immigrants*; Tichenor, *Dividing Lines*; and Fleegler, *Ellis Island Nation*.

29 Daniels, *Coming to America*, 113.

30 For histories of nativism, see Daniels, *Coming to America*, 265–84; Archdeacon, *Becoming American*, xvii; Higham, *Strangers in the Land*; Oxx, *The Nativist Movement in America*; Burgquist, "The Concept of Nativism," 125–41; Daniels, "Changes in Immigration Law," 159–80; Allerfeldt, *Race, Radicalism, Religion, and Restriction*; Ross, *Forging New Freedoms*; Petit, *The Men and Women We Want*; Zeidel, *Immigrants, Progressives, and Exclusion Politics*; Benton-Cohen, *Inventing the Immigration Problem*; De León, *They Called Them Greasers*; Montejano, *Anglos and Mexicans*; Gordon, *The Great Arizona Orphan Abduction*; Guerin-Gonzales, *Mexican Workers and American Dreams*; Hoffman, *Unwanted Mexican Americans*; Jacobson, *The New Nativism*; Chan, *Entry Denied*; Lew-Williams, *The Chinese Must Go*; Hirobe, *Japanese Pride, American Prejudice*; Kinzer, *An Episode in Anti-Catholicism*; Bennett, *The Party of Fear*; Jacobson, *Barbarian Virtues*; Hirota, *Expelling the Poor*; Ngai, *Impossible Subjects*; Borstelmann, *Just Like Us*; and Okrent, *The Guarded Gate*.

31 Billington, *The Protestant Crusade*. See also Shea, *The Lion and the Lamb*.

32 Lee, *America for Americans*.

33 Gaston, *Imagining Judeo-Christian America*, 3–4.

34 Fleegler explicates this well in *Ellis Island Nation*.

35 For more on the histories of race, ethnicity, and immigration in the United States, see Kraut, "A Century of Scholarship," 134–37; Jacobson, *Whiteness of a Different Color*; Roediger, *The Wages of Whiteness*; Horsman, *Race and Manifest Destiny*; and Gerstle, *American Crucible*.

36 Grant, *The Passing of the Great Race*, 228. See also Spiro, *Defending the Master Race*.

37 Jacobson, *Whiteness of a Different Color*. For more on white American designations of racial/ethnic "outsiders," see Roediger, *Working Toward Whiteness*; Fleegler, *Ellis Island Nation*; and Guglielmo, *White on Arrival*.

38 See Cheng, *Citizens of Asian America*; Buff, *Immigrant Rights*; Ngai, *Impossible Subjects*, 227–30, 240; Tichenor, *Dividing Lines*, 212–13; Findlay, *Church People in the Struggle*; Chappell, *A Stone of Hope*; Alvis, *Religion and Race*; Shattuck, *Episcopalians and Race*; Willis, *All According to God's Plan*; and Newman, *Getting Right with God*.

39 Gabaccia, *From the Other Side*; Gardner, *The Qualities of a Citizen*. See also Petit, *The Men and Women We Want*.

40 Jane H. Hunter, "Women's Mission in Historical Perspective: American Identity and Christian Internationalism," in Reeves-Ellington, Sklar, and Shemo, *Competing Kingdoms*, 19–42. See also Derek Chang, "Imperial Encounters at Home: Women, Empire, and the Home Mission Project in Late Nineteenth-Century America," in Reeves-Ellington, Sklar, and Shemo, *Competing Kingdoms*, 293–317.

41 See Turpin, *A New Moral Vision*; Kunzel, *Fallen Women, Problem Girls*; Edwards and Gifford, *Gender and the Social Gospel*.

42 Kenny, "The World Day of Prayer," 129–58. The work of historian Melody Maxwell on Southern Baptist settlement house work among Italians in Birmingham, Alabama, is a good example of a gradual shift toward male control of home mission work. Maxwell, "'We Are Happy to Co-Operate,'" 249–65. Other studies of Protestant women's home mission work include Reeves-Ellington, Sklar, and Shemo, *Competing Kingdoms*; Yohn, *A Contest of Faiths*.

43 Key studies on the notion of America as a "Christian nation" include Green, *Inventing a Christian America*; Kruse, *One Nation Under God*; and Hamburger, *Separation of Church and State*.

44 For a history of the civil rights movement and Cold War foreign policy, see Dudziak, *Cold War Civil Rights*.

CHAPTER 1. SETTLING INTO RESTRICTION

1 Leach, "The Next Forty Years," 414–19; first quote from 416; second quote from 414; third quote from 419; fourth quote from 417.

2 Ibid., first quote from 414; second quote from 419.

3 Zolberg provides a comprehensive overview of American immigration policy during this period in *A Nation by Design*, 200–201, 238–67. See also Marinari, *Unwanted*, 36–80.

4 Watson, *Year Book of the Churches, 1921–22*, 250; US Department of Commerce, Bureau of the Census, *Religious Bodies: 1926, Vol. I, Summary and Detailed Tables*, 15–16.

5 Daniels, *Coming to America*, 124.

6 I especially appreciate the sources related to the social gospel and home missions to immigrants identified by Olivier Zunz in *Why the American Century?*, 231n48.

7 Dr. W. M. Gilbert, "Dr. Gilbert's Address," *Woman's Home Missions* 39 (December 1922), 18.

8 Burgess, *Foreign-Born Americans*, 25.

9 Selected, "God Is Sending Them," *Missionary Review of the World* 47 (June 1924), 466.

10 HMC, *Thirteenth Annual Meeting*, 12–26, 96, 99, 100–102; PHS, "Biographical Note/ Administrative History," HMC of North America Records, NCC RG 26, Presbyterian Historical Society, www.history.pcusa.org; Thomson, *Enter the Mexican*, 7.

11 HMC and CWHM, *Fifteenth Annual Meeting*, 189–92; "Christian Workers at Ellis Island," *Woman's Home Missions* 40 (June 1923), 10; "Since eighty per cent," *Woman's Home Missions* 39 (November 1922), 16; Henry M. Bowden, "Ellis Island Today," *American Missionary* 76 (May 1921), 76–77.

12 "CHMS, 1925," 18.6.3 Box 9, CLA.

13 PEC, *Living Church Annual, Churchman's Year Book, and American Church Almanac, 1924*, 97.

14 Millicent M. McCorkle, "How They Celebrated Christmas," *Woman's Home Missions* 39 (March 1922), 10–11.

15 MECS, *Missionary Yearbook* (1930), 34; "All Along the Gulf Coast," *Missionary Voice* 16 (August 1926), 29; "Immigration Service at Galveston," *Missionary Voice* 17 (April 1927), 27; John E. Reifschneider, "Serving at a Gateway," *Missionary Voice* 17 (October 1927), 26.

16 Higham, *Strangers in the Land*, 121.

17 H. Campbell-Duncan, "Creating Wealth Out of Waste," *The Baptist*, May 31, 1924, 423–25; first quote from 423; second quote from 423; third quote from 423–24; fourth quote from 424. See also Charles L. White, "Tracing the Spiritual Growth of a Great Society," *The Baptist*, May 31, 1924, 433. Northern Baptists had a long tradition of ministry to immigrants. During the late nineteenth and early twentieth centuries, Baptists in the North and Midwest sponsored work in urban centers and labored to meet both the spiritual and physical needs of the immigrants, while also demonstrating a strong impulse to Americanize the newcomers. See Davis, *Immigrants, Baptists, and the Protestant Mind in America*; Phalen, *American Evangelical Protestantism and European Immigrants, 1800–1924*.

18 Landis, *Protestant Experience*, 21–22. See also "New Day of Home Missions," *Missionary Voice* 13 (March 1923), 87; "The Little Scotch Bride," *Missionary Voice* 16 (December 1926), 19.

19 PCUSA, *One Hundred Sixteenth Annual Report*, 19–20. See also "Articles, 1922–24," UPCUSA Board of National Missions Dept. of Mission Development Records, box 10, folder 1, RG 301.7.10.1, PHS.

20 "Review of the year in figures, Board of Church Erection," *The Presbyterian*, May 19, 1921, 18. For more on Presbyterian work among Mexican American communities, see Brackenridge and García-Treto, *Iglesia Presbiteriana*; Yohn, *A Contest of Faiths*; and Banker, *Presbyterian Missions and Cultural Interaction*. See also McLean and Williams, *Old Spain in New America*.

21 Thomson, *Enter the Mexican*, 8.

22 PCUSA, *Minutes of the General Assembly of the Presbyterian Church in the U.S.A.*, vol. 1, part 1 (1922), 287.

23 For earlier Episcopal work among immigrants and society, see Holmes, *A Brief History*, 87–91; Prichard, *A History*, 224–30.

24 Burgess, *Foreign-Born Americans*, quote from 23.

25 Foreign-Born Americans Division, National Council of the PEC, *How to Reach the Foreign-Born*, first quote from 10; second quote from 11; third quote from 11; fourth quote from 4; fifth quote from 16; sixth quote from 17; seventh quote from 19; final block quote from 18, AEC. See also Burgess, Gilbert, and Bridgeman, *Foreigners or Friends*.

26 For early twentieth-century Congregational home mission work among immigrants, see Pruitt, "American Sojourners," 6–13.

27 "CHMS, 1925," 18.6.3 Box 9, CLA.

28 CHMS, "Summary of Work: 1924," 18.6.3 Box 9, CLA.

29 "Filipinos in the United States," *American Missionary* 79 (November 1925), 304.

30 "The Farthest-Reaching Kindergarten in the World," *American Missionary* 79 (March 1925), 500–503.

31 For Southern Baptist social ministry during the late nineteenth and early twentieth centuries, see Harper, *The Quality of Mercy*. See also Holcomb, "The Kingdom at Hand."

32 "Broad Field Open to Home Missions," *Campaign Talking Points*, November 1, 1923, 1; see also W. H. Knight, "Christianizing the Homeland," *Baptist Standard*, March 9, 1922, 12–13. This article stated that the Southern Baptist Home Mission Board was ministering to Swedes, Germans, Italians, Cubans, French, and Mexicans in various states.

33 Alldredge, *Southern Baptist Handbook 1924*, 203–204.

34 BGCT, *Annual of the Baptist General Convention of Texas* (1921), 22.

35 Loyd Carter, "Good Will Center Work" and Sara Taylor, "Good Will Centers in Missions," in *Encyclopedia of Southern Baptists*, 569–70; Maxwell, "'We Are Happy to Co-operate,'" 249–65. See also frequent attention to immigrants in *Royal Service* at this time.

36 BGCT, *Annual of the Baptist General Convention of Texas* (1924), 121–22.

37 Dawson, *The Spiritual Conquest of the Southwest*, 157.

38 For historical work on this movement, see Evans, *The Social Gospel in American Religion*; Carter, *Union Made*; Curtis, *A Consuming Faith*; Carter, *The Decline and Revival*; Miller, *American Protestantism and Social Issues, 1919–1939*; May, *Protestant Churches and Industrial America*; Hopkins, *The Rise of the Social Gospel*; White and Hopkins, *The Social Gospel*; Evans, *The Social Gospel Today*; Luker, *The Social Gospel in Black and White*; White, *Liberty and Justice for All*; Edwards and Gifford, *Gender and the Social Gospel*; and Hutchison, "The Americanness of the Social Gospel," 367–81.

39 AMA, *Seventy-Eighth Annual Report*, 92.

40 For a helpful introduction into the European origins of these concepts and their usage among American religious leaders at the turn of the century, see Wattles, *The Golden Rule*, 90–104. See also David Mislin's argument that late nineteenth-century liberal Protestantism inspired Christian notions of "brotherhood" during the twentieth century. Mislin, *Saving Faith*, 11–12.

41 Henry C. Adams, "Introduction," in Addams et al., *Philanthropy and Social Progress*, xi; Jane Addams, "The Subjective Necessity for Social Settlements," 2, quote from 6, in Addams et al., *Philanthropy and Social Progress*.

42 Kittelstrom, "The International Social Turn," 245, 251–52; Mislin, *Saving Faith*, 60, 70; Wattles, *The Golden Rule*, 91, 94.

43 Katharine Lee Bates, "America," *The Congregationalist*, July 4, 1895, 17; "The Listener," *Boston Evening Transcript*, November 19, 1904, 19; Collins, *Songs Sung Red, White, and Blue*, 13–21. See also Bates's poem "To My Country," in which she wrote: "Climb to the light. Imperiled Pioneer; Of Brotherhood among the nations, seal; Our faith with thy sublime." In Bates, *America the Beautiful and Other Poems*, 34.

44 By the mid-twentieth century, its more universal inference would be used once again in the spirit of global peace and cooperation following two world wars. Sociologist Will Herberg would conclude in 1955 that the brotherhood of man, along with the Fatherhood of God and the "dignity of the individual human being," were "spiritual values" in American society. Herberg, *Protestant, Catholic, Jew*, 38–39.

45 Morris, *The Task That Challenges*, 84. See also the chapter titled "America, The Melting Pot," 159–86.

46 Wattles, *The Golden Rule*, 93.

47 Barker, *The Social Gospel and the New Era*, 15.

48 Grose, *Aliens or Americans?* 297.

49 Burgess, Gilbert, and Bridgeman, *Foreigners or Friends*, 48.

50 National Council of the CCUS, *The Congregational Year-Book*, Vol. 47, 18.

51 Evans, *The Social Gospel in American Religion*, 11; Darryl M. Trimiew, "The Social Gospel Movement and the Question of Race," in Evans, *The Social Gospel Today*, 27–37; Luker, *The Social Gospel in Black and White*; White, *Liberty and Justice for All*.

52 "How Long Will America Be American?" *Christian Century*, August 23, 1917, 6. The article also reflected a callous nativist viewpoint of immigrant childbirth and parenting. "There is, of course, some offset to this [population statistic]. Among these people less intelligence is used in the rearing of children and the infantile death rate is also higher. It is not enough, however, to make up the difference."

53 Richard H. Edmonds, "The South a Great Mission Field," *Baptist Standard*, May 1, 1924, 7, 37.

54 "Urge Government Action," *The Presbyterian*, April 24, 1924, 22. For historical context on ethnicity and immigration in Arizona at the turn of the twentieth century, see Gordon, *The Great Arizona Orphan Abduction*.

55 Thomson, *Enter the Mexican*.

56 Edith Terry Bremer, "Half Brothers from Across the Border," *Missionary Voice* 18 (February 1928), 22.

57 Foreign-Born Americans Division, National Council of the PEC, *How to Reach the Foreign-Born*, 3, AEC.

58 "A Moron Militant," *Independent*, August 21, 1926, 198.

59 Erdmann D. Beynon, "The Country Church and the Foreigner," *Methodist Review* (January 1927), 84.

60 Strong, *The Challenge of the City*, 149.

61 Gordon, *Assimilation in American Life*, 137–38; Lissak, *Pluralism and Progressives*.

62 Kallen, "Democracy Versus the Melting-Pot," February 18, 1915, 190–94; February 25, 1915, 217–20; first quote from 219; second quote from 220. See also Kaufman, *Horace Kallen Confronts America*. Kallen would over the course of his career continue to advance a positive interpretation of cultural pluralism. See Kallen, *Culture and Democracy in the United States*; and Kallen, *Cultural Pluralism and the American Idea*.

63 Mislin, *Saving Faith*, 8–9, 60, 160.

64 Ibid., 11–12, 60, 70, 147, 162. See also Schultz, *Tri-Faith America*.

65 "Worshiping God at the Gates of Entry," *Missionary Voice* 13 (February 1923), 52.

66 Marinari, *Unwanted*, 91–92.

67 Truett, "Baptists and Religious Liberty," 66.

68 Burgess, *Foreign-Born Americans*. In 1919, Northern Baptist women formed a Christian Americanization program through the WABHMS that initiated work among immigrants. Carlson, "Chronology of the American Baptist Churches, USA," 146; "11/14/55," Publicity, Christian Friendliness, WABHMS, box 32, folder 6, ABHS; Kinney, *The World at My Door*, 167–77. The New York Diocese's Social Service Commission sponsored an Americanization Committee as of 1921. Burgess, Gilbert, and Bridgeman, "Preface," *Foreigners or Friends*; Diocese of New York, *Journal of the One Hundred and Thirty-Eighth Convention*, 227, AEC.

69 Chang, "'Brought Together,'" 41; Chang, *Citizens of a Christian Nation*.

70 Higham, *Strangers in the Land*, 260–63. Both Sidney Gulick and Charles Brooks suggested Americanization was not a complete success by the 1920s. Sidney L. Gulick, "A Comprehensive Immigration Policy and Program," *Scientific Monthly* 6 (March 1918), 214; Brooks, *Christian Americanization*, 5–6.

71 Kallen, "Democracy Versus the Melting-Pot," February 18, 1915, 192.

72 Craig, *America, God's Melting-Pot*, see 80 for a brief reference to "the brotherhood-of-man viewpoint." See also Harkness, *The Church and the Immigrant*.

73 Laura S. Copenhagen, "A Hymn of Christian Americanization," *Missionary Voice* 14 (July 1924), 29.

74 Brooks, *Christian Americanization*. Even Southern Baptists, by no means ecumenical, referenced the book in their own handbook on immigrant ministry published in the 1930s. Plainfield, *The Stranger within Our Gates*, 87. The HMC also promoted material for young adults that included books with accompanying pictures of immigrants. The Council even suggested for its Protestant readers a drama production titled "A Pageant of Democracy." Brooks, *Christian Americanization*, 161. See also Brooks, *The Church and the Foreigner*; Brooks, *Through*

the Second Gate; and Florence E. Quinlan, "Some Samples from 'The New Line,'" *Missionary Review of the World* 42 (August 1919), 612–14.

75 Brooks, *Christian Americanization*, 5–6, 9–12.

76 Ibid., 32–33.

77 Ibid., 30–31. See also Phalen, *American Evangelical Protestantism and European Immigrants, 1800–1924*, 177–78.

78 "The Task of the Church at Home," *Missionary Voice* 13 (May 1923), 131.

79 Burgess, *Foreign-Born Americans*, 19.

80 Brooks, *Christian Americanization*, first quote from 98; second quote from 147.

81 Mrs. W. H. Hickman, "Immigration," *Woman's Home Missions* 39 (November 1922), 14–15.

82 "What about Immigration?" *Missionary Voice* 13 (November 1923), 324.

83 "A Hyphenated Allegiance," *The Presbyterian*, February 15, 1917, 12. See also "The Immigrant Problem in Chicago," *Missionary Voice* 13 (February 1923), 48.

84 MECS, *Seventy-Eighth Annual Report*, 24–25.

85 Alldredge, *Southern Baptist Handbook 1924*, first quote from 43; second quote from 39. See also W. H. Knight, "Christianizing the Homeland," *Baptist Standard*, March 9, 1922, 12.

86 L. M. Martucci, "Our Italian People," *Baptist Standard*, January 31, 1918, 26.

87 MECS, *Seventy-Ninth Annual Report*, 20.

88 Alldredge, *Southern Baptist Handbook 1924*, 43; "Chit-Chat on a Dining Car," *World Outlook* 25 (October 1935), 28.

89 MECS, *Missionary Yearbook* (1930), 33, 385, 390–91, 395; Thomson, *Enter the Mexican*, 1; Elmer T. Clark, "Methodist Mexicans of the Southwest," *World Outlook* 29 (January 1939), 4. For the consequences that these racial views had on social welfare for Mexican and European immigrants, see Fox, *Three Worlds of Relief*.

90 AMA, *The Eighty-First Annual Report*, 33; AMA, *The Eighty-Second Annual Report*, 39–40.

91 "Jews and Christians Agree on Definition of 'Americanization,'" *Federal Council Bulletin* 3 (April 1920), 66.

92 Machen, *Christianity and Liberalism*, 149.

93 Brooks, *Christian Americanization*, 78.

94 "The Literacy Test Bill Becomes a Law," *The Presbyterian*, February 15, 1917, 4.

95 Phalen, *American Evangelical Protestantism and European Immigrants, 1800–1924*, 186, 188.

96 *Christian Century*, May 5–June 30, 1921.

97 "Limited Immigration in Force Here," *Christian Advocate*, June 9, 1921, 749.

98 G.B.F. Hallock, "Young People's Prayer-Meeting," *The Presbyterian*, April 21, 1921, 13.

99 "What about Immigration?" *Missionary Voice* 13 (November 1923), 323–24.

100 AMA, *Seventy-Eighth Annual Report*, 31.

101 Hirobe, *Japanese Pride, American Prejudice*, 3–13.

102 Ibid., 5, 12–13; Taylor, *Advocate of Understanding*; Phalen, *American Evangelical Protestantism and European Immigrants, 1800–1924*, 183; Gulick, "A Comprehensive Immigration Policy," 214–23. See also Gulick, *Should Congress Enact Special Laws*. For more on Gulick and also the central role the YMCA played in advocating for Asian Americans throughout the first half of the twentieth century, see Griffith, *The Fight for Asian American Civil Rights*.

103 Cavert, *The Churches Allied*, 183, quote from 186.

104 Ibid., 187–89, quote from 189.

105 McClatchy, *Japanese Immigration and Colonization*, 51–52, quote from 51.

106 For the Catholic response to immigration restriction during this time, see Gribble, "The Immigration Restriction Debate, 1917–1929."

107 "The Trend of Events," *Herald of Gospel Liberty* 116 (October 1924), 989. See also *The Baptist*, May 31, 1924, 436–37; "Exclusion and Missions," *Missionary Review of the World* 47 (September 1924), 742; Axling, *Japan Wonders Why?*; and Disciples of Christ, *1925 Year Book*, 104. See also MECS, *Seventy-Eighth Annual Report*, 256; MECS, *Seventy-Ninth Annual Report*, 13, 99, 101; "Adult Program—March, Japan Missions and Immigration," *Missionary Voice* 16 (February 1926), 29; Julia McGowan, "Missions and International Relations," *Missionary Voice* 19 (January 1929), 16.

108 "'The Gentleman's Agreement' with Japan," *The Presbyterian*, April 24, 1924, 13.

109 "The Japanese Army and Navy," *The Presbyterian*, May 1, 1924, 13.

110 AMA, *Seventy-Eighth Annual Report*, 30.

111 "Immigration and Assimilation," *The Baptist*, April 26, 1924, 296.

112 James H. Franklin, "As Others See Us," *The Baptist*, May 17, 1924, 383.

113 Corwin S. Shank, "Annual Address of the President of the Northern Baptist Convention," *The Baptist*, June 7, 1924, 447–50; "The Eighteenth Annual Meeting of the Northern Baptist Convention," *The Baptist*, June 14, 1924, 475. Southern Baptist E. C. Routh, editor of the *Baptist Standard*, affirmed his northern counterpart's criticism of the 1924 law. E. C. Routh, "The Northern Baptist Convention," *Baptist Standard*, June 5, 1924, 7.

114 "The Trend of Events," *Herald of Gospel Liberty* 116 (April 1924), 317. Brooks also recognized this in his book on Americanization. He wrote, "As a nation we are committed irrevocably to the separation of church and state; but that does not involve the divorcement of religion from the national life." Brooks, *Christian Americanization*, 155.

115 "Editorial," *Woman's Home Missions* 39 (November 1922), 16.

116 "Editorial Notes," *Home Mission Monthly* 37 (April 1922), 131.

117 "The Japanese Exclusion Measure," "Facing the Future," *Missionary Voice* 14 (October 1924), 4–5, 22.

118 Hirobe notices this as well, *Japanese Pride, American Prejudice*, 225. The executive secretary of the World Student Christian Federation did suggest quota laws should be adjusted to allow more foreign students to come to America. Muriel Day, "The Foreign Student in America," *Woman's Home Missions* 40 (December 1923), 8.

119 E. H. Zaugg, "The Present Race Problem," *Reformed Church Review* 3 (July 1924), 281.

120 "American Prejudice against Japan," *Missionary Voice* 16 (May 1926), 21.

121 Phalen, *American Evangelical Protestantism and European Immigrants, 1800–1924*, 76–81.

122 For a Japanese Congregational perspective on exclusion, see Seizo Abe, "An Evangelistic Tour Along the Pacific Coast," *American Missionary* 79 (June 1925), 113.

123 Executive Committee, FCC, *Declaration Regarding Asiatic Exclusion*, December 11, 1925, FCC Records, box 35, folder 14, NCC RG 18.35.14, PHS.

124 PEC, *Journal of the General Convention* (1928), 126, 145, quote from 126.

125 SBC, *Annual of the Southern Baptist Convention* (1925), 125–26.

126 National Council of the CCUS, *Twenty-Second Regular Meeting*, 230.

127 General Council of the CCC, *Digest Minutes*, 218.

128 "Regional Conference, Western Division, Meets," *Missionary Voice* 16 (September 1926), 26.

129 For the election of 1928 and responses to Al Smith's candidacy, see Hankins, *Jesus and Gin*, 187–212.

130 Steiner, *The Making of a Great Race*, 29.

131 For interwar Protestant fundamentalism, see Carpenter, *Revive Us Again*.

CHAPTER 2. THE TRYING THIRTIES

1 Steiner referred to culture as "the result of a certain form of spiritual life in the three dominant religious groups in the United States—Jews, Roman Catholics, and Protestants—and, to a lesser degree, culture as an expression of racial inheritance and national tradition." Steiner, *The Making of a Great Race*, 7–8; Steiner, *From Alien to Citizen*.

2 Messmore Kendall, "America's Place in International Affairs," *Vital Speeches of the Day*, December 15, 1938, 159.

3 See Morse, *Home Missions Today and Tomorrow*, 123–24.

4 Together, the church membership of these denominations reflected nearly 10% of the US population during the 1930s. This percentage is based on the 1936 Census of Religious Bodies and overall 1940 Census for the Continental United States. US Department of Commerce, Bureau of the Census, *Religious Bodies: 1936, Vol. I, Summary and Detailed Tables*, 19; US Department of Commerce, Bureau of the Census, *Historical Statistics of the United States, 1789–1945*, 25.

5 Kinney, *The World at My Door*, 76.

6 Morse, *Toward a Christian America*, 162.

7 PEC, "Church Settlements," *Living Church Annual, Year Book of the Episcopal Church, 1935*, 137.

8 Diocese of New York, *Journal of the One Hundred and Fifty-Sixth Convention*, 146, AEC; Woman's Home Missionary Society of the MEC, *Fifty-Fifth Annual Report*, 159.

9 PEC, *Journal of the General Convention of the Protestant Episcopal Church in the United States of America, 1931*, 546.

10 Morse, *Toward a Christian America*, iv, 105; Morse, *Home Missions Today and Tomorrow*, viii–ix, 122–61. I would like to especially thank historian Mark Edwards for bringing Morse and the HMC to my attention.

11 "A Vital Gospel," *Home Missions* 9 (February 1938), 2.

12 For the Methodist Department of Evangelism and General Conference Commission on Evangelism, see MEC, *Journal of the Thirty-First Delegated General Conference*, 575, 713–15; MEC, *Journal of the Thirty-Second Delegated General Conference*, 967.

13 The report identified the following categories: Open-Air, Printed Page, Laymen, Industrial and Social, Personal, Rural, Pastoral and Visitation, Preaching Mission, Educational Evangelism, and Youth. Morse, *Home Missions Today and Tomorrow*, 265–75, quote from 269.

14 Ibid., 269.

15 Carter, *Union Made*; Curtis, *A Consuming Faith*; Kenny, "The World Day of Prayer," 129–58.

16 Bowman, *The Urban Pulpit*. Quote from 110.

17 Board of National Missions, PCUSA, *The Church in the Changing City* (New York: Board of National Missions, PCUSA, 1938), 27, UPCUSA Board of National Missions Dept. of Mission Development Records, box 10, folder 5, RG 301.7.10.5, PHS.

18 Thomson, *Enter the Mexican*, 7.

19 Harper argues in *The Quality of Mercy* that Southern Baptists practiced multiple forms of "social Christianity" in their missions work at the turn of the twentieth century.

20 See Plainfield, *The Stranger Within Our Gates*. See also Una Roberts Lawrence, "Kingdom News," *Home Missions* 9 (March 1938), 4.

21 Morse, *Toward a Christian America*, 163; see also Morse, *Home Missions Today and Tomorrow*, 136.

22 Jenkins, *The Next Christendom*.

23 The report was sponsored by the Federation of Churches of Greater New York and Brooklyn Church and Mission Federation and published by the Board of National Missions of the PCUSA. Jones, *The Evangelical Movement*, 4.

24 Everett C. Parker, "New York City; Spanish-Speaking Churches," *Christian Century*, April 12, 1961, 466–67. A scathing rejoinder by a Puerto Rican member of the First Spanish Presbyterian Church of Washington Heights was printed a few months later. Alicia Cotto-Thorner, "Reader's Response: Those Spanish-Speaking Churches," *Christian Century*, June 28, 1961, 801–802.

25 The February issue of *Home Missions* in 1938 provided a good example of the many fronts of Southern Baptist work among immigrants. *Home Missions* 9 (February 1938).

26 Wheeler, "Southern Baptists and Their Missions to Jews"; Jacob Gartenhaus Collection, AR 759, SBHLA. Gartenhaus wrote often within *Home Missions* during the 1930s and also published several books. For examples of Jewish responses to his work, see Chas. H. Joseph, "Random Thoughts," *Jewish Criterion*, August 23,

1929, 12–13; Chas. H. Joseph, "Random Thoughts," *Jewish Criterion*, September 20, 1929, 8–9; Chas. H. Joseph, "Random Thoughts," *Jewish Criterion*, April 1, 1932, 6, 39; Chas. H. Joseph, "Random Thoughts," *Jewish Criterion*, May 13, 1932, 6.

27 Lawrence, *Winning the Border*, 125–29. See also "D. Ruiz Describes Fruitful Months in Mexican Missions," *Home Missions* 9 (April 1938), 6; "Home Missionaries on the Air," *Home Missions* 9 (April 1938), 15.

28 Plainfield, *The Stranger Within Our Gates*, 11–13; Joseph Frank Plainfield Papers, AR 821, SBHLA. Plainfield wrote periodically in *Home Missions*; see especially "Heart Hungers Brought Europeans to America," *Home Missions* 9 (March 1938), 10–12. For a response to his book *The Stranger Within Our Gates*, see "Helps for a Home Mission Program," *Home Missions* 9 (February 1938), 15.

29 Plainfield, *The Stranger Within Our Gates*, 10, 19–21, 29, 41, 85–87, 100, 114–15, first quote from 11; second quote from 55.

30 "New Missionaries of the Home Mission Board Among the Italians in Kansas City," box 13, folder 7; Mrs. Jerry Culbertson and Miss Louise Barnes to J. B. Lawrence, May 23, 1940; Una R. Lawrence to Tenette Lavender, May 24,1940, box 13, folder 10, Una Roberts Lawrence Collection, AR 631, SBHLA.

31 Una R. Lawrence to O. J. Wade, June 10, 1940, box 13, folder 10, Una Roberts Lawrence Collection, AR 631, SBHLA.

32 See Jones, *The Evangelical Movement*.

33 "Foreign Language Churches and Missions," August 16, 1933; A. Di. Domenica, "Retrospect and Prospect of Our Work," 35th Annual Convention Italian Baptist Association, Brooklyn, NY, September 12–14, 1933, "Protestant Home Missions to Catholic Immigrants," ABHMS, box 43, folder 3, ABHS.

34 Carlson, "Chronology of the American Baptist Churches, USA," 146; "11/14/55," Publicity, Christian Friendliness, WABHMS, box 32, folder 6, ABHS; Kinney, *The World at My Door*, 20, 167–77, quote from 176.

35 Board of National Missions, PCUSA, *The Church in the Changing City*, 3, 10–20, 24–32; first quote from 12; second quote from 13; UPCUSA Board of National Missions Dept. of Mission Development Records, box 10, folder 5, RG 301.7.10.5, PHS.

36 Diocese of New York, *Journal of the One Hundred and Fifty-First Convention*, 202; Diocese of New York, *Journal of the One Hundred and Fifty-Sixth Convention*, 146, AEC.

37 PEC, "National Council, Department of Domestic Missions," in *Living Church Annual, Year Book of the Episcopal Church, 1935*, 443–44. See also Thomas Burgess, "Decennial Report of the Foreign-Born Americans Division" and W. C. Emhardt, "Report of the Field Director, Foreign-Born Americans Division," in PEC, *Domestic and Foreign Missionary Society of the Protestant Episcopal Church in the United States of America, Original Minutes, Meeting of the National Council, Apr. 30, May 1, 1930*, 66–73.

38 MEC, *Journal of the Thirty-First Delegated General Conference*, 575, 1252–1304, 1480–81, first quote from 1260, second quote from 1284; MEC, *Journal of the*

Thirty-Second Delegated General Conference, 953–1013. See also Maude M. Scudder, "Finding Ways of Service Among the Orientals," *World Outlook* 28 (December 1938), 16–17, 31.

39 MEC, *Journal of the Thirty-First Delegated General Conference*, 1252–1304, second quote from 756; MEC, *Journal of the Thirty-Second Delegated General Conference*, 953–1013, first quote from 1010; Jay S. Stowell, "Churches of All Nations," *World Outlook* 29 (August 1939), 4–7, 31.

40 Paul W. Shankweiler, "The Settlement in a Changing Order," *World Outlook* 25 (October 1935), 18–26, 39; Nettie Stroup, "Glimpsing Our Work at St. Mark's Community Center New Orleans," *World Outlook* 25 (August 1935), 15–20.

41 MECS, *Missionary Yearbook* (1930), 27–28, 32–33, 385–401, 444–47; "All Along the Gulf Coast," *Missionary Voice* 16 (August 1926), 29; Bertha Ellison, "Cuban Work in Tampa," *Missionary Voice* 20 (October 1930), 16–17; C. Lazos de la Vega, "Work Among the Mexicans," *Missionary Voice* 21 (January 1931), 34–35; Elmer T. Clark, "Methodist Mexicans of the Southwest," *World Outlook* 29 (January 1939), 4–5, 41–42.

42 MECS, *Missionary Yearbook* (1930), 402–18, 444–46, quote from 410.

43 Board of National Missions, PCUSA, *The Church in the Changing City*, 12, UP-CUSA Board of National Missions Dept. of Mission Development Records, box 10, folder 5, RG 301.7.10.5, PHS.

44 Plainfield, *The Stranger Within Our Gates*, 96.

45 "Foreign Churches in America with Which the Episcopal Church Is Co-operating," in PEC, *Living Church Annual, Churchman's Year Book, and American Church Almanac, 1931*; Burgess, "Decennial Report," and Emhardt, "Report of the Field Director," in PEC, *Domestic and Foreign Missionary Society of the Protestant Episcopal Church in the United States of America, Original Minutes, Meeting of the National Council, Apr. 30, May 1, 1930*, 68, 72–73.

46 Geffert, *Eastern Orthodox and Anglicans*; "Churches Continue Vigorous Efforts for Near East," *Federal Council Bulletin* 6 (December 1922–January 1923), 6–7. Episcopal attempts to collaborate with Eastern Orthodox churches resembled their earlier efforts at the turn of the century to bring together Protestants and Catholics. Mislin, *Saving Faith*, 127–29.

47 PEC, *The Annual Report of the National Council for the Year 1933*, 75; Diocese of New York, *Journal of the One Hundred and Fifty-First Convention*, 102, AEC.

48 See North American Home Missions Congress, *Reports of Commissions*. For home missions to immigrants, see x–xi, 34–35, 75–79, 83, 91–96, 114–15. See also Casselman, *Making America Christian*, 47–51, 68–72.

49 HMC and CWHM, *Findings of the Interdenominational Conference on the City and the Church in the Present Crisis, Chicago, Illinois, November 29, 30, December 1, 2, 1932*, quote from 7, UPCUSA Board of National Missions Dept. of Mission Development Records, box 10, folder 2, RG 301.7.10.2, PHS.

50 MEC, *Journal of the Thirty-Second Delegated General Conference*, 439. See also 976–77, 994.

51 Lawrence, *Winning the Border*, 52–53.

52 Hansen, *The Problem of the Third Generation Immigrant*; Dolan, "Immigration and American Christianity," 126–27; Shenton and Kenny, "Ethnicity and Immigration," 363; Kivisto and Blanck, *American Immigrants and Their Generations*. See also Hansen and Schlesinger, *The Immigrant in American History*.

53 See Presbyterian work among Chinese youth on Pacific Coast. Board of National Missions, PCUSA, *Orientals in an Occidental Church* (New York: Board of National Missions, PCUSA, 1938), UPCUSA Board of National Missions Dept. of Mission Development Records, box 10, folder 21, RG 301.7.10.21; Board of National Missions, PCUSA, *The Church in the Changing City*, 3, 10–20, 24–32, UPCUSA Board of National Missions Dept. of Mission Development Records, box 10, folder 5, RG 301.7.10.5, PHS. See also Jones, *The Evangelical Movement*, 29, 31, 36–37.

54 Kinney, *The World at My Door*, 150. See also 18.

55 A similar logic was still being used nearly 30 years later, evident in home missions work in New York City among the Puerto Rican population. Frederick L. Whitam, "New York's Spanish Protestants," *Christian Century*, February 7, 1962, 162–64.

56 MEC, *Journal of the Thirty-Second Delegated General Conference*, 976–77.

57 HMC and CWHM, *Findings of the Interdenominational Conference*, 14, UPCUSA Board of National Missions Dept. of Mission Development Records, box 10, folder 2, RG 301.7.10.2; Board of National Missions, PCUSA, *The Church in the Changing City*, 14, UPCUSA Board of National Missions Dept. of Mission Development Records, box 10, folder 5, RG 301.7.10.5, PHS.

58 Evans, *The Social Gospel in American Religion*, 146–47; Rebecca Brenner Graham, "No Refuge," *Contingent Magazine*, August 23, 2019, https://contingentmagazine. org; Marinari, *Unwanted*, 85, 93–94, 101. For more on American religion during the Great Depression, see Kruse, *One Nation Under God*; Greene, *No Depression in Heaven*; and Lowe, *Baptized with the Soil*.

59 Daniels, *Coming to America*, 288.

60 PEC, *Domestic and Foreign Missionary Society of the Protestant Episcopal Church in the United States of America, Original Minutes, Meeting of the National Council, Feb. 12–13, 1930*, 112–13; PEC, *Domestic and Foreign Missionary Society of the Protestant Episcopal Church in the United States of America, Original Minutes, Meeting of the National Council, Apr. 25, 26, 1939*, 55; PEC, *The Annual Report of the National Council for the Year 1930*, 7, 13, 15; PEC, *The Annual Report of the National Council for the Year 1924*, 13. See also PEC, "National Council, Department of Domestic Missions," in *Living Church Annual, Year Book of the Episcopal Church, 1935*, 443–46.

61 Lawrence, *History of the Home Mission Board*, 110, 114–28, 133–34; Lawrence, *Winning the Border*, 139–41; SBC, *Annual of the Southern Baptist Convention* (1927), 325; SBC, *Annual of the Southern Baptist Convention* (1935), 288, 290.

62 MEC, *Journal of the Thirty-First Delegated General Conference*, 1277, 1296, 1299; MEC, *Journal of the Thirty-Second Delegated General Conference*, 967, 991, 1001.

The Methodist Church merged "bilingual" work into the "Departments of City and Rural Work."

63 AMA, *The Eighty-Sixth Annual Report*, 8, 18; AMA, *Review of Mission Field for Year 1933–1934*, 57.

64 HMC and CWHM, *Findings of the Interdenominational Conference*, 14, UPCUSA Board of National Missions Dept. of Mission Development Records, box 10, folder 2, RG 301.7.10.2, PHS.

65 Daniels, *Coming to America*, 288. See Di. Domenica, "Retrospect and Prospect of Our Work," 6, "Protestant Home Missions to Catholic Immigrants," ABHMS, box 43, folder 3, ABHS.

66 Kinney, *The World at My Door*, 23; see also 21–23.

67 "Outline and Illustration for a Mission Talk," *Home Missions* 9 (February 1938), 6.

68 PEC, "National Council, Department of Domestic Missions," in *Living Church Annual, Year Book of the Episcopal Church*, 1935, 445–46.

69 For specific studies of religion, internationalism, and diplomatic history, see Nurser, *For All Peoples and All Nations*; Preston, *Sword of the Spirit*; Thompson, *For God and Globe*; Paul Boyer, "Piety, International Politics, and Religious Pluralism in the American Experience," in Cohen and Numbers, *Gods in America*, 320–46; Burnidge, *A Peaceful Conquest*; Edwards, *Faith and Foreign Affairs*; and Turek, *To Bring the Good News*.

70 Bertha Condé, "Women Facing a New Task," *Missionary Voice* 17 (February 1927), 19; Julia McGowan, "Missions and International Relations," *Missionary Voice* 19 (January 1929), 16; Kenny, "The World Day of Prayer," 129–31, 151n2.

71 Morse, *Toward a Christian America*, 190.

72 Chang, *Citizens of a Christian Nation*.

73 MEC, "Report of the Executive Secretary," in *Reports Presented at the 1936 Annual Meeting*, 5.

74 PEC, *The Annual Report of the National Council for the Year 1933*, 11.

75 "The American Peril," *Home Missions* 9 (April 1938), 3.

76 Kruse, *One Nation Under God*. See Morse, *Home Missions Today and Tomorrow*, 5.

77 PEC, "National Council, Department of Domestic Missions," in *Living Church Annual, Year Book of the Episcopal Church*, 1935, 443–44.

78 HMC and CWHM, *Findings of the Interdenominational Conference*, 3–4, UPCUSA Board of National Missions Dept. of Mission Development Records, box 10, folder 2, RG 301.7.10.2, PHS.

79 Morse, *Home Missions Today and Tomorrow*, 153.

80 Plainfield, *The Stranger Within Our Gates*, 95.

81 For historical analysis of the relationship between Protestant missions and the ideal of domesticity, see Hunter, "Women's Mission in Historical Perspective" in Reeves-Ellington, Sklar, and Shemo, *Competing Kingdoms*, 19–42

82 Nettie Stroup, "Glimpsing Our Work at St. Mark's Community Center New Orleans," *World Outlook* 25 (August 1935), 17–18. See also Thomson, *Enter the Mexican*, 6.

83 Tenette Lavender, "Our Italian Women," Una Roberts Lawrence Collection, box 13, folder 10, AR 631, SBHLA.

84 Kinney, *The World at My Door*, 43–44, 167–68, 170–71, 174; first quote from 167; second quote from 171.

85 Thomson, *Enter the Mexican*, 6.

86 Kinney, *The World at My Door*, first quote from 128; second quote from 171; "Books and Literature: *The Well Baby Primer*," *Journal of Home Economics* 11 (October 1919), 467–68.

87 MEC, *Journal of the Thirty-Second Delegated General Conference*, 976–77.

88 Morse, *Home Missions Today and Tomorrow*, 124.

89 C. A. Richardson, "Department of City Work," in MEC, *Reports Presented at the 1936 Annual Meeting*, 73–75; Morse, *Home Missions Today and Tomorrow*, 134; Essick, "The International Baptist Seminary," 96–103.

90 Mabel A. Brown, "Aliens a la Mode," *Christian Century*, October 15, 1930, 1247–49.

91 Kinney, *The World at My Door*, 175–76.

92 AMA, *The Eighty-Third Annual Report*, 8.

93 Morse, *Home Missions Today and Tomorrow*, 139.

94 Chicago Presbytery, *Presbyterian Progress in 100 Years*, University of Chicago Library, www.lib.uchicago.edu.

95 Woman's Home Missionary Society of the MEC, *Fifty-Fifth Annual Report*, 157.

96 Nettie Stroup, "Glimpsing Our Work at St. Mark's Community Center New Orleans," *World Outlook* 25 (August 1935), 19.

97 Lawrence, *Winning the Border*, first quote from 34; second quote from 51; third quote from 131.

98 Fleegler, *Ellis Island Nation*.

99 Kinney, *The World at My Door*, first quote from 150; second quote from 12.

100 Thomson, "What Church Members Can Do," in *Enter the Mexican*.

101 Ibid., 70.

102 Mislin, *Saving Faith*; Schultz, *Tri-Faith America*; Hedstrom, *The Rise of Liberal Religion*.

103 Morse, *Home Missions Today and Tomorrow*, 227–29. See also 134 for how they believed the Catholic Church had adopted Protestant measures to reach Italians. See also Plainfield's take on this matter in *The Stranger Within Our Gates*, 114–16.

104 Morse, *Home Missions Today and Tomorrow*, 134, 152, 228–29. For a description of an Italian Catholic community during this time, see Orsi, *The Madonna of 115th Street*. See also Dolan, *The American Catholic Experience*.

105 Abel, *Protestant Home Missions*, viii, 103.

106 Morse, *Home Missions Today and Tomorrow*, 125–26.

107 "Protestant Home Missions to Catholic Immigrants," ABHMS, box 43, folders 2, 3, ABHS.

108 Ibid.

109 "Protestant Home Missions to Catholic Immigrants," ABHMS, box 43, folder 3, ABHS. See also Essick, "The International Baptist Seminary," 100.

110 MEC, *Journal of the Thirty-First Delegated General Conference*, 1294, 1303. See also 648, 1759, and "Memorial to the General Conference of the Methodist Episcopal Church at Atlantic City, May, 1932," State of the Church V—Immigration, 1932, Records of the General Conference, 1345-2-1:3, UMAHC.

111 MEC, *Journal of the Thirty-Second Delegated General Conference*, 521. See also 617, 1206.

112 Ibid., 620.

113 An exception was Presbyterian home missionary Robert N. McLean's searing critique published in *The Nation* concerning the deportations and fickle nature of white American labor needs. McLean, "The Mexican Return" (1932), 201–204. See also McLean, *That Mexican!*. Mount Hollywood Church also offered material relief to Mexicans being repatriated. Balderrama and Rodríguez, *Decade of Betrayal*, 129, 146–48.

114 Una Roberts Lawrence noted the challenges the Great Depression posed for Mexican immigrants, including their inability to access New Deal relief, and acknowledged, without comment, that deportation occurred. But she implied many more voluntarily returned or were victims of impersonal economic forces. Lawrence, *Winning the Border*, 65–68, quote from 66. In Benson Y. Landis's 1961 recounting of Protestant work among immigrants over the last several decades, missions to Mexican immigrants is neglected entirely, along with any political positions on immigration policy concerning repatriation and deportations during the 1930s. Landis, *Protestant Experience*. For histories of the 1930s deportations and repatriation initiatives, see Sánchez, *Becoming Mexican American*, 209–26; Balderrama and Rodríguez, *Decade of Betrayal*; Guerin-Gonzales, *Mexican Workers and American Dreams*; Hernández, *Migra!*, 80–81; Kang, *The INS on the Line*, 66–70; Ngai, *Impossible Subjects*, 72–75; Enciso, *They Should Stay There*; and Daniels, *Coming to America*, 307, 310.

115 National Council of the CCUS, *Minutes, Twenty-Third Regular Meeting*, 43–44.

116 "Putting Mexicans under the Quota System," *Christian Century*, May 28, 1930, 675–76.

117 PHS, "Biographical Note/Administrative History," FCC Records, NCC RG 18, Presbyterian Historical Society, www.history.pcusa.org; Sidney L. Gulick to Bureau of Immigration, March 29, 1933; Harry E. Hull to Gulick, April 3, 1933; A. R. Archibald to Gulick, August 9, 1933; Gulick to Commissioner of Immigration, September 6, 1933; D. W. MacCormack to Gulick, September 19, 1933; Gulick to Secretary of State, November 27, 1933; Charles E. Wyzanski, Jr., to Gulick, December 1, 1933; Benedict M. English to Gulick, December 2, 1933; Albert Levitt to Gulick, December 6, 1933; Gulick to Charles E. Wyzanski, Jr., December 6, 1933, FCC Records, box 33, folder 18, NCC RG 18.33.18, PHS.

118 PHS, "Biographical Note/Administrative History"; Walter W. Van Kirk to Daniel W. McCormack, November 23, 1933; D. W. MacCormack to Van Kirk, December 4, 1933; Van Kirk to MacCormack, December 15, 1933; MacCormack to Van Kirk,

December 21, 1933, FCC Records, box 33, folder 18, NCC RG 18.33.18, PHS. See also MEC, *Journal of the Thirty-First Delegated General Conference*, 648.

119 General Secretary to Benedict M. English, December 8, 1933; "On Amending the Naturalization Law"; "Conscience and Citizenship, Administrative Committee, May 23, 1930," FCC Records, box 33, folder 18, NCC RG 18.33.18, PHS.

120 Spear, "The United States and the Persecution of Jews," 226; Marinari, *Unwanted*, 92–94.

121 Deportation of Immigrants (Kerr Bill), FCC Records, box 50, folder 15, NCC RG 18.50.15, PHS, quotes from Worth M. Tippy to Pastors, Church Officials and Councils of Churches, February 20, 1936; D. W. MacCormack, February 21, 1936.

122 Deportation of Immigrants (Kerr Bill), FCC Records, box 50, folder 15, NCC RG 18.50.15, PHS, quote from "Joint Statement on Kerr Bill."

123 Tillich, "Christianity and Emigration," 13, 16. See also Tillich, "Mind and Migration," 295–305.

124 "Churches Continue Vigorous Efforts for Near East," *Federal Council Bulletin* 6 (December 1922–January 1923), 6; "Bill Introduced Supporting Federal Council Position," *Christian Century*, January 18, 1923, 93. For more on refugee relief at this time, see Curtis, *Holy Humanitarians*; Bon Tempo, *Americans at the Gate*, 11–16; and Miglio, "The Near Eastern Front," 43–70.

125 Burgess, *The League of Nations and the Refugees*, 83–84; Curti, *American Philanthropy Abroad*, 383; Victoria Barnett, "Christian and Jewish Interfaith Efforts during the Holocaust: The Ecumenical Context," in Mazzenga, *American Religious Responses*, 21–22; Kyle Jantzen, "'The Fatherhood of God and Brotherhood of Man': Mainline American Protestants and the Kristallnacht Pogrom," in Mazzenga, *American Religious Responses*, 49–50; General Council of the CCC, *Minutes, Third Regular Meeting*, 115–16.

126 "Luccock Wants German Jews Admitted Here," *World Outlook* 29 (February 1939), 36.

127 "Immigration Figures Speak," *World Outlook* 29 (August 1939), 25.

128 "11/14/55," Publicity, Christian Friendliness, WABHMS, box 32, folder 6, ABHS.

129 PEC, "National Council—Department of Christian Social Relations," *Living Church Annual, Year Book of the Episcopal Church, 1941*, 50; "Call to Aid German Refugees," *Spirit of Missions* 104 (March 1939), 24; "G.F.S. Helps German Refugees," *Spirit of Missions* 104 (March 1939), 30; PEC, *Domestic and Foreign Missionary Society of the Protestant Episcopal Church in the United States of America, Original Minutes, Meeting of the National Council, December 13, 14, 15, 1938*, 142–43, 164; *Domestic and Foreign Missionary Society of the Protestant Episcopal Church in the United States of America, Original Minutes, Meeting of the National Council, February 14, 15, 16, 1939*, 148–49; *Domestic and Foreign Missionary Society of the Protestant Episcopal Church in the United States of America, Original Minutes, Meeting of the National Council, April 25, 26, 1939*, 133, 154; *Domestic and Foreign Missionary Society of the Protestant Episcopal Church in the United States of America, Original Minutes, Meeting of the National Council, Oct. 10, 11, 12, 1939*,

196; *Domestic and Foreign Missionary Society of the Protestant Episcopal Church in the United States of America, Original Minutes, Meeting of the National Council, Dec. 5, 6, 7, 1939*, 200.

130 Wepman, "di Donato, Pietro,"; Di Donato, *Christ in Concrete*.

131 PEC, "National Council—Department of Domestic Missions," in *Living Church Annual, Year Book of the Episcopal Church, 1941*, 48.

132 Morse, *Toward a Christian America*, 188.

133 Bennett, *The Party of Fear*, 3.

134 Roland Q. Leavell, "Wider Evangelistic Visions," *Home Missions* 9 (April 1938), 5.

CHAPTER 3. THE HUDDLED MASSES THE WAR PRODUCED

1 Nixon, *Protestantism's Hour of Decision*, first quote from 27; second and third quotes from 50; fourth quote from 143; Dorrien, *Soul in Society*, 75–77.

2 Nixon, *Protestantism's Hour of Decision*, 72.

3 Gleason, "American Identity and Americanization," 50; Fleegler, *Ellis Island Nation*. See also Higham, *Hanging Together*, and Borstelmann, *Just Like Us*.

4 For more on the prominence of toleration and emphasis on a common humanity during World War II, see Fleegler's chapter "The Quest for Tolerance and Unity" in *Ellis Island Nation*, 59–84.

5 SBC, *Annual of the Southern Baptist Convention* (1948), 170.

6 Jacob A. Long, *Scotch, Irish, AND—* (New York: Board of National Missions, PCUSA, 1943), 35, UPCUSA Board of National Missions Dept. of Mission Development Records, box 10, folder 5, RG 301.7.10.5, PHS; Gleason, "American Identity and Americanization," 47–52; Bennett, *The Party of Fear*, 3. Southern Baptists, however, still reflected anti-Catholic concerns as well when listing subversive ideologies: "communism, fascism, political ecclesiasticism, and anti-Semitism." SBC, *Annual of the Southern Baptist Convention* (1948), 57.

7 See for example Woman's Division of Christian Service, Methodist Church, *First Annual Report*, 100.

8 Methodist Church, *Composite Annual Report*, 15–17; first quote from 16; second and third quotes from 17.

9 See for example Long, *Scotch, Irish, AND—*, 13, PHS.

10 Ibid., 40.

11 See for example ibid., 36–39.

12 Carolyn G. Henderson, "The Report of the Social Service Committee," in Maryland Baptist Union Association, *Minutes of the One Hundred and Seventh Annual Session*, 34–35.

13 Long, *Scotch, Irish, AND—*, 37, PHS.

14 For helpful histories of Asian and Korean Americans, see Lee, *The Making of Asian America*, and Yoo, *Contentious Spirits*.

15 Methodist Church, *Composite Annual Report*, 83–87; Davis, *The Methodist Unification*; Methodist Church, *Mid-Century Report*, 142–49; MEC, "Boundaries of Annual Conferences" (1920), UMAHC.

16 Diocese of California, *Journal of the Ninety-Third Convention*, 66–67, AEC; PEC, "National Council—Department of Domestic Missions," in *Living Church Annual, Year Book of the Episcopal Church, 1941*, 48.

17 H. Paul Douglass, "Report on Presbyterian Oriental Churches on the Pacific Coast," 2, UPCUSA Board of National Missions Dept. of Mission Development Records, box 12, folder 33, RG 301.7.12.33, PHS.

18 Jung, Margaret (Chinese in Phoenix, Arizona), 1939, Una Roberts Lawrence Collection, box 15, folder 51, AR 631, SBHLA.

19 Cohen, *Braceros*; Sánchez, *Becoming Mexican American*. For Protestant home mission programs to Mexican American communities in Chicago, see Jones and Wilson, *The Mexican in Chicago*.

20 Long, *Scotch, Irish, AND—*, 27–29, PHS; Methodist Church, *Composite Annual Report*, 67–73, 89–91; PEC, *Living Church Annual, Year Book of the Episcopal Church, 1941*, 48; SBC, *Annual of the Southern Baptist Convention* (1947), 148–49; *Annual of the Southern Baptist Convention* (1948), 178–79, 182; *Annual of the Southern Baptist Convention* (1949), 177–79, 183.

21 Mrs. J. I. Freeman, "Mingling with the Mexicans," *Southern Baptist Home Missions* 14 (April 1943), 10–11.

22 SBC, *Annual of the Southern Baptist Convention* (1949), 177–78.

23 For an example of Southern Baptist attention to local Catholic resistance, see Ann Huguley, "Home Missions Made Vital," *Royal Service* 40 (May 1946), 9; "The Work of Two Missionaries in New Bedford, Mass.," UPCUSA Board of National Missions Dept. of Mission Development Records, box 12, folder 26, RG 301.7.12.26, PHS.

24 UPCUSA Board of National Missions Dept. of Mission Development Records, box 11, folder 54, RG 301.7.11.54, PHS.

25 SBC, *Annual of the Southern Baptist Convention* (1948), 170.

26 Ibid., 178–179.

27 Stowe, *Immigration and the Growth of the Episcopal Church*, 3, 6, 35–36; first quote from 6; second and third quotes from 35; fourth quote from 36.

28 SBC, *Annual of the Southern Baptist Convention* (1946), 336.

29 SBC, *Annual of the Southern Baptist Convention* (1949), 170–71, 178. See also SBC, *Annual of the Southern Baptist Convention* (1947), 141; *Annual of the Southern Baptist Convention* (1946), 336.

30 For a comprehensive study of the cultural ramifications of mainline Protestant foreign missionaries who returned to the United States, see Hollinger, *Protestants Abroad*.

31 Methodist Church, *Composite Annual Report*, 15–16.

32 PEC, "Forward in Service," in *Living Church Annual, Year Book of the Episcopal Church, 1945*, 42.

33 "Mrs. Mayflower and Mrs. Quota Talk It Over," Christian Friendliness, WAB-HMS, box 90, folder 12, ABHS. Fleegler refers to this as a "modified version of Zangwill's melting pot" in *Ellis Island Nation*, 105, 124.

34   For more on the interwar refugee crisis, see Erbelding, *Rescue Board*; Coser, *Refugee Scholars in America*; Breitman and Lichtman, *FDR and the Jews*; and Garland, *After They Closed the Gates.*

35   The FCC did indicate in 1943 its support for a bill proposed by Representative Samuel Dickstein on relocating some Jewish refugees to America. Samuel McCrea Cavert to Samuel Dickstein, September 28, 1943, FCC Records, box 11, folder 8, NCC RG 18.11.8; UPCUSA Board of National Missions Dept. of Mission Development Records, box 15, folders 43, 46, RG 301.7.15.43, 46, PHS. See also Ross, *So It Was True.*

36   Mrs. W. J. Cox, "My Alabaster Box," *Royal Service* 36 (February 1942), 7.

37   PEC, *Living Church Annual, Year Book of the Episcopal Church, 1941*, 50; *Living Church Annual, Year Book of the Episcopal Church, 1943*, 73–74.

38   Long, *Scotch, Irish, AND—*, 20–21, 24, 40–41, PHS.

39   PEC, *Living Church Annual, Year Book of the Episcopal Church, 1943*, 74; October 2, 1944, American Christian Committee for Refugees, Inc., Records of the War Refugee Board, 1944–1945, box 1, folder 10, Franklin D. Roosevelt Presidential Library and Museum, www.fdrlibrary.marist.edu/. The organization was also consulted for Saenger, *Today's Refugees, Tomorrow's Citizens*, xiii.

40   Blankenship, *Christianity, Social Justice, and the Japanese American Incarceration*; Beth Hessel, "Keeping Silence: Executive Order 9066 at 75," Presbyterian Historical Society, www.history.pcusa.org. For general surveys of this topic, see Reeves, *Infamy*; Robinson, *By Order of the President.*

41   Shaffer, "Opposition to Internment," 597–619.

42   Frances Priest, *Christian Friendliness* (New York: ABHMS, WABHMS, 1948), Christian Friendliness, WABHMS, box 90, folder 12, ABHS. See also "11/14/55," Publicity, Christian Friendliness, WABHMS, box 32, folder 6, ABHS.

43   Gordon K. Chapman, "Meeting the Unexpected," 2, UPCUSA Board of National Missions Dept. of Mission Development Records, box 12, folder 3, RG 301.7.12.3, PHS; Frank Herron Smith, "Some Results Achieved by the Protestant Commission for Japanese Service, February—December, 1942," UPCUSA Board of National Missions Dept. of Mission Development Records, box 12, folder 11, RG 301.7.12.11, PHS.

44   Fern M. Colborn to John Sherman Cooper, May 19, 1948, UPCUSA Board of Christian Education, Council on Church and Society Records, box 12, folder 23, RG 78.12.23, PHS.

45   Chapman, "Meeting the Unexpected," 3, PHS.

46   Fellowship of Reconciliation, *American Refugees*, 8, Japanese Relocation, 1942, Records of the UMC General Board of Higher Education and Ministry, 2628-6-2:13, UMAHC. See also Miller, *Harry Emerson Fosdick.*

47   Chapman, "Meeting the Unexpected," first quote from 10; second quote from 12, PHS.

48   H. D. Bollinger to Hideo Hashimoto, October 6, 1942, Japanese Relocation, 1942, Records of the UMC General Board of Higher Education and Ministry, 2628-6-

2:13, UMAHC. See also the extensive collection of Methodist and other Protestant material on Japanese internment in Roll No. 115, Japan Conf., Missionary Files: Methodist Church, 1912–1949, UMAHC.

49 General Council of the CCC, *Digest Minutes*, 174.

50 Griffith, *The Fight for Asian American Civil Rights*, 103–126.

51 Long, *Scotch, Irish, AND*—, 34–35, PHS; Chapman, "Meeting the Unexpected," 8, PHS; box 12, folder 4, RG 301.7.12.4; box 11, folder 42, RG 301.7.11.42, UPCUSA Board of National Missions Dept. of Mission Development Records, PHS; PEC, *Living Church Annual, Year Book of the Episcopal Church, 1943*, 72; Diocese of California, *Journal of the Ninety-Third Convention*, 67–69, AEC. See also Roll No. 115, Japan Conf., Missionary Files: Methodist Church, 1912–1949, UMAHC.

52 Smith, "Some Results Achieved by the Protestant Commission," box 12, folder 11, RG 301.7.12.11; box 11, folder 42, RG 301.7.11.42, UPCUSA Board of National Missions Dept. of Mission Development Records, PHS.

53 These two Protestant organizations maintained a tenuous relationship in part over authority and lack of coordination. Mark A. Dawber to Gordon K. Chapman, October 16, 1942; Mark A. Dawber to Members of the Committee on Administration of Japanese Christian Work, January 26, 1943; "Minutes of the Committee on Administration of Japanese Work," UPCUSA Board of National Missions Dept. of Mission Development Records, box 12, folder 4, RG 301.7.12.4, PHS.

54 Diocese of California, *Journal of the Ninety-Third Convention*, 67–68, AEC; Chapman, "Meeting the Unexpected," 3–10, PHS. See also Japanese minister Hideo Hashimoto's description of Protestant work in "Dear Friends," September 23, 1942, Japanese Relocation, 1942, Records of the UMC General Board of Higher Education and Ministry, 2628-6-2:13, UMAHC.

55 Chapman, "Meeting the Unexpected," 4, PHS; PEC, *Domestic and Foreign Missionary Society of the Protestant Episcopal Church in the United States of America, Original Minutes, Meeting of the National Council, Dec. 4, 5, 6, 1945*, 115–16.

56 PEC, *Domestic and Foreign Missionary Society of the Protestant Episcopal Church in the United States of America, Original Minutes, Meeting of the National Council, Feb. 8, 9, 10, 1944*, 114; "To Wesley Foundations and Methodist Colleges on the West Coast"; Elizabeth F. Johnson to Harvey C. Brown, November 27, 1942, Japanese Relocation, 1942, 2628-6-2:13; Japanese Re-Location, 1943–1944, 2598-5-1:24; 1941 Student Refugee Scholarship Fund, 1941–1942, 2594-6-3:45, Records of the UMC General Board of Higher Education and Ministry, UMAHC; *Japanese American Student Relocation: An American Challenge*, UPCUSA Board of National Missions Dept. of Mission Development Records, box 11, folder 67, RG 301.7.11.67, PHS. Baptists also sponsored a Buddhist student at Drake University. Hideo Hashimoto to H. D. Bollinger, October 9, 1942, Japanese Relocation, 1942, Records of the UMC General Board of Higher Education and Ministry, 2628-6-2:13, UMAHC. See also "Christian Friendliness, State Summary Sheet, April 1944–April 1945," WABFMS, box 23, folder 7, ABHS.

57 Committee on Resettlement of Japanese Americans, "Relocating the Dislocated"; Gracia D. Booth, *How Can We Help Japanese American Evacuees?: Suggestions for Church Women* (New York: Committee on Resettlement of Japanese Americans, 1944), UPCUSA Board of National Missions Dept. of Mission Development Records, box 12, folder 4, RG 301.7.12.4, PHS.

58 UPCUSA Board of National Missions Dept. of Mission Development Records, box 11, folder 64, RG 301.7.11.64, PHS. See also PEC, *Living Church Annual, Year Book of the Episcopal Church, 1945*, 50.

59 Board of Home Missions, CCC, "The Board of Home Missions—Postwar Emergency Program Financial Statement—Japanese Appropriations—Acct. A-2," September 28–29, 1948; Stanley U. North, "Department of City Work," n.d., 1, Board of Home Missions of Congregational and Christian Records, 1943–1954, box 1, folder 1, RG 1282, CLA. See also Board of Home Missions War Emergency Committee Minutes 1943–1946, box 2, RG 1282.

60 Fern M. Colborn to John S. Cooper, March 11, 1948; Ina Sugihara to Fern Colburn, April 20, 1948; Fern M. Colborn to John Sherman Cooper, May 19, 1948, UPCUSA Board of Christian Education, Council on Church and Society Records, box 12, folder 23, RG 78.12.23, PHS.

61 "Program, Nisei Summer Assembly, Corpus Christi, Texas, August 26–29, 1948, For Nisei and Their Friends," Una Roberts Lawrence Collection, box 20, folder 22, AR 631, SBHLA.

62 Billington, *The Protestant Crusade*, 234.

63 See PEC, *Living Church Annual, Year Book of the Episcopal Church, 1945*, 49; Race Relations—Folder 1, 1942–1950, 2583-2-3:7; Charter for Racial Policies, 1948–1962, 2587-6-5:1, Records of the Women's Division of the General Board of Global Ministries, UMAHC. See also NCC, "Brethren—Dwell Together in Unity," Race Relations Sunday, February 13, 1955, The King Center, www.thekingcenter.org.

64 "Prescription," "Will You Help," Christian Friendliness, WABHMS, box 90, folder 12, ABHS.

65 Mrs. W. J. Neel, "With Jesus through the Homeland," *Royal Service* 36 (February 1942), 6. Concerning Southern Baptists, see also *Royal Service* 40 (May 1946); Maston, *"Of One"*; Newman, *Getting Right with God*, 72–73, 112, 172.

66 "Portent of Storm," *Christian Century*, June 23, 1943, 735–36.

67 "Our Race Riots Create an International Incident," *Christian Century*, July 28, 1943, 861.

68 "Ten Tips to Tactful Talkers," Christian Friendliness, WABHMS, box 90, folder 12, ABHS.

69 Eakin, *Getting Acquainted*, 12.

70 Priest, *Christian Friendliness*, ABHS.

71 Ibid.; Booth, *How Can We Help*, 11, PHS. For material on war brides, see Albaugh, *Who Shall Separate Us?*, 43; "Bible Class for Brides," *Home Missions* 31 (October 1960), 24–25.

72 "Will You Help," ABHS.

73 Booth, *How Can We Help*, 12, PHS.

74 Eugene H. Kone, "Incubator of Democracy," *Parents' Magazine* 22 (January 1947), 26–27, 81–82.

75 On mainline Protestant family values, see Bendroth, *Growing Up Protestant*.

76 "C.F. Conference, February 15–17," 3, WABFMS, box 23, folder 7, ABHS.

77 Benson Y. Landis to Dr. Barnes, December 17, 1948, FCC Records, box 33, folder 19, NCC RG 18.33.19, PHS.

78 Schultz, *Tri-Faith America*, 65–66, 69, 75, 78, 105; Fleegler, *Ellis Island Nation*, 38, 43–44, 69–70, 74, 76–77.

79 *Pattern for Peace: Catholic, Jewish and Protestant Declaration on World Peace* (New York: Church Peace Union, World Alliance for International Friendship through the Churches, 1943), W. E. B. Du Bois Papers (MS 312), Special Collections and University Archives, University of Massachusetts Amherst Libraries, http://credo.library.umass.edu/; "Religious Leaders Issue Peace Plan," *New York Times*, October 7, 1943.

80 For a comprehensive account of this movement, see Hong, *Opening the Gates*.

81 Wynn C. Fairfield to Walter W. Van Kirk, September 2, 1941; William Ernest Hocking to Henry St. George Tucker, March 14, 1943, FCC Records, box 34, folder 1, NCC RG 18.34.1, PHS.

82 Francis B. Sayre to Van Kirk, November 7, 1942; "To the Members of the Committee on International Relations of the Foreign Missions Conference of N.A.," April 22, 1943; L. J. Shafer to Van Kirk, February 15, 1943; George Gleason, "Dr. Walter W. Van Kirk—#2"; Henry A. Atkinson to Van Kirk, June 2, 1943, FCC Records, box 34, folder 1, NCC RG 18.34.1, PHS.

83 Fawcett, *Liberalism*, xix–xxi.

84 See also Kittelstrom, *The Religion of Democracy*, 3, 8.

85 FCC Records, box 34, folder 1, NCC RG 18.34.1; "Resolution adopted by the Executive Committee . . . May 18th, 1943," FCC Records, box 33, folder 18, NCC RG 18.33.18, PHS.

86 Van Kirk to George Gleason, March 22, 1943, and passim, FCC Records, box 34, folder 1, NCC RG 18.34.1, PHS.

87 George Gleason to Van Kirk, June 11, 1943, FCC Records, box 34, folder 1, NCC RG 18.34.1, PHS.

88 FCC, "For Immediate Release," May 28, 1943, FCC Records, box 11, folder 8, NCC RG 18.11.8, PHS.

89 Luman J. Shafer, May 28, 1943; Wisconsin Council of Churches to Samuel Dickstein, June 22, 1943; Wisconsin Council of Churches to Alexander Wiley, June 22, 1943, FCC Records, box 34, folder 1, NCC RG 18.34.1, PHS.

90 U. G. Murphy to Roswell P. Barnes, June 28, 1943, FCC Records, box 11, folder 8, NCC RG 18.11.8, PHS.

91 James Myers to Barnes, June 17, 1943; to William Green, June 17, 1943; William Green to Roswell P. Barnes, July 2, 1943, FCC Records, box 11, folder 8, NCC RG 18.11.8, PHS.

92 Albert Lee to Van Kirk, February 4, 1943; Van Kirk to U. G. Murphy, April 28, 1943; "To the Members of the Committee on International Relations of the Foreign Missions Conference of N.A.," April 22, 1943; Van Kirk to George Gleason, March 22, 1943, FCC Records, box 34, folder 1, NCC RG 18.34.1; Walter H. Judd to Roswell P. Barnes, March 4, 1943; Barnes to U. G. Murphy, June 15, 1943, FCC Records, box 11, folder 8, NCC RG 18.11.8, PHS; Calkins, "Judd, Walter H.," 155–56; Hollinger, *Protestants Abroad*, 31, 146, 184–85.

93 "News of Christian Friendliness Coast to Coast," March 1949, 1, Christian Friendliness, 1949–1951, WABHMS, box 53, folder 18, ABHS.

94 Samuel McCrea Cavert to Secretaries of Councils of Churches, July 14, 1943; Mrs. Lester P. Wager to Cavert, September 18, 1943; General Convention, PEC, "Chinese Exclusion Act"; Charles F. Boss Jr., October 14, 1943; Van Kirk, October 11, 1943; and passim, FCC Records, box 34, folder 2, NCC RG 18.34.2; "To the Congress of the United States of America"; FCC Records, box 34, folder 3, NCC RG 18.34.3; Samuel McCrea Cavert to Basil Mathews, October 8, 1943, FCC Records, box 11, folder 8, NCC RG 18.11.8, PHS.

95 FCC, "A petition signed by 800," October 21, 1943; Raymond E. Willis to Cavert, November 1, 1943; Walter H. Judd to Luman J. Shafer, November 1, 1943; and passim, FCC Records, box 34, folder 2, NCC RG 18.34.2, PHS.

96 FCC Records, box 34, folder 5, NCC RG 18.34.5; Van Kirk, "Statement made before the House Committee," March 7, 1945, FCC Records, box 34, folder 3, NCC RG 18.34.3; "Action of the Woman's Division," September 2, 1948, FCC Records, box 33, folder 19, NCC RG 18.33.19; "Luce-Celler Bills HR1584 and HR 173," FCC Records, box 33, folder 20, NCC RG 18.33.20, PHS. See also Sirdar J. J. Singh, President, India League of America, "Memorandum on Proposed Legislation," South Asian American Digital Archive, www.saada.org/.

97 U.S. House of Representatives, *To Grant a Quota*, 12–17.

98 Read Lewis to Van Kirk, February 14, 1946; Van Kirk to Social Action Secretaries, February 19, 1946; Leland Rex Robinson to John Lesinski, February 26, 1946; G. Bromley Oxnam to Lesinski, March 19, 1946, FCC Records, box 33, folder 18, NCC RG 18.33.18; Van Kirk to Beverly Boyd, June 28, 1948; "Action of the Woman's Division," September 2, 1948, FCC Records, box 33, folder 19, NCC RG 18.33.19, PHS.

99 Van Kirk to Judd, January 22, 1946, FCC Records, box 33, folder 18, NCC RG 18.33.18, PHS.

100 FCC, clipping, "Resolution Adopted by the Executive Committee of the Federal Council of Churches, November 18, 1947"; and passim, FCC Records, box 34, folder 3, NCC RG 18.34.3. See also FCC Records, box 35, folder 14, NCC RG 18.35.14; box 33, folders 18, 19, NCC RG 18.33.18, 19, PHS.

101 "Lifting the Immigration Ban," *New York Times*, March 4, 1949; Methodist Church, *Journal of the 1948 General Conference*, 741–42. For other denominational responses, see "Re Elimination of Considerations of Race and Color from Immigration and Naturalization Laws," FCC Records, box 33, folder 19, NCC RG 18.33.19, PHS.

102 Ruth Isabel Seabury to Van Kirk, October 30, 1947, FCC Records, box 33, folder 18, NCC RG 18.33.18, PHS.

103 Dudziak, *Cold War Civil Rights*; Cheng, *Citizens of Asian America*; Zubovich, "For Human Rights Abroad," 267–90.

104 Judd to Van Kirk, April 15, 1948; Robert M. Cullum to John Foster Dulles, June 16, 1948, FCC Records, box 33, folder 19, NCC RG 18.33.19, PHS.

105 Judd to Van Kirk, April 21, 1948; Mike Masaoka to Van Kirk, April 29, 1948, FCC Records, box 33, folder 19, NCC RG 18.33.19, PHS.

106 Beverley M. Boyd to Robert E. Bondy, June 18, 1948, FCC Records, box 33, folder 19, NCC RG 18.33.19, PHS.

107 Van Kirk, "Statement made before the Staff of the Senate Subcommittee," July 8, 1948, FCC Records, box 33, folder 19, NCC RG 18.33.19, PHS.

108 Alson J. Smith, "Testimony," July 14, 1948, FCC Records, box 33, folder 19, NCC RG 18.33.19, PHS.

109 Howard J. Baumgartel to Louis Ludlow, March 20, 1948, FCC Records, box 33, folder 19, NCC RG 18.33.19, PHS.

110 Bedros Baharian to Richard B. Wigglesworth, March 24, 1948; Baharian to Van Kirk, March 24, 1948; Kenneth I. Clawson to Paul J. Kilday, April 21, 1948; G. Weir Hartman to Walter Judd, April 21, 1948; John C. Mayne to Van Kirk, April 23, 1948; Virgil F. Dougherty to Dept. of International Justice and Goodwill, FCC, May 27, 1948, FCC Records, box 33, folder 19, NCC RG 18.33.19, PHS.

111 "Resolutions Adopted by the Program Board of the Council of Churches of Buffalo and Erie County," April 7, 1948, FCC Records, box 33, folder 19, NCC RG 18.33.19, PHS.

112 Judd to Van Kirk, April 1, 1949; Thoburn T. Brumbaugh to Board Member, April 26, 1949; Van Kirk to Ina Sugihara, April 27, 1949; Van Kirk to Judd, April 27, 1949; Van Kirk to J. Howard McGrath, July 14, 1949; "Statement by Dr. Walter W. Van Kirk," July 20, 1949, FCC Records, box 33, folder 20, NCC RG 18.33.20, PHS. See also FCC Records, box 58, folder 7, NCC RG 18.58.7, PHS.

113 Harry S. Truman, "Address in Columbus at a Conference of the Federal Council of Churches," March 6, 1946, *American Presidency Project*, edited by Gerhard Peters and John T. Woolley, www.presidency.ucsb.edu; Chesly Manly, "Truman Pleads for a Rebirth of Golden Rule," *Chicago Daily Tribune*, March 7, 1946.

114 Coffman, The Christian Century, 175–81; Edwards, *The Right of the Protestant Left*, 1–2; "This Nation under God," *Christian Century*, December 13, 1950, 1478–79; "Inaugural Message of the National Council," *Christian Century*, December 13, 1950, 1484–85.

CHAPTER 4. STRANGERS IN MAYBERRY

1 *The Tourist* (1993–126), UMC 6027-3-4:10, UMAHC. Demonstrating the inroads Protestant denominations were making into the film industry, this episode included other prominent midcentury actors and was directed by William F. Claxton, who later helped direct the TV series *Bonanza* and *Little House on the*

Prairie, and was produced by Wilbur T. Blume, who won an Academy Award the following year.

2 Historian David Hollinger makes a similar argument for this period in relation to foreign missions, immigration more broadly, and "contact theory." Hollinger, *Protestants Abroad*, 296–98.

3 Hermann N. Morse, "Evangelizing a Procession," *Christian Century*, November 21, 1951, 1337.

4 Ellen M. Studley, "Stranded Intellectuals: The Case of the Chinese Student in America," *motive* 13 (January 1953), 20–26. Some Protestant leaders were also members of the Aid Refugee Chinese Intellectuals, Inc. See *Aid Refugee Chinese Intellectuals* pamphlet, NCC Division of Christian Life and Mission Records, box 20, folder 21, NCC RG 6.20.21, PHS.

5 Roswell P. Barnes to Roy G. Ross, October 21, 1958; R. H. Edwin Espy to Wilbur C. Parry, February 19, 1959, NCC Division of Christian Life and Mission Records, box 2, folder 17, NCC RG 6.2.17; Fern M. Colborn to John Sherman Cooper, May 19, 1948, UPCUSA Board of Christian Education, Council on Church and Society Records, box 12, folder 23, RG 78.12.23, PHS.

6 Blair, Lively, and Trimble, *Spanish-Speaking Americans*; Committees: Spanish American Work, Records of the National Division of the General Board of Global Ministries, 2540-3-5:7, UMAHC; UPCUSA Board of National Missions Dept. of Mission Development Records, box 19, folder 36, RG 301.7.19.36, box 24, folder 5, RG 301.7.24.5, PHS; Willis, *All According to God's Plan*, 121–48. For general historical overviews of Southern Baptist Mexican missions, see McBeth, *The Baptist Heritage*, 735–44; McBeth, *Texas Baptists*; Grijalva, "The Story of Hispanic Southern Baptists," 40–47; Grijalva, *A History of Mexican Baptists*; Rodríguez, "The Cultural Context." For Southern Baptist work among braceros in Texas, see Taylor, *God's Messengers*.

7 Glen W. Trimble, comp., "Responses to the Brief Survey of Church Related Spanish American Work in the Continental United States," January 10, 1961, UPCUSA Board of National Missions Dept. of Mission Development Records, box 24, folder 6, RG 301.7.24.6, PHS.

8 Gladys Creed to Miss Minkler, February 20, 1951, Methodist Mexican Work, Port Arthur, Texas 1950–1952, Records of the National Division of the General Board of Global Ministries, 2572-5-3:5, UMAHC.

9 Thomas Alfred Tripp, "El Divino Salvador: Spanish-American Congregational Church, Gallup, New Mexico," 6–8, Town and Country Minutes 1950–1953, Board of Home Missions of Congregational and Christian Records, 1943–1954, box 2, RG 1282, CLA.

10 For histories of Operation Wetback, see Hernández, *Migra!*, 171–95; Kang, *The INS on the Line*, 139–67; Ngai, *Impossible Subjects*, 147–58; and Daniels, *Coming to America*, 312.

11 Helen Kenyon, "Present Need in Home Missions," *Christian Century*, January 6, 1954, 24–25.

12 Department of the Church and Economic Life, Division of Christian Life and Work, NCC, "Draft of a Resolution Regarding the Future of Public Law 78 (82nd Congress)," January 15, 1960, 4, NCC Division of Christian Life and Mission Records, box 20, folder 23, NCC RG 6.20.23, PHS.

13 *Presbyterian Journal*: "The NCC and Public Law 78," November 11, 1964, 12; "Across the Editor's Desk," November 18, 1964, 3; "Mailbag: The NCC and Public Law 78," December 16, 1964, 2; "Spokesman for Council Asks Higher Farm Pay," December 23, 1964, 5; "Wire to President," March 10, 1965, 4–5; "Let Everybody In?" March 24, 1965, 14–15; "Executives of Councils Hit Foreign Farm Help," April 7, 1965, 4; "Most Americans Oppose Immigration Changes," August 4, 1965, 6; "Clydie Goes for 'Action,'" August 11, 1965, 8; "A Sorry Record," August 25, 1965, 13.

14 May, *Protestant Churches and Industrial America*; Carter, *The Decline and Revival*; Miller, *American Protestantism and Social Issues, 1919–1939*. Christopher H. Evans has also demonstrated persuasively the continuation of the social gospel following the early years of the twentieth century in Evans, *The Social Gospel in American Religion*.

15 Diocese of New York, *Journal of the One Hundred and Sixty-Seventh Convention*, 151; *Journal of the One Hundred and Seventy-Third Convention*, 139, AEC.

16 Woman's Division of Christian Service, Methodist Church, *Patterns for Peace*, 116.

17 Carl G. Karsch, "The Lady Who Adopted a Neighborhood," *Presbyterian Life*, April 26, 1952, 10–12.

18 PEC, "Settlements and Community Centers," *Episcopal Church Annual, 1960*, 103–104; Woman's Division of Christian Service, Methodist Church, "Community Centers," *Twenty-First Annual Report*, 81–82; first quote from Woman's Division of Christian Service, Methodist Church, *Patterns for Peace*, 128; Loyd Carter, "Good Will Center Work"; Sara Taylor, "Good Will Centers in Missions," in *Encyclopedia of Southern Baptists*, 569–70; second quote from 570.

19 "Signposts in Christian Social Relations, Objectives in Christian Social Relations, 1954–1955," Christian Friendliness Lit Resources, 1954–55, ABHMS/National Missions, box 224, folder 22, ABHS.

20 "Mission: Stranger in the Midst," 1962, National Ministries, box 231, folder 24, ABHS.

21 Dorothy O. Bucklin, "A Missionary's Notebook," 5, 10, Christian Friendliness, WABHMS, box 90, folder 12, ABHS.

22 "Happenings Along the Highways," ABHMS/National Missions, box 224, folder 22, ABHS.

23 Paul L. Warnshois, "A Presbyterian Look at the Puerto Rican Situation," UPCUSA Board of National Missions Dept. of Mission Development Records, box 19, folder 31, RG 301.7.19.31, PHS. See also Lyle Saunders, "Anglos and Spanish-Speaking: Contrasts and Similarities," July 16, 1959, Committees: Spanish American Work, Records of the National Division of the General Board of Global Ministries, 2540-3-5:7, UMAHC.

24 SBC, *Annual of the Southern Baptist Convention* (1956), 196.

25 Woman's Division of Christian Service, Methodist Church, *Patterns for Peace*, 129.

26 Blair, Lively, and Trimble, *Spanish-Speaking Americans*, quote from 222.

27 "Committee on Spanish American Work," June 15, 1959; "Cantares de mi Tierra," Committees: Spanish American Work, Records of the National Division of the General Board of Global Ministries, 2540-3-5:7, UMAHC; SBC, *Annual of the Southern Baptist Convention* (1942), quote from 284. For more information on radio broadcasts, see SBC, *Annual of the Southern Baptist Convention* (1941), 298; McBeth, *Texas Baptists*, 298; Grijalva, *A History of Mexican Baptists*, 80.

28 SBC, *Annual of the Southern Baptist Convention* (1948), 179. See also Caylor, *Our Neighbors of Many Tongues*.

29 Blair, Lively, and Trimble, *Spanish-Speaking Americans*, 114.

30 For example, see Woman's Division of Christian Service, Methodist Church, *Patterns for Peace*, 8.

31 Grijalva, *A History of Mexican Baptists*, 110–21. Similar developments were occurring among Mexican Americans and Anglos in Presbyterian and Methodist denominations as well. Sylvest, "Hispanic American Protestantism," 124–25.

32 BGCT, *Annual of the Baptist General Convention of Texas* (1961), 429.

33 Grijalva, *A History of Mexican Baptists*, 183. Barton affirms this conclusion in *Hispanic Methodists, Presbyterians, and Baptists*, 5–6.

34 Blair, Lively, and Trimble, *Spanish-Speaking Americans*, 4, 6–8, 10, 32–33, 123–28.

35 Historian Mark Wild, however, notes that in the area of urban renewal, white mainline Protestants largely "clung to black/white dichotomies," at the expense of other racial/ethnic designations. Wild, *Renewal*, 10. For an earlier example of racial categorizations among immigrant groups, see Thomson, *Enter the Mexican*, 1–2.

36 "Committee on Spanish American Work," June 15, 1959, 3, Committees: Spanish American Work, Records of the National Division of the General Board of Global Ministries, 2540-3-5:7, UMAHC.

37 Gladys Keith, "Is It Jus' For Whites?" Home Mission Board Communication Division Collection, box 2, folder 10, AR 631-7, SBHLA.

38 Methodist Church, *Mid-Century Report*, 234–36, quote from 235; Willis, *All According to God's Plan*, 121–48.

39 Georgia Harkness, *O Worship the Lord* (New York: NCC, 1952), 5, UCW Resources, 1948–1955, Church Women United Records, 1222-4-2:7, UMAHC.

40 "Because We Are . . . 'A City Set on a Hill': National Missions Seeks to Make America a Light to the World," *Presbyterian Life*, October 18, 1952, 11–13. For a more nuanced position, see "National Purpose and Christian Mission," *Christian Century*, January 6, 1960, 3–5.

41 SBC, *Annual of the Southern Baptist Convention* (1949), 178.

42 Dallas P. Lee, "Foreword," in Taylor, *God's Messengers*.

43 Methodist Church, *Mid-Century Report*, 146.

44 Herberg, *Protestant, Catholic, Jew*. For an example of conversation on this form of religious pluralism at the time, see United Student Christian Council, "Religious

Pluralism on the College Campus," Aug. 1955, NCC Division of Christian Education Records, box 77, folder 26, NCC RG 9.77.26, PHS. This document also demonstrates reserve over the concept of "brotherhood" in the context of religious pluralism. Allyn P. Robinson, "An Introductory Statement," 33.

45 Schultz, *Tri-Faith America*.

46 Will Herberg, "Protestantism in a Post-Protestant America," *Christianity and Crisis* 22 (February 5, 1962), 3.

47 Taylor, *God's Messengers*, 22, 71. See also John D. Gearing, "Cotton-Picking Braceros in Arkansas," *Home Missions* 31 (March 1960), 26.

48 E. S. James, "Separation of Church and State," in SBC, *News Copy, For Release: 3:40 P.M., Friday, May 26, 1961*, Baptist Press Archives from 1948 to 1996, Southern Baptist Historical Library and Archives, www.sbhla.org.

49 SBC, *Annual of the Southern Baptist Convention* (1946), 36.

50 For an assessment of anti-Catholicism among midcentury public intellectuals, see McGreevy, *Catholicism and American Freedom*, 166–88, 213.

51 "Our Mission in New Mexico," *Presbyterian Life* 5 (February 2, 1952), 20–25; Christopher Fullman, "'I Think We Can Agree,'" *Presbyterian Life* 5 (March 29, 1952), 5; William N. Wysham, "Disagrees with Father Fullman," *Presbyterian Life* 5 (May 10, 1952), 3.

52 Paul L. Warnshois, "A Presbyterian Look at the Puerto Rican Situation," UPCUSA Board of National Missions Dept. of Mission Development Records, box 19, folder 31, RG 301.7.19.31, PHS.

53 Thomas Alfred Tripp, "El Divino Salvador: Spanish-American Congregational Church, Gallup, New Mexico," 5, Town and Country Minutes 1950–1953, Board of Home Missions of Congregational and Christian Records, 1943–1954, box 2, RG 1282, CLA.

54 Diocese of California, *Journal of the One Hundred Third Convention*, 62, AEC.

55 T. A. Patterson, "The Bracero and Texas Baptists," *Baptist Standard*, July 1, 1964, 8.

56 Methodist Church, *Mid-Century Report*, 75.

57 Dwight D. Eisenhower, "Text of the President's Appeal to the World Council of Churches," *New York Times*, August 20, 1954.

58 Ibid.

59 Hartzell Spence, "They Put Christianity to Work," *Saturday Evening Post*, July 24, 1954, 25, 96–98.

60 Grodka and Hennes, *Homeless No More*, vi.

61 CWS, "DPs, Our Urgent Christian Obligation," quote from this source; CWS, "You Wanted to Know: Some Questions and Answers about the Resettlement of Displaced Persons," Central Congregational Church (Newton, Mass.) Records, box 33, folder 1, RG 4680, CLA.

62 Daniels, *Coming to America*, 331, 336. See also Bon Tempo, *Americans at the Gate*.

63 Religious News Service, "Federal Council Urges Amendment of Immigration Laws," December 9, 1946; American Christian Committee for Refugees, Inc., "Joint Meeting of the Executive Committee and the Committee on Overseas

Program," February 15, 1946; American Christian Committee for Refugees, Inc., "Meeting of the Board of Directors," February 20, 1946, FCC Records, box 33, folder 18, NCC RG 18.33.18, PHS.

64 NCC, "United States Immigration and Naturalization Policy," March 21, 1952, NCC Division of Christian Life and Mission Records, box 20, folder 19, NCC RG 6.20.19, PHS.

65 Daniels, *Coming to America*, 331; Marinari, *Unwanted*, 104–5, 108, 110.

66 Methodist Church, *Journal of the 1948 General Conference*, 741.

67 "The Refugees: Free Nations Make Plans," *Presbyterian Life*, January 5, 1952, 24–26; quote from John H. Marion to Ethel Hamilton, October 1, 1948, FCC Records, box 33, folder 19, NCC RG 18.33.19, PHS.

68 Diocese of New York, *Journal of the One Hundred and Seventy-Second Convention*, 75–76, 84, AEC.

69 SBC, *Annual of the Southern Baptist Convention* (1947), 51. See also SBC, *Annual of the Southern Baptist Convention* (1949), 55. In 1946 the SBC funded CWS $275,300 and the American Christian Committee for Refugees $5,000, though these funds were disbursed by the Foreign Mission Board and were probably seen as helping refugees overseas. SBC, *Annual of the Southern Baptist Convention* (1947), 138.

70 "News of Christian Friendliness Coast to Coast," March 1949, 3, Christian Friendliness, 1949–1951, WABHMS, box 53, folder 18, ABHS.

71 General Board, NCC, "Resolution on Refugee Legislation," May 20, 1953, NCC Division of Christian Life and Mission Records, box 20, folder 21, NCC RG 6.20.21, PHS.

72 Elliott, "Article on Refugees," PHS.

73 Roland Elliott to Robert A. Taft, March 4, 1953; NCC, "Information Memorandum #3-Emergency Legislation," May 5, 1953, NCC Division of Christian Life and Mission Records, box 20, folder 21, NCC RG 6.20.21, PHS.

74 Walter W. Van Kirk to Social Action Secretaries, April 27, 1953, NCC Division of Christian Life and Mission Records, box 20, folder 21, NCC RG 6.20.21, PHS.

75 Walter W. Van Kirk, "Statement on Behalf of the National Council of the Churches of Christ in the U.S.A. and the National Lutheran Council Respecting the Emergency Migration Act of 1953," May 27, 1953, 1–6, first quote from 3; second quote from 4; Walter W. Van Kirk to Social Action Secretaries, June 3, 1953, NCC Division of Christian Life and Mission Records, box 20, folder 21, NCC RG 6.20.21, PHS.

76 Reimers, "An Unintended Reform," 13.

77 General Board, NCC, "Resolution on Refugee Act of 1953," September 16, 1953, NCC Division of Christian Life and Mission Records, box 20, folder 21, NCC RG 6.20.21, PHS. For a critical assessment of the implementation of the Refugee Act of 1953, see Charles H. Seaver, "Who Is My Neighbor?" *Social Action* 21 (May 1955), 28–31; Charles H. Seaver, "The Refugee Situation," *Social Action* 22 (December 1955), 20–24.

78 Leech, "The Forgotten Crisis," 45–46, 106.

79 General Board, NCC, "The Need for New Legislation for Refugee Immigration to the U.S.A.," December 4–5, 1956, NCC Division of Christian Life and Mission Records, box 20, folder 23, NCC RG 6.20.23, PHS; "Churches Move Fast in Hungarian Crisis," *Presbyterian Life*, December 8, 1956, 17–18; Bon Tempo, *Americans at the Gate*, 66–71.

80 General Assembly, NCC, "Concerning Refugees," December 1–6, 1957, NCC Division of Christian Life and Mission Records, box 2, folder 6, NCC RG 6.2.6, PHS; Bon Tempo, *Americans at the Gate*, 70–75.

81 Cuba—Correspondence and Report on Refugee Work, 1960–64, UPCUSA Board of National Missions Dept. of Mission Development Records, box 24, folder 7, RG 301.7.24.7, PHS; James MacCracken, "Statement of James MacCracken, Associate Executive Director, Church World Service," in US Senate, *Hearings before the Subcommittee to Investigate*, Part 2, 350–52; Donald Harris, Alfonso Rodriguez, and Russell Stevens, "The Ministry of the United Presbyterian Church to the Spanish Speaking Community of Miami, with Special Reference to the Cuban Refugee," June 1962, UPCUSA Board of National Missions Dept. of Mission Development Records, box 24, folder 8, RG 301.7.24.8, PHS.

82 SBC, *Annual of the Southern Baptist Convention* (1963), 160; SBC, *Annual of the Southern Baptist Convention* (1965), 170.

83 See, for example, Roland Elliott, "How to Resettle a Refugee," *Christian Century*, December 8, 1954, 1488–89.

84 "New Life for Them If We Help!" Citizen-Immigration Material-Refugee Resettlement, 1953–1954, WABHMS, box 76, folder 5, ABHS.

85 *The Fence*, revised edition, November 1959, UPCUSA Board of Christian Education, Council on Church and Society Records, box 12, folder 1, RG 78.12.1, PHS; American Jewish Committee to Clifford Earle, October 6, 1959, UPCUSA Board of Christian Education, Council on Church and Society Records, box 12, folder 2, RG 78.12.2, PHS. See also Nicholas T. Pruitt, "The Fence: Mainline Protestants and Immigration Sixty Years Ago," August 7, 2017, *Religion in American History*, http://usreligion.blogspot.com.

86 "What Is Happening in Christian Friendliness," Christian Friendliness, WABHMS, box 90, folder 12, ABHS.

87 Albaugh, *Who Shall Separate Us?*

88 Night Call, "What Can I Do to Help Cuban Refugees?" December 3, 1965, DA-1424, Historical UM Media, United Methodist Archives and History Center-General Commission on Archives and History, http://catalog.gcah.org.

89 James Breetveld, *This Citadel of Faith* (New York: United Council of Church Women, 1949), UCW Resources, 1948–1955, Church Women United Records, 1222-4-2:7, UMAHC.

90 Grodka and Hennes, *Homeless No More*, 114, 116. For other books on the refugee crisis published at this time, see Cirtautas, *The Refugee*; Chandler, *The High Tower of Refuge*.

91 S. Franklin Mack, "More for Peace," *Presbyterian Life*, May 24, 1952, 29–31.

92 Dept. of Inter-Church Aid and Service to Refugees, World Council of Churches, "Inter-Church Aid Newsletter," January 3, 1952, 13–14, NCC Division of Christian Life and Mission Records, box 20, folder 18, NCC RG 6.20.18, PHS.

93 Robson E. Taylor, First Presbyterian Church of Berkeley, Calif. to Dept. of International Affairs, NCC, May10, 1957, NCC Division of Christian Life and Mission Records, box 20, folder 23, NCC RG 6.20.23, PHS.

94 Travis A. Warlick to Joanna Podberezka, January 28, 1960, Refugee Resettlement Program, 1957–1960, Records of the United Methodist Committee on Relief, 2041-4-2:1, UMAHC.

95 Geoffrey Pond, "Ex-D.P.'s Salute Success in Jersey," *New York Times*, February 22, 1960.

96 Flora Wester to Dr. Neigh, et al., March 12, 1963, UPCUSA Board of National Missions Dept. of Mission Development Records, box 24, folder 7, RG 301.7.24.7, PHS.

97 "Refugee Lawyer Here," *Honolulu Star-Bulletin*, January 26, 1962, UPCUSA Board of National Missions Dept. of Mission Development Records, box 24, folder 8, RG 301.7.24.8, PHS.

98 WABHMS, "Tabea Korjus"; "Tabea Korjus," September 11, 1951, Korjus, Tabea-Christian Friendliness, WABHMS, box 31, folder 9, ABHS; Albaugh, *Who Shall Separate Us?* 39.

99 Central Congregational Church (Newton, Mass.) Records, box 33, folders 1–2, RG 4680, CLA. First quote from Teodors Dreimanis to Central Congregational Church of Newton, July 27, 1975; second quote from Kenneth A. Bernard, "Some Notes of Interest on the 'Human Side' of Our Displaced Persons Experience after World War II," September 1, 1975, 3, folder 2.

100 "What Can I Do to Help Cuban Refugees?" UMAHC.

101 Diocese of New York, *Journal of the One Hundred and Seventy-Second Convention*, 84, AEC.

102 Paul M. Corson to Gaither P. Warfield, September 25, 1957; Gaither P. Warfield to Paul M. Corson, October 1, 1957, Refugee Resettlement Program, 1957–1960, Records of the United Methodist Committee on Relief, 2041-4-2:1, UMAHC.

103 Gaither P. Warfield to A. Raymond Grant, September 28, 1959; "Why Refugee Committee Is Needed at This Point," Refugee Resettlement Program, 1957–1960, Records of the United Methodist Committee on Relief, 2041-4-2:1, UMAHC.

104 Barbara T. Coogan to American Consulate General, Rotterdam, The Netherlands, August 11, 1960, Missions, Missionaries, and Refugees Correspondence, Newton, Massachusetts, First Church (Congregational), Records, 1773–1972, box 25, RG 0132, CLA.

105 Roland Elliott to Church Leaders Interested in Immigration, January 28, 1954, NCC Information Memorandum #7, NCC Division of Christian Life and Mission Records, box 20, folder 22, NCC RG 6.20.22, PHS.

106 Roland Elliott to Walter W. Van Kirk, November 23, 1951, box 20, folder 18, NCC RG 6.20.18; Roland Elliott to John W. Gibson, January 14, 1952, box 2, folder 6, NCC RG 6.2.6, NCC Division of Christian Life and Mission Records, PHS.

107 Diocesan Press Service, "Protestants—Catholics Cooperate," June 5, 1963, XI-4, Archives of the Episcopal Church, www.episcopalarchives.org.

108 *Resettlement Re-Cap*, January 1963, UPCUSA Board of National Missions Dept. of Mission Development Records, box 24, folder 7, RG 301.7.24.7, PHS.

109 Diocese of New York, *Journal of the One Hundred and Sixty-Seventh Convention*, 144, AEC.

110 Ralph E. Smeltzer, "For Justice in Immigration," *Christian Century*, June 4, 1952, 666. See also "C.W.S.-N.L.C. Proposals Re Special Emergency Refugee Legislation," NCC Division of Christian Life and Mission Records, box 20, folder 21, NCC RG 6.20.21, PHS.

111 Grodka and Hennes, *Homeless No More*, 53. A brief perusal of the United Methodist records of refugee resettlement reveal that Methodists sponsored not only Methodist refugees, but also Muslim, Lutheran, Catholic, Orthodox, Georgian Orthodox, Dutch Reformed, Mennonite, and "none." Refugee Arrivals by Refugee Concluded (V-Z), 1950–1970, 2041-6-4.1; Refugee Arrivals by Public Law 316, 1950–1960, 2041-6-4.2; Refugee Arrivals by Public Law 648, 1950–1960, 2041-6-4.3; Refugee Arrivals by Public Law 892, 1959–1961, 2041-6-4.4; Refugee Arrivals by Quota, 1955–1974, 2041-6-4.6, Records of the United Methodist Committee on Relief, UMAHC.

112 "Good News on the Interfaith Front," *Christian Century*, August 19, 1959, 942.

113 *The Gates Swing Wide, for a World Friendship Group of Girls, in the Commission on Missions and World Friendship to Study the Work of the Woman's Society of Christian Service, September 1951 through August 1952*, 24, The Gates Swing Wide, 1951–1952, Records of the Women's Division of the General Board of Global Ministries, 2601-4-4:29, UMAHC.

114 Roland Elliott to Walter W. Van Kirk, November 23, 1951, NCC Division of Christian Life and Mission Records, box 20, folder 18, NCC RG 6.20.18, PHS.

115 General Assembly, NCC, "Concerning Refugees," December 1–6, 1957, NCC Division of Christian Life and Mission Records, box 2, folder 6, NCC RG 6.2.6, PHS.

116 Mislin, *Saving Faith*, 120, 147.

117 Fleegler, *Ellis Island Nation*.

118 Grodka and Hennes, *Homeless No More*, 17–18.

119 Lee and Kulisz, *The Methodist Program* 1, 13.

120 "Changing America: A Social Perspective for the Churches in Their Christian Life and Work," *Social Progress: Changing America* 47 (April 1957), 7, Rapid Social Change-Folder 2, 1955–1963, Records of the Women's Division of the General Board of Global Ministries, 2597-3-5:5, UMAHC.

121 United States Committee for Refugees, *News*, September 28, 1959, UPCUSA Board of Christian Education, Council on Church and Society Records, box 12, folder 2, RG 78.12.2, PHS; PEC, *Domestic and Foreign Missionary Society of the Protestant Episcopal Church in the United States of America, Original Minutes, Meeting of the National Council, Apr. 26, 27, 28, 1960*, 81; *Domestic and Foreign Missionary Society of the Protestant Episcopal Church in the United States of*

America, Original Minutes, Meeting of the National Council, Oct. 13, 14, 15, 1959,
119; General Board, NCC, "Resolution on Refugees and Immigration," December
3, 1959, NCC Division of Christian Life and Mission Records, box 20, folder 23,
NCC RG 6.20.23, PHS; Francis B. Sayre, Jr., "A Litany for Refugees," and other material, World Refugee Year, 1959–1960, Records of the United Methodist Committee on Relief, 2041-4-7:7, UMAHC; Francis B. Sayre, Jr., "The World Refugee Year,"
Christian Century, June 10, 1959, 695–97; Dillon Wesley Throckmorton, "From
the Minister's Study: World Refugee Year," *Methodist Messenger*, November 6,
1959, Refugee Resettlement Program, 1957–1960, Records of the United Methodist Committee on Relief, 2041-4-2:1, UMAHC; "Refugee Relief Goal Unreached,"
Christian Century, August 24, 1960, 965. See also Rees, *We Strangers and Afraid*.

122 For more on this incongruity, see Gleason, "American Identity and Americanization," 50; and Fleegler, *Ellis Island Nation*. For a thorough exposition of the themes
of pluralism and shared national identity in US history, see Higham, *Hanging
Together*.

123 For the increasingly secular orientation of some liberal Protestants after the mid-
twentieth century, see Gaston, *Imagining Judeo-Christian America*; and Hollinger,
After Cloven Tongues of Fire, 23–24, 29.

124 General Assembly, NCC, "Concerning Refugees," December 1–6, 1957, NCC Division of Christian Life and Mission Records, box 2, folder 6, NCC RG 6.2.6, PHS.

CHAPTER 5. PAVING THE WAY FOR PLURALISM

1 Benson Y. Landis and Constant H. Jacquet, Jr., "Immigration Programs and
Policies of Churches of the United States," December, 1957, 58, NCC Office of
Planning and Program Records, box 17, folder 26, NCC RG 14.17.26, PHS. On Su-
preme Court jurisprudence and "neutrality," see Witte, *Religion and the American
Constitutional Experiment*, 193–96.

2 Mrs. C. A. Bender to Mrs. W. F. Hartwig, October 30, 1961, Immigration—Folder
One, 1960–1965, Records of the Women's Division of the General Board of Global
Ministries, 2599-5-3:6, UMAHC. See also F.S.S., "Updating Immigration Policy,"
Christianity and Crisis, February 22, 1965, 16.

3 Roswell P. Barnes to Walter Van Kirk, March 27, 1952; "Statement on Immigration
Policy"; "Proposed Joint Statement on Immigration"; Roland Elliott to Walter W.
Van Kirk and Wynn C. Fairfield, March 19, 1952; "A Joint Statement on Immigra-
tion Refugees Surplus Populations," March 19, 1952, NCC Division of Christian
Life and Mission Records, box 20, folder 19, NCC RG 6.20.19, PHS; Walter W. Van
Kirk, April 18, 1952; Walter W. Van Kirk, Simon G. Kramer, and Paul C. Empie,
"A Joint Statement on Immigration Refugees Surplus Populations," NCC Division
of Christian Life and Mission Records, box 20, folder 20, NCC RG 6.20.20, PHS;
Committee to Improve U.S. Immigration Law, *U.S. Immigration Policy, Statements
of Position by Major Religious, Labor, Civic and Nationality Organization* (New
York: Committee to Improve U.S. Immigration Law, 1952), 24–25, NCC Division
of Christian Life and Mission Records, box 20, folder 21, NCC RG 6.20.21, PHS.

4 Committee to Improve U.S. Immigration Law, *U.S. Immigration Policy*, 37–38.

5 Mildred H. Taylor to Walter Van Kirk, March 13, 1953, NCC Division of Christian Life and Mission Records, box 20, folder 21, NCC RG 6.20.21, PHS.

6 Roland Elliott to Wynn C. Fairfield, et al., May 7, 1953, NCC Division of Christian Life and Mission Records, box 20, folder 21, NCC RG 6.20.21, PHS; Walter W. Van Kirk, *The Immigration and Nationality Act of 1952 (McCarran-Walter Act): What It Means in Terms of Our Foreign Policy and What It Means to Social Work* (New York: Community Relations Service, 1954), UPCUSA Board of Christian Education, Council on Church and Society Records, box 12, folder 1, RG 78.12.1, PHS; American Immigration and Citizenship Conference, "*We Must Open Opportunity . . .*" (New York: American Immigration and Citizenship Conference, 1965); Committee on Integration, American Immigration and Citizenship Conference, "The Integration of Immigrants: A Digest of Source Material," February 1963 (see list of committee members at the back of the booklet), Immigration—Folder One, 1960–1965, Records of the Women's Division of the General Board of Global Ministries, 2599-5-3:6, UMAHC.

7 Committee for Equality in Naturalization, March 21, 1951, NCC Division of Christian Life and Mission Records, box 20, folder 18, NCC RG 6.20.18, PHS.

8 Advertisement: "Nations, like men, sometimes find a rare opportunity . . .," *New York Times*, April 24, 1952.

9 A. D. Willis to R. P. Barnes, March 4, 1953; Walter Van Kirk to A. D. Willis, March 6, 1953, NCC Division of Christian Life and Mission Records, box 20, folder 21, NCC RG 6.20.21, PHS.

10 Zolberg, *A Nation by Design*, 311–15; Marinari, *Unwanted*, 111–24.

11 Francis E. Walter to Walter W. Van Kirk, January 11, 1951; Van Kirk to Walter, January 19, 1951, NCC Division of Christian Life and Mission Records, box 20, folder 18, NCC RG 6.20.18, PHS.

12 Central Department of Research and Survey, NCC, "Fourth Report on Activities of the 82nd Congress, Revision of Immigration Statutes," *Information Service*, February 23, 1952, NCC Division of Christian Life and Mission Records, box 20, folder 19, NCC RG 6.20.19, PHS.

13 Walter W. Van Kirk to Herbert H. Lehman, et al., March 12, 1952, NCC Division of Christian Life and Mission Records, box 20, folder 19, NCC RG 6.20.19, PHS.

14 Walter W. Van Kirk to Herbert H. Lehman, April 1, 1952, NCC Division of Christian Life and Mission Records, box 20, folder 20, NCC RG 6.20.20, PHS.

15 Thelma Stevens to Walter W. Van Kirk, April 10, 1952, NCC Division of Christian Life and Mission Records, box 20, folder 20, NCC RG 6.20.20, PHS.

16 Herbert H. Lehman to J. Henry Carpenter, July 17, 1951; J. Henry Carpenter to Walter Van Kirk, November 1, 1951, NCC Division of Christian Life and Mission Records, box 20, folder 18, NCC RG 6.20.18, PHS.

17 NCC, "A Pronouncement: A Policy Statement of the National Council of the Churches of Christ in the United States of America; United States Immigration and Naturalization Policy, Adopted by the General Board March 21, 1952," 18.1-1-2,

NCC Division of Christian Life and Mission Records, box 20, folder 19, NCC RG 6.20.19, PHS.

18 Walter W. Van Kirk to Jules Cohen, March 21, 1952; Paul Hartmann to Van Kirk, March 26, 1952; Van Kirk to Francis E. Walter, March 27, 1952, NCC Division of Christian Life and Mission Records, box 20, folder 19, NCC RG 6.20.19; Van Kirk to Herbert H. Lehman, April 1, 1952, NCC Division of Christian Life and Mission Records, box 20, folder 20, NCC RG 6.20.20, PHS.

19 Herbert H. Lehman to Walter W. Van Kirk, April 4, 1952, NCC Division of Christian Life and Mission Records, box 20, folder 20, NCC RG 6.20.20, PHS.

20 Arthur Greenleigh to Walter W. Van Kirk, April 3, 1952, NCC Division of Christian Life and Mission Records, box 20, folder 20, NCC RG 6.20.20, PHS.

21 Owen E. Pence to Walter Van Kirk, New York City, April 5, 1952, NCC Division of Christian Life and Mission Records, box 20, folder 20, NCC RG 6.20.20, PHS. See also Eugene J. McCarthy to Walter W. Van Kirk, April 21, 1952.

22 Charles R. Howell to Walter W. Van Kirk, April 22, 1952, NCC Division of Christian Life and Mission Records, box 20, folder 20, NCC RG 6.20.20, PHS.

23 Francis E. Walter to Walter W. Van Kirk, April 3, 1952, NCC Division of Christian Life and Mission Records, box 20, folder 20, NCC RG 6.20.20, PHS.

24 Samuel McCrea Caver to Senators Ives, et al., May 7, 1952, NCC Division of Christian Life and Mission Records, box 20, folder 20, NCC RG 6.20.20, PHS.

25 William F. Hastings to Paul Hutchinson, May 17, 1952, NCC Division of Christian Life and Mission Records, box 20, folder 20, NCC RG 6.20.20, PHS.

26 Zolberg, *A Nation by Design*, 311–17; Marinari, "Divided and Conquered," 9–40; Daniels, *Coming to America*, 328–29, 332–33; Reimers, "An Unintended Reform," 12. See also Walter W. Van Kirk to M. Moran Weston, April 23, 1952, NCC Division of Christian Life and Mission Records, box 20, folder 20, NCC RG 6.20.20, PHS.

27 "Immigration Laws to Be Revised?" *Christian Century*, August 15, 1951, 932; "What Should Be Done About Immigration?" *Christian Century*, May 14, 1952, 580; "Church Forces Continue to Fight McCarran Bill," *Christian Century*, May 28, 1952, 635–36; "The Senate Passes the McCarran Bill," *Christian Century*, June 4, 1952, 661; "McCarran Immigration Bill Become Law," *Christian Century*, July 16, 1952, 820–21; "Churches and the McCarran Law," *Christian Century*, November 12, 1952, 1308–9. See also Ralph E. Smeltzer, "For Justice in Immigration," *Christian Century*, June 4, 1952, 666–68.

28 "McCarran Act Revision a Church Priority," *Christian Century*, March 11, 1953, 275–76; Pat McCarran, "From Senator McCarran," *Christian Century*, April 8, 1953, 419; Rosenfield, "The Prospects for Immigration Amendments," 412–16. The *Christian Century* reported in 1956, "Our foreign relations have suffered enough from this act, but our self-respect as a free and humane people has suffered more." "Creaking McCarran Act Should Be Amended," *Christian Century*, February 22, 1956, 227.

29 Herbert Hackett, "These Are the Platforms," Supplement to *motive* 13 (October 1952), 3-S.

30 Roland Elliott to Colleague, June 20, 1952; Walter W. Van Kirk to Harry S. Truman, June 6, 1952, NCC Division of Christian Life and Mission Records, box 20, folder 21, NCC RG 6.20.21, PHS.

31 Herbert H. Lehman to Walter W. Van Kirk, June 12, 1952, NCC Division of Christian Life and Mission Records, box 20, folder 21, NCC RG 6.20.21, PHS.

32 Abraham J. Multer to Walter Van Kirk, May 12, 1952, NCC Division of Christian Life and Mission Records, box 20, folder 20, NCC RG 6.20.20, PHS.

33 Harry S. Truman, "Text of Truman's Message to House on Veto of Immigration Bill," *New York Times*, June 26, 1952.

34 Walter W. Van Kirk to "those to be invited to testify . . . ," September 26, 1952, NCC Division of Christian Life and Mission Records, box 20, folder 21, NCC RG 6.20.21, PHS; "Churchmen Question New Immigration Law," *Presbyterian Life*, November 29, 1952, 16.

35 Myron W. Fowell to Walter Van Kirk, October 1, 1952, NCC Division of Christian Life and Mission Records, box 20, folder 21, NCC RG 6.20.21, PHS.

36 Photocopy of Mitchell, "McCarran Smears Religious Leaders," *S.D. Daily Republic*, January 10, 1953, UPCUSA Board of Christian Education, Council on Church and Society Records, box 12, folder 1, RG 78.12.1, PHS; President's Commission on Immigration and Naturalization, *Whom We Shall Welcome*, 80; Edward D. Auchard, "A Statement Presented to the President's Commission on Immigration and Naturalization," October 11, 1952, UPCUSA Board of Christian Education, Council on Church and Society Records, box 12, folder 3, RG 78.12.3, PHS.

37 "Statement to be Submitted by Dr. Walter W. Van Kirk, National Council of the Churches of Christ in the U.S.A., To the President's Commission on Immigration and Naturalization, Washington, D.C., October 28, 1952," NCC Division of Christian Life and Mission Records, box 20, folder 21, NCC RG 6.20.21, PHS; Appendix I: The Immigration and Nationality Act of 1952; Statement by Walter W. Van Kirk, before the President's Commission on Immigration and Naturalization, Washington, Oct. 28, 1952, in "As We Do Unto Others: Immigrants, Alien Residents, Naturalized Citizens," April 20, 1954, 31–32, NCC Division of Christian Life and Mission Records, box 20, folder 22, NCC RG 6.20.22, PHS.

38 President's Commission on Immigration and Naturalization, *Whom We Shall Welcome*, xi, xiv–xv; first quote from xi; second quote from xiv; third quote from 9, see also 80; Fleegler, *Ellis Island Nation*.

39 NCC, "Information Memorandum," February 3, 1953, 1, NCC Division of Christian Life and Mission Records, box 20, folder 21, NCC RG 6.20.21, PHS.

40 The NCC educated its constituents through periodic memoranda and informational bulletins. See multiple examples in NCC Division of Christian Life and Mission Records, box 20, folder 21, NCC RG 6.20.21, PHS.

41 "Churchmen Question New Immigration Law," *Presbyterian Life*, November 29, 1952, 16.

42 Rosenfield, "The Prospects for Immigration Amendments," 414; "Immigration Law," 1953, *CQ Almanac*, online ed., https://library.cqpress.com. See also Thelma

Stevens to Maurice Gross, December 29, 1961, Immigration—Folder One, 1960–1965, Records of the Women's Division of the General Board of Global Ministries, 2599-5-3:6, UMAHC.

43 Episcopal Diocese of Michigan, "Resolution at 120th Convention, February 5, 1953," in American Immigration Conference, *American Immigration Policy*, 20.

44 Diocese of New York, *Journal of the One Hundred and Seventy-Second Convention*, 75, AEC.

45 Peter K. Emmons, March 30, 1953, NCC Division of Christian Life and Mission Records, box 20, folder 21, NCC RG 6.20.21, PHS.

46 Dwight D. Eisenhower, "Text of Eisenhower's State of the Union Message on New Domestic and Foreign Policies," *New York Times*, February 3, 1953; Walter W. Van Kirk to Clark P. Garman, February 27, 1953; "Joint Position (June 17, 1953) of the National Lutheran Council and the National Council of the Churches of Christ in the U.S.A."; Roland Elliott to Agencies Interested in Emergency Legislation for Refugees, June 23, 1953; Joseph B. Mow to Don Bolles, July 27, 1953, NCC Division of Christian Life and Mission Records, box 20, folder 21, NCC RG 6.20.21, PHS.

47 Jules Cohen to Roland Elliott, March 24, 1953, NCC Division of Christian Life and Mission Records, box 20, folder 21, NCC RG 6.20.21, PHS.

48 Clifford Earle to William N. Wysham, October 28, 1953, UPCUSA Board of Christian Education, Council on Church and Society Records, box 12, folder 3, RG 78.12.3, PHS.

49 Bennett, *The Party of Fear*, 3.

50 "Revision of M'Carran Act," *New York Times*, January 20, 1953.

51 Landis, *Protestant Experience*, 53.

52 Sherwood E. Wirt, "American Baptists Quell Revolt Over NCC Tie," *Christianity Today*, June 20, 1960, 25.

53 Gaston, *Imagining Judeo-Christian America*; Hollinger, *After Cloven Tongues of Fire*, 23–24, 29. See also Arthur H. Matthews, "The Cloud Over NCC," *Christianity Today*, March 26, 1965, 45–46.

54 Ivan H. Peterman to Board of Christian Education, PCUSA, February 21, 1956, UPCUSA Board of Christian Education, Council on Church and Society Records, box 12, folder 3, RG 78.12.3, PHS.

55 Emily Keenan to Woman's Division of Christian Service, April 24, 1957; Thelma Stevens to Emily Keenan, May 3, 1957, Immigration, 1957–1959, Records of the Women's Division of the General Board of Global Ministries, 2583-2-2:15, UMAHC.

56 Frank Farrell, "NCC and the Freedom Riders," *Christianity Today*, July 3, 1961, 29.

57 Maurice Gross to Bishop; Thelma Stevens to Maurice Gross, December 29, 1961, Immigration—Folder One, 1960–1965, Records of the Women's Division of the General Board of Global Ministries, 2599-5-3:6, UMAHC.

58 Franklin Hichborn, *Reply to Pastor's View of Immigration Laws*, Santa Clara, California, April 1958, UPCUSA Board of Christian Education, Council on Church and Society Records, box 12, folder 1, RG 78.12.1, PHS.

59 Photocopy of Mitchell, "McCarran Smears Religious Leaders," PHS; Pat McCarran, "Statement by Senator McCarran Regarding the Report by the President's Commission," in Ziegler, *Immigration*, 113.

60 "McCarran Act Revision a Church Priority," *Christian Century*, March 11, 1953, 275.

61 Pat McCarran, "From Senator McCarran," *Christian Century*, April 8, 1953, 419.

62 Roy, *Communism and the Churches*, 228–30, 234, 264, 419–20; Landis, *Protestant Experience*, 60–61; Hargis, *Facts about Communism*, 125–26.

63 Carpenter, *Revive Us Again*; Dochuk, *From Bible Belt to Sun Belt*; Dochuk, *Anointed with Oil*. See for example Editorial, "Foundations: Tilt to the Left," *Christianity Today*, April 28, 1958, 21.

64 "Immigr.," S. F. Mack to Kenneth L. Maxwell, July 24, 1957, NCC Division of Christian Life and Mission Records, box 20, folder 23, NCC RG 6.20.23, PHS. See also Rafael Cepeda to Editor, *Christianity Today*, September 26, 1960, UPCUSA Board of National Missions Dept. of Mission Development Records, box 24, folder 7, RG 301.7.24.7, PHS; and "Most Americans Oppose Immigration Changes," *Presbyterian Journal*, August 4, 1965, 6.

65 National Association of Evangelicals, "Immigration Laws 1957," *National Association of Evangelicals*, www.nae.net.

66 "Immigration Bill," *Christianity Today*, July 22, 1957, 29.

67 Gaston, *Imagining Judeo-Christian America*.

68 Committee on Un-American Activities, US House of Representatives, *100 Things You Should Know About Communism and Religion* (Washington, DC: US Government Printing Office, 1948), 15, Communism and Religion—House on Un-American Activities Committee, 1948–1952, Records of the Methodist Federation for Social Action, 2136-2-3:12, UMAHC.

69 Roy, *Communism and the Churches*, 312–16, 319.

70 For a biographical treatment of Oxnam, see Miller, *Bishop G. Bromley Oxnam*.

71 "Bishop Oxnam—Committee Hearing," *U.S. News and World Report*, August 7, 1953, 116–17; Roy, *Communism and the Churches*, 254–60; G. Bromley Oxnam, "The Impact of the American City Upon the World Scene," Urban Pamphlet No. 8, in *Convocation: Urban Life in America, Washington, D.C., February 18–20, 1958* (Philadelphia: Department of City Work, Division of National Missions, Methodist Church, 1958), Urban Church, 1956–1962, Records of the Women's Division of the General Board of Global Ministries, 2597-3-6:2, UMAHC.

72 Seaver, *As We Do unto Others*, quote from 9.

73 For more on midcentury immigration reform, race, and civil rights, see Cheng, *Citizens of Asian America*; Buff, *Immigrant Rights*; Ngai, *Impossible Subjects*, 227–30, 240.

74 Quote from John W. Schauer to Kenneth Maxwell, January 19, 1965; NCC, "Background Information on the Proposed Resolution on the Churches and United States Immigration Policy," NCC Division of Christian Life and Mission Records, box 20, folder 24, NCC RG 6.20.24, PHS.

75 "The Churches and Race: Report from Department of Racial and Cultural Relations and Division of Christian Life and Work," NCC Division of Christian Life and Mission Records, box 2, folder 17, NCC RG 6.2.17, PHS.

76 PEC, *Episcopal Church Annual, 1963*, 124.

77 "Statement of the Council of Bishops of the Methodist Church; Adopted November 13, 1963, Detroit, Michigan," Racial Questionnaire (Prelude to Charters), 1948–1969, Records of the Women's Division of the General Board of Global Ministries, 2594-2-3:10, UMAHC.

78 Kate Bullock Helms, "How Christian Is America?" *Royal Service* 44 (February 1950), 23, 29.

79 Fleegler, *Ellis Island Nation*; Jacobson, *Whiteness of a Different Color*; Roediger, *Working Toward Whiteness*; and Guglielmo, *White on Arrival*.

80 CWS, "You Wanted to Know: Some Questions and Answers about the Resettlement of Displaced Persons," Central Congregational Church (Newton, Mass.) Records, box 33, folder 1, RG 4680, CLA.

81 Dwight D. Eisenhower, "Text of President Eisenhower's Annual Message to Congress on the State of the Union," *New York Times*, January 6, 1956.

82 Kenneth L. Maxwell to Denominational Executives in Christian Social Education and Action, July 16, 1957, NCC Division of Christian Life and Mission Records, box 20, folder 23, NCC RG 6.20.23, PHS; Zolberg, *A Nation by Design*, 325.

83 Methodist Board of Missions, "Resolution at Annual Meeting, January 18, 1957," in American Immigration Conference, *American Immigration Policy*, 20–21.

84 Kenneth L. Maxwell to Lyndon B. Johnson, June 17, 1957; Johnson to Maxwell, June 20, 1957, NCC Division of Christian Life and Mission Records, box 20, folder 23, NCC RG 6.20.23, PHS.

85 "United Church Women Action Taken on Immigration and Refugees"; Esther W. Hymer to Lyndon Johnson, June 24, 1957, NCC Division of Christian Life and Mission Records, box 20, folder 23, NCC RG 6.20.23, PHS.

86 "Authorization from General Board NCCUSA," October 5–6, 1955; To Denominational Executives with Responsibilities for Christian Social Education and Action, November 4, 1955, NCC Division of Christian Life and Mission Records, box 20, folder 23, NCC RG 6.20.23, PHS.

87 "Statement to Be Made by President Eugene Carson Blake for the National Council of Churches of Christ at the Projected Hearings Before the Senate Judiciary Committee on Immigration, Washington, D.C., November 21, 1955," NCC Division of Christian Life and Mission Records, box 20, folder 23, NCC RG 6.20.23, PHS. See also Eugene Carson Blake, "National Council of Churches of Christ in the U.S.A., Dr. Eugene Carson Blake, President, November 21, 1955," in American Immigration Conference, *American Immigration Policy*, 21–22.

88 "Conversation Between K. L. Maxwell and Roland Elliot—Jan 24, 1957," NCC Division of Christian Life and Mission Records, box 20, folder 23, NCC RG 6.20.23, PHS.

89 Quote from Kenneth L. Maxwell to Paul C. Empie, July 19, 1957; see also "Immigr.," phone conversation with Jules Cohen, May 31, 1957, NCC Division of Christian Life and Mission Records, box 20, folder 23, NCC RG 6.20.23, PHS.

90 Gerald H. Kennedy, "Statement Presented to the Committee on Platform and Resolutions of the Democratic Party," July 5, 1960, NCC Division of Christian Life and Mission Records, box 20, folder 23, NCC RG 6.20.23, PHS.

91 NCC, *Witness for Immigration*. On several occasions, some mainline Protestant leaders still considered Walter an ally. See Roland Elliot to Francis E. Walter, January 26, 1953, NCC Division of Christian Life and Mission Records, box 20, folder 19, NCC RG 6.20.19; Kenneth L. Maxwell to Francis E. Walter, May 2, 1962, NCC Division of Christian Life and Mission Records, box 20, folder 24, NCC RG 6.20.24, PHS.

92 NCC, *Witness for Immigration*, 93–94. See also NCC, "Resolution, Study of Immigration Policy, Approved by the General Board, June 8–9, 1961," NCC Division of Christian Life and Mission Records, box 20, folder 24, NCC RG 6.20.24, PHS.

93 Kenneth L. Maxwell to Robert F. Kennedy, April 17, 1962, NCC Division of Christian Life and Mission Records, box 20, folder 24, NCC RG 6.20.24, PHS.

94 Francis E. Walter to Kenneth L. Maxwell, May 8, 1962, NCC Division of Christian Life and Mission Records, box 20, folder 24, NCC RG 6.20.24, PHS.

95 NCC, "A Pronouncement: A Policy Statement of the National Council of the Churches of Christ in the United States of America; The Churches and Immigration, Adopted by the General Board, February 27, 1962," 18.2-1-3, NCC Division of Christian Life and Mission Records, box 20, folder 24, NCC RG 6.20.24, PHS.

96 Ibid.

97 Kennedy's booklet later led to the book *A Nation of Immigrants* published posthumously. Concerning its usage among immigration reform efforts, see the American Immigration and Citizenship Conference pamphlet "We must open opportunity . . . ," Immigration—Folder One, 1960–1965, Records of the Women's Division of the General Board of Global Ministries, 2599-5-3:6, UMAHC; John F. Kennedy, "A Nation of Immigrants," *New York Times*, August 4, 1963; Zolberg, *A Nation by Design*, 318–19, 324–29.

98 "Statement by Congressman Herman Toll at Hearings of Subcommittee No. 1 on Immigration and Nationality, Committee on the Judiciary, U.S. House of Representatives, June 25, 1964," 3–4, UPCUSA Board of Christian Education, Council on Church and Society Records, box 12, folder 3, RG 78.12.3, PHS.

99 Zolberg, *A Nation by Design*, 329–33; "Administration's Immigration Proposals Not Enacted," 1964, *CQ Almanac*, online ed., https://library.cqpress.com; "National Quotas for Immigration to End," 1965, *CQ Almanac*, online ed., https://library.cqpress.com.

100 Zolberg, *A Nation by Design*, 323, 328–30.

101 Lyndon B. Johnson, "Texts of Johnson's State of the Union Message and His Earlier Press Briefing," *New York Times*, January 9, 1964.

102 Marinari, *Unwanted*, 159–61.

103 John W. Schauer to R. H. Edwin Espy, Memorandum, "Statement to be Presented before the Subcommittee on Immigration and Nationality of the House Judiciary Committee," June 11, 1964, NCC Division of Christian Life and Mission Records, box 20, folder 24, NCC RG 6.20.24, PHS; "Administration's Immigration Proposals Not Enacted," 1964, *CQ Almanac*.

104 *I Lift My Lamp* (Cincinnati, OH: Board of Missions, Methodist Church, 1964), Immigration—Folder Two, 1960–1965, Records of the Women's Division of the General Board of Global Ministries, 2599-5-3:7, UMAHC.

105 Zolberg, *A Nation by Design*, 329–33; Marinari, *Unwanted*, 159–67; "Administration's Immigration Proposals Not Enacted," 1964, *CQ Almanac*; "National Quotas for Immigration to End," 1965, *CQ Almanac*. See also Wagner, "The Lingering Death"; and Koed, "The Politics of Reform."

106 NCC, "Resolution on the Churches and United States Immigration Policy, Adopted by the General Board on February 24, 1965"; Kenneth L. Maxwell to Jon L. Regier and Norman Baugher, February 19, 1965; Ken to Thelma Stevens, February 20, 1965, NCC Division of Christian Life and Mission Records, box 20, folder 24, NCC RG 6.20.24; "Portland, Ore., Feb. 26," NCC General Board Roundup, 4–5, NCC Broadcasting and Film Commission Records, box 12, folder 32, NCC RG 16.12.32, PHS.

107 Council for Christian Social Action, "IX: United States Immigration Policy," *Social Action* 31 (April 1965), 24.

108 Robert D. Bulkley to Church and Society Chairmen, "Proposed Amendments to the Immigration and Nationality Act," March 17, 1965, UPCUSA Board of Christian Education, Council on Church and Society Records, box 12, folder 3, RG 78.12.3, PHS.

109 Only an outline of that program has survived; thus, it is assumed that the program was aired. "Pilgrimage, May 9, 1965," NCC Broadcasting and Film Commission Records, box 12, folder 32, NCC RG 16.12.32, PHS.

110 "The Churches and Immigration," *Social Action* 31 (May 1965), quote from 3.

111 "Churchmen Roam," *Wall Street Journal*, March 5, 1965.

112 US Senate, *Hearings before the Subcommittee on Immigration*, Parts 1 and 2, 159, 872, 875–79, 890, 907–908, 910–11, 917–19.

113 Ibid., 759–63, quote from 760.

114 Ibid., 775–76.

115 "The NCC and Public Law 78," *Presbyterian Journal*, November 11, 1964, 12; "Across the Editor's Desk," *Presbyterian Journal*, November 18, 1964, 3; "Mailbag: The NCC and Public Law 78," *Presbyterian Journal*, December 16, 1964, 2; "Spokesman for Council Asks Higher Farm Pay," *Presbyterian Journal*, December 23, 1964, 5; "Wire to President," *Presbyterian Journal*, March 10, 1965, 4–5; "Let Everybody In?" *Presbyterian Journal*, March 24, 1965, 14–15; "Executives of Councils Hit Foreign Farm Help," *Presbyterian Journal*, April 7, 1965, 4; "Most Americans Oppose Immigration Changes," *Presbyterian Journal*, August 4, 1965, 6; "Clydie Goes for 'Action,'" *Presbyterian Journal*, August 11, 1965, 8; "A Sorry Record," *Presbyterian Journal*, August 25, 1965, 13.

116 Harold B. Kuhn, "Current Religious Thought," *Christianity Today*, December 18, 1964, 48.

117 National Association of Evangelicals, "Immigration Laws 1965," *National Association of Evangelicals*, www.nae.net.

118 Concerning the conservative evangelical embrace of "Judeo-Christian" rhetoric by the late twentieth century, see Gaston, *Imagining Judeo-Christian America*.

119 Lyndon B. Johnson, "Remarks at the Signing of the Immigration Bill, Liberty Island, New York," October 3, 1965, LBJ Presidential Library, www.lbjlib.utexas.edu.

120 Zolberg, *A Nation by Design*, 329–38; Yang, *One Mighty and Irresistible Tide*, 230–60; Daniels, *Coming to America*, 338–44; Reimers, "An Unintended Reform," 9–28.

121 "Churches Oppose Braceros Program," *Christian Century*, December 23, 1964, 1580–81.

122 Zolberg, *A Nation by Design*, 337–39.

123 Baltzell, *The Protestant Establishment*, x, 22–23, 159–61, 387.

124 Landis and Jacquet, "Immigration Programs and Policies," 59.

125 For late twentieth-century religious pluralism in America, see Eck, *A New Religious America*.

CONCLUSION

1 "Protestantism on the Wane?" *Christianity and Crisis* 22 (February 5, 1962), 2–10. See also Frederick L. Whitam, "New York's Spanish Protestants," *Christian Century*, February 7, 1962, 162.

2 Gleason, "American Identity and Americanization," 50; Fleegler, *Ellis Island Nation*; Higham, *Hanging Together*.

3 "Changing America: A Social Perspective for the Churches in Their Christian Life and Work," *Social Progress: Changing America* 47 (April 1957), 7, Rapid Social Change-Folder 2, 1955–1963, Records of the Women's Division of the General Board of Global Ministries, 2597-3-5:5, UMAHC.

4 Herberg, *Protestant, Catholic, Jew*. See also Gunnar Myrdal, "American Dilemma Still Remains in Our Intentions of Democracy and What We Do About Our Serious Race Problem," *motive* 9 (January 1949), 15–16, 44.

5 One still sees this in 1962 in Littell, *From State Church to Pluralism*.

6 Hutchison, *Religious Pluralism in America*, 6, 8–9.

7 US Senate, *Hearings before the Subcommittee on Immigration*, Part 2, 775–76.

8 "Changing America," 22, UMAHC.

9 Will Herberg, "Protestantism in a Post-Protestant America," *Christianity and Crisis* 22 (February 5, 1962), 3.

10 Wagner, "The Lingering Death," 478.

11 Susan Jacoby, "The Law Changed in 1965," *New York Times*, June 8, 1975.

12 Pew Research Center, "Racial and Ethnic Composition," "Immigrant Status," *Religious Landscape Study*, 2014, www.pewforum.org.

13 "Changing America," 23, UMAHC.

14 R. Stephen Warner, "Coming to America: Immigrants and the Faith They Bring," *Christian Century*, February 10, 2004, 20.

15 Paul Lehmann and Ira Gollobin, "The Stranger Within the Gate: Two Stories for the American Conscience," *Christian Century*, November 15, 1972, 1149–52.

16 Mark Day, "Rounding Up the Aliens," *Christian Century*, July 18, 1973, 748–49. See also Jim Castelli, "The Year of the Immigrants," *Christian Century*, November 12, 1975, 1031–1033; and Jorge Prieto, "The Challenge of the U.S.-Mexico Border," *Christian Century*, December 27, 1978, 1258–62.

17 Prichard, *A History*, 359.

18 American Baptist Churches USA, "Immigration Letter," May 14, 2010, *American Baptist Churches USA*, www.abc-usa.org.

19 Gradye Parsons, "Stated Clerk Issues Letter to Trump on refugees, immigrants," October 2, 2015, *Presbyterian Church (USA)*, www.pcusa.org.

20 David A. Hollinger, "After Cloven Tongues of Fire: Ecumenical Protestantism and the Modern American Encounter with Diversity," in *After Cloven Tongues of Fire*, 18–55. For more on US evangelical responses to immigration, see Stockhausen, "'The Strangers in Our Midst'"; Melkonian-Hoover and Kellstedt, *Evangelicals and Immigration*. For recent examples of evangelical work, see Callie Stevens, "Welcome to the Table," *NCM Magazine* (Winter 2016), 21–23, https://issuu.com/ncm.magazine; Nazarene Compassionate Ministries, "Refugee and Immigrant Support," *Nazarene Compassionate Ministries*, www.ncm.org; Mission to North America, Presbyterian Church in America, "Refugee and Immigrant Ministry," *Mission to North America, Presbyterian Church in America*, https://pcamna.org; and Evangelical Immigration Table, https://evangelicalimmigrationtable.com. See also Joe Maxwell, "The Alien in Our Midst," *Christianity Today*, December 13, 1993, 48–51; "Evangelicals Speak Out on Immigration," *Christianity Today* 53 (December 2009), 14.

21 Don Bjork, "Foreign Missions: Next Door and Down the Street," *Christianity Today*, July 12, 1985, 17–21.

22 Tim Stafford, "Here Comes the World," *Christianity Today*, May 15, 1995, 18–25; Letters to the Editor: Chinkook Lee, Timothy Tseng, and Leon G. Johnson, "From Melting Pot to Salad Bowl," *Christianity Today*, July 17, 1995, 6.

23 Chad Hayward, et al. to President Trump and Vice President Pence, January 29, 2017, http://static.politico.com (accessed April 22, 2017).

24 Russell Moore, "Exclusive: The Letter Russell Moore will Send Trump about the Refugee Order," *Washington Post*, January 30, 2017.

25 Pew Research Center, "Wide gaps by race, education, religious affiliation in views of immigration policy," in Alec Tyson, "Public backs legal status for immigrants brought to U.S. illegally as children, but not a bigger border wall," January 19, 2018, *Pew Research Center*, www.pewresearch.org.

26 Robert McAfee Brown, "Protestantism on the Wane?" *Christianity and Crisis* 22 (February 5, 1962), 2.

BIBLIOGRAPHY

MANUSCRIPT COLLECTIONS

American Baptist Historical Society Archives, Atlanta, Georgia
    American Baptist Home Mission Society Collection
    Woman's American Baptist Home Mission Society Collection
Archives of the Episcopal Church, Austin, Texas
    Diocese of California. *Journal of the Ninety-Third Convention of the Protestant Episcopal Church in the Diocese of California, Grace Cathedral, San Francisco, February 2–3, 1943.*
    ———. *Journal of the One Hundred Third Convention of the Protestant Episcopal Church in the Diocese of California, Grace Cathedral, San Francisco, February 3–4, 1953.*
    Diocese of New York. *Journal of the One Hundred and Thirty-Eighth Convention of the Diocese of New York, New York: Synod Hall, May 11, 12, 13, 1921.*
    ———. *Journal of the One Hundred and Fifty-First Convention of the Diocese of New York, New York: Synod Hall, May 8, 9, 1934.*
    ———. *Journal of the One Hundred and Fifty-Sixth Convention of the Diocese of New York, New York: Synod Hall, May 9, 10, 1939.*
    ———. *Journal of the One Hundred and Sixty-Seventh Convention of the Diocese of New York, New York: Synod Hall, May 10, 1949.*
    ———. *Journal of the One Hundred and Seventy-Second Convention of the Diocese of New York, New York: Synod Hall, May 12, 1953.*
    ———. *Journal of the One Hundred and Seventy-Third Convention of the Diocese of New York, Held on May 11, 1954.*
    Foreign-Born Americans Division, National Council of the Protestant Episcopal Church. *How to Reach the Foreign-Born: A Practical Parish Program of American Fellowship.* Bulletin No. 45. New York: Department of Publicity, 1924.
Congregational Library and Archives, Boston, Massachusetts
    18.6.3 Box 9
    Board of Home Missions of Congregational and Christian Records, 1943–1954
    Central Congregational Church (Newton, Massachusetts) Records
    Newton, Massachusetts. First Church (Congregational) Records, 1773–1972
Presbyterian Historical Society, Philadelphia, Pennsylvania
    Federal Council of the Churches of Christ in America Records
    National Council of the Churches of Christ in the United States of America

Broadcasting and Film Commission Records
National Council of the Churches of Christ in the United States of America
Division of Christian Education Records
National Council of the Churches of Christ in the United States of America
Division of Christian Life and Mission Records
National Council of the Churches of Christ in the United States of America
Office of Planning and Program Records
United Presbyterian Church in the U.S.A. Board of Christian Education
Council on Church and Society Records
United Presbyterian Church in the U.S.A. Board of National Missions
Department of Mission Development Records
Southern Baptist Historical Library and Archives, Nashville, Tennessee
Home Mission Board Communication Division Collection
Jacob Gartenhaus Collection
Joseph Frank Plainfield Papers
Una Roberts Lawrence Collection
United Methodist Archives and History Center–General Commission on Archives and
History,
Madison, New Jersey
"Boundaries of Annual Conferences" (1920)
Church Women United Records
Missionary Files: Methodist Church, 1912–1949, Japan Conf., Roll No. 115
Night Call. "What Can I Do to Help Cuban Refugees?" December 3, 1965. DA-1424.
Historical UM Media. http://catalog.gcah.org/DigitalArchives.
Records of the General Conference
Records of the Methodist Federation for Social Action
Records of the National Division of the General Board of Global Ministries
Records of the United Methodist Church General Board of Higher Education
and Ministry
Records of the United Methodist Committee on Relief
Records of the Women's Division of the General Board of Global Ministries
The Tourist (1993–126)

NEWSPAPERS AND PERIODICALS
American Missionary
The Baptist
Baptist Standard
Boston Evening Transcript
Campaign Talking Points
Chicago Daily Tribune
Christian Advocate
Christian Century
Christianity and Crisis

Christianity Today
The Congregationalist
Federal Council Bulletin
Herald of Gospel Liberty
Home Mission Monthly
Home Missions
Independent
Jewish Criterion
Journal of Home Economics
Methodist Review
Missionary Review of the World
Missionary Voice
motive
New York Times
Parents' Magazine
The Presbyterian
Presbyterian Journal
Presbyterian Life
Reformed Church Review
Royal Service
Saturday Evening Post
Scientific Monthly
Social Action
Southern Baptist Home Missions
Spirit of Missions
U.S. News and World Report
Vital Speeches of the Day
Wall Street Journal
Washington Post
Woman's Home Missions
World Outlook

BOOKS, ARTICLES, AND PUBLIC DOCUMENTS

Abbreviations are identified in frontmatter.

Abel, Theodore. *Protestant Home Missions to Catholic Immigrants.* New York: Institute of Social and Religious Research, 1933.

Addams, Jane, et al. *Philanthropy and Social Progress.* New York: Thomas Y. Crowell & Co., 1893.

Albaugh, Dana M. *Who Shall Separate Us?: A New Dimension in Christian Witness; Relief, Resettlement, Rehabilitation, Reconstruction.* Valley Forge, PA: Judson Press, 1962.

Alldredge, E. P. *Southern Baptist Handbook 1924.* Nashville, TN: Baptist Sunday School Board, 1924.

Allerfeldt, Kristofer. *Race, Radicalism, Religion, and Restriction: Immigration in the Pacific Northwest, 1890–1924*. Westport: Praeger, 2003.

Alvis, Joel L. *Religion and Race: Southern Presbyterians, 1946–1983*. Tuscaloosa: University of Alabama Press, 1994.

American Immigration Conference, ed. *American Immigration Policy: Selected Statements*. New York: American Immigration Conference, 1957.

American Missionary Association. *Seventy-Eighth Annual Report*. New York: American Missionary Association, 1924. CLA.

———. *The Eighty-First Annual Report*. New York: American Missionary Association, 1927. CLA.

———. *The Eighty-Second Annual Report*. New York: American Missionary Association, 1928. CLA.

———. *The Eighty-Third Annual Report*. New York: American Missionary Association, 1929. CLA.

———. *The Eighty-Sixth Annual Report*. New York: American Missionary Association, 1932. CLA.

———. *Review of Mission Field for Year 1933–1934*. New York: American Missionary Association, 1934. CLA.

Archdeacon, Thomas. *Becoming American: An Ethnic History*. New York: Free Press, 1983.

Axling, William. *Japan Wonders Why?: A Challenging Chapter in American Japanese Relations*. New York: Commission on International Justice and Goodwill, Federal Council of the Churches of Christ in America, 1924. ABHS.

Balderrama, Francisco E., and Raymond Rodríguez. *Decade of Betrayal: Mexican Repatriation in the 1930s*, rev. ed. Albuquerque: University of New Mexico Press, 2006.

Baltzell, E. Digby. *The Protestant Establishment: Aristocracy and Caste in America*. 1964. Reprint, New Haven, CT: Yale University Press, 1987.

Banker, Mark T. *Presbyterian Missions and Cultural Interaction in the Far Southwest, 1850–1950*. Urbana: University of Illinois Press, 1993.

Baptist General Convention of Texas. *Annual of the Baptist General Convention of Texas*. Dallas, 1921.

———. *Annual of the Baptist General Convention of Texas*. Dallas, 1924.

———. *Annual of the Baptist General Convention of Texas*. Dallas, 1961.

Barker, John Marshall. *The Social Gospel and the New Era*. New York: Macmillan Co., 1919.

Barton, Paul. *Hispanic Methodists, Presbyterians, and Baptists in Texas*. Austin: University of Texas Press, 2006.

Bates, Katharine Lee. *America the Beautiful and Other Poems*. New York: Thomas Y. Crowell Co., 1911.

Bebbington, David. "Evangelicalism and Cultural Diffusion." In *British Evangelical Identities Past and Present*, Vol. 1, *Aspects of the History and Sociology of Evangelicalism in Britain and Ireland*, edited by Mark Smith. Eugene, OR: Wipf and Stock, 2009.

Bendroth, Margaret. *Growing Up Protestant: Parents, Children, and Mainline Churches*. New Brunswick, NJ: Rutgers University Press, 2002.

———. *The Last Puritans: Mainline Protestants and the Power of the Past*. Chapel Hill: University of North Carolina Press, 2015.

Bennett, David H. *The Party of Fear: From Nativist Movements to the New Right in American History*. Chapel Hill: University of North Carolina Press, 1988.

Benton-Cohen, Katherine. *Inventing the Immigration Problem: The Dillingham Commission and Its Legacy*. Cambridge, MA: Harvard University Press, 2018.

Billington, Ray Allen. *The Protestant Crusade: A Study of the Origins of American Nativism, 1800–1860*. 1938. Reprint, Chicago: Quadrangle Books, 1964.

Blair, Bertha, Anne O. Lively, and Glen W. Trimble. *Spanish-Speaking Americans: Mexicans and Puerto Ricans in the United States*. Home Missions Division, National Council of Churches of Christ in the U.S.A., 1959.

Blankenship, Anne M. *Christianity, Social Justice, and the Japanese American Incarceration during World War II*. Chapel Hill: University of North Carolina Press, 2016.

Bodnar, John. *The Transplanted: A History of Immigrants in Urban America*. Bloomington: Indiana University Press, 1987.

Bon Tempo, Carl J. *Americans at the Gate: The United States and Refugees During the Cold War*. Princeton, NJ: Princeton University Press, 2008.

Borstelmann, Thomas. *Just Like Us: The American Struggle to Understand Foreigners*. New York: Columbia University Press, 2020.

Bowman, Matthew. *The Urban Pulpit: New York City and the Fate of Liberal Evangelicalism*. New York: Oxford University Press, 2014.

Brackenridge, R. Douglas, and Francisco O. García-Treto. *Iglesia Presbiteriana: A History of Presbyterians and Mexican Americans in the Southwest*, 2nd ed. San Antonio, TX: Trinity University Press, 1987.

Breitman, Richard, and Allan J. Lichtman. *FDR and the Jews*. Cambridge, MA: Belknap Press, Harvard University Press, 2013.

Brooks, Charles Alvin. *Christian Americanization: A Task for the Churches*. Council of Women for Home Missions and Missionary Education Movement of the United States and Canada, 1919.

———, ed. *The Church and the Foreigner: A Christian Service Program for the Local Church*. New York: American Baptist Home Mission Society, n.d.

———. *Through the Second Gate: Baptists in Action among New Americans*. New York: American Baptist Home Mission Society, 1922.

Buff, Rachel Ida, ed. *Immigrant Rights in the Shadows of Citizenship*. New York: New York University Press, 2008.

Burgess, Greg. *The League of Nations and the Refugees from Nazi Germany: James G. McDonald and Hitler's Victims*. London: Bloomsbury Academic, 2016.

Burgess, Thomas. *Foreign-Born Americans and Their Children: Our Duty and Opportunity for God and Country from the Standpoint of the Episcopal Church*. New York: Department of Missions and Church Extension of the Episcopal Church, 1922.

Burgess, Thomas, Charles Kendall Gilbert, and Charles Thorley Bridgeman. *Foreigners or Friends: The Churchman's Approach to the Foreign-Born and Their Children*. New York: Department of Missions and Church Extension, 1921.

Burgquist, James M. "The Concept of Nativism in Historical Study Since *Strangers in the Land*." *American Jewish History* 76, no. 2 (December 1986): 125–41.

Burnidge, Cara Lea. *A Peaceful Conquest: Woodrow Wilson, Religion, and the New World Order*. Chicago: University of Chicago Press, 2016.

Butler, Jon. "God, Gotham, and Modernity." *Journal of American History* 103, no. 1 (June 2016): 19–33.

Calkins, Laura M. "Judd, Walter H. 1898–1994." In *Encyclopedia of Chinese-American Relations*, edited by Yuwu Song. Jefferson, NC: McFarland and Co., 2009.

Carlson, Beverly. "Chronology of the American Baptist Churches, USA." *American Baptist Quarterly* 14, no. 2 (June 1995): 106–85.

Carpenter, Joel A. *Revive Us Again: The Reawakening of American Fundamentalism*. New York: Oxford University Press, 1997.

Carter, Heath W. *Union Made: Working People and the Rise of Social Christianity in Chicago*. New York: Oxford University Press, 2015.

Carter, Paul A. *The Decline and Revival of the Social Gospel: Social and Political Liberalism in American Protestant Churches, 1920–1940*. Ithaca, NY: Cornell University Press, 1956.

Casselman, Arthur V. *Making America Christian: A Guide in the Study of the Home Mission of the Church Based on the Research and Findings of the North American Home Missions Congress, Washington, D.C., December 1–5, 1930*. New York: Council of Women for Home Missions and Missionary Education Movement, 1930.

Cavert, Samuel McCrea, ed. *The Churches Allied for Common Tasks: Report of the Third Quadrennium of the Federal Council of the Churches of Christ in America, 1916–1920*. New York: Federal Council of the Church of Christ in America, 1921.

Caylor, John. *Our Neighbors of Many Tongues: Resource Book on 1954 Home Mission Series*. Atlanta, GA: Home Mission Board, SBC, 1954.

Chan, Sucheng, ed. *Entry Denied: Exclusion and the Chinese Community in America, 1882–1943*. Philadelphia, PA: Temple University Press, 1991.

Chandler, Edgar H. S. *The High Tower of Refuge: The Inspiring Story of Refugee Relief Throughout the World*. New York: Frederick A. Praeger, 1959.

Chang, Derek. "'Brought Together upon Our Own Continent': Race, Religion, and Evangelical Nationalism in American Baptist Home Missions, 1865–1900." In *Immigrant Faiths: Transforming Religious Life in America*, edited by Karen I. Leonard, et al. Walnut Creek, CA: Altamira Press, 2005.

———. *Citizens of a Christian Nation*. Philadelphia: University of Pennsylvania Press, 2010.

Chappell, David L. *A Stone of Hope: Prophetic Religion and the Death of Jim Crow*. Chapel Hill: University of North Carolina Press, 2004.

Cheng, Cindy I-Fen. *Citizens of Asian America: Democracy and Race during the Cold War*. New York: New York University Press, 2013.

Cirtautas, K. C. *The Refugee: A Psychological Study*. Boston: Meador Publishing, 1957.

Coffman, Elesha J. *The Christian Century and the Rise of the Protestant Mainline*. New York: Oxford University Press, 2013.

Cohen, Charles L., and Ronald L. Numbers, eds. *Gods in America: Religious Pluralism in the United States*. New York: Oxford University Press, 2013.

Cohen, Deborah. *Braceros: Migrant Citizens and Transnational Subjects in the Postwar United States and Mexico*. Chapel Hill: University of North Carolina Press, 2011.

Collins, Ace. *Songs Sung Red, White, and Blue: The Stories Behind America's Best-Loved Patriotic Songs*. New York: HarperCollins, 2003.

Coser, Lewis A. *Refugee Scholars in America: Their Impact and Their Experiences*. New Haven, CT: Yale University Press, 1984.

Craig, Laura Gerould. *America, God's Melting-Pot: A Parable-Study*. New York: Fleming H. Revell Co., 1913.

Curti, Merle. *American Philanthropy Abroad*. 1963. Reprint, New York: Routledge, 2017.

Curtis, Heather D. *Holy Humanitarians: American Evangelicals and Global Aid*. Cambridge, MA: Harvard University Press, 2018.

Curtis, Susan. *A Consuming Faith: The Social Gospel and Modern American Culture*. Baltimore, MD: Johns Hopkins University Press, 1991.

Daniels, Roger. "Changes in Immigration Law and Nativism since 1924." *American Jewish History* 76, no. 2 (December 1986): 159–80.

———. *Coming to America: A History of Immigration and Ethnicity in American Life*. 2nd ed. New York: Harper Perennial, 2002.

Davis, Lawrence. *Immigration, Baptists, and the Protestant Mind in America*. Urbana: University of Illinois Press, 1973.

Davis, Morris L. *The Methodist Unification: Christianity and the Politics of Race in the Jim Crow Era*. New York: New York University Press, 2008.

Dawson, J. M. *The Spiritual Conquest of the Southwest*. Nashville, TN: Sunday School Board of the Southern Baptist Convention, 1927.

De León, Arnoldo. *They Called Them Greasers: Anglo Attitudes Toward Mexicans in Texas, 1821–1900*. Austin: University of Texas Press, 1987.

Di Donato, Pietro. *Christ in Concrete*. Indianapolis, IN: Bobbs-Merrill, 1939.

Dinnerstein, Leonard, and David Reimers. "Strangers in the Land: Then and Now." *American Jewish History* 76, no. 2 (December 1986): 107–16.

Diocesan Press Service. "Protestants—Catholics Cooperate." June 5, 1963. XI-4. Archives of the Episcopal Church. www.episcopalarchives.org.

Disciples of Christ. *1925 Year Book*. St. Louis, MO: United Christian Missionary Society, 1925.

Dochuk, Darren. *From Bible Belt to Sun Belt: Plain-Folk Religion, Grassroots Politics, and the Rise of Evangelical Conservatism*. New York: W. W. Norton, 2012.

———. *Anointed with Oil: How Christianity and Crude Made Modern America*. New York: Basic Books, 2019.

Dolan, Jay P. *The American Catholic Experience: A History from Colonial Times to the Present*. Garden City, NY: Doubleday, 1985.

———. "Immigration and American Christianity: A History of Their Histories." In *A Century of Church History: The Legacy of Philip Schaff*, edited by Henry W. Bowden. Carbondale: Southern Illinois University Press, 1988.

Dorrien, Gary. *Soul in Society: The Making and Renewal of Social Christianity*. Minneapolis, MN: Fortress Press, 1995.

Dudziak, Mary L. *Cold War Civil Rights: Race and the Image of American Democracy*. Princeton, NJ: Princeton University Press, 2011.

Eakin, Mildred Moody. *Getting Acquainted with Jewish Neighbors: A Guide Book for Church School Leaders of Children*. New York: Macmillan, 1945.

Eck, Diana L. *A New Religious America: How a "Christian Country" Has Become the World's Most Religiously Diverse Nation*. New York: HarperSanFrancisco, 2001.

Edwards, Mark Thomas. *The Right of the Protestant Left: God's Totalitarianism*. New York: Palgrave Macmillan, 2012.

———. *Faith and Foreign Affairs in the American Century*. Lanham, MD: Lexington Books, 2019.

Edwards, Wendy J. Deichmann, and Carolyn De Swarte Gifford, eds. *Gender and the Social Gospel*. Urbana: University of Illinois Press, 2003.

Enciso, Fernando Saúl Alanís. *They Should Stay There: The Story of Mexican Migration and Repatriation during the Great Depression*, translated by Russ Davidson. Chapel Hill: University of North Carolina Press, 2017.

Encyclopedia of Southern Baptists. Vol. 1. Nashville, TN: Broadman Press, 1958.

Erbelding, Rebecca. *Rescue Board: The Untold Story of America's Efforts to Save the Jews of Europe*. New York: Doubleday, 2018.

Essick, John D. "The International Baptist Seminary: A Baptist Attempt at Americanization, Education, and Missions in East Orange, New Jersey." *Baptist History and Heritage* 40, no. 1 (Winter 2005): 96–103.

Evans, Christopher H., ed. *The Social Gospel Today*. Louisville, KY: Westminster John Knox Press, 2001.

———. *The Social Gospel in American Religion: A History*. New York: New York University Press, 2017.

Fawcett, Edmund. *Liberalism: The Life of an Idea*. Princeton, NJ: Princeton University Press, 2015.

Findlay, James F. *Church People in the Struggle: The National Council of Churches and the Black Freedom Movement, 1950–1970*. New York: Oxford University Press, 1993.

Fleegler, Robert L. *Ellis Island Nation: Immigration Policy and American Identity in the Twentieth Century*. Philadelphia: University of Pennsylvania Press, 2013.

Fox, Cybelle. *Three Worlds of Relief: Race, Immigration, and the American Welfare State, from the Progressive Era to the New Deal*. Princeton, NJ: Princeton University Press, 2012.

Gabaccia, Donna. *From the Other Side: Women, Gender, and Immigrant Life in the U.S., 1820–1990*. Bloomington: Indiana University Press, 1994.

Gardner, Martha. *The Qualities of a Citizen: Women, Immigration, and Citizenship, 1870–1965*. Princeton, NJ: Princeton University Press, 2005.

Garland, Libby. *After They Closed the Gates: Jewish Illegal Immigration to the United States, 1921–1965*. Chicago: University of Chicago Press, 2014.

Gaston, K. Healan. *Imagining Judeo-Christian America: Religion, Secularism, and the Redefinition of Democracy*. Chicago: University of Chicago Press, 2019.

Geffert, Bryn. *Eastern Orthodox and Anglicans: Diplomacy, Theology, and the Politics of Interwar Ecumenism*. Notre Dame, IN: University of Notre Dame Press, 2010.

General Council of the Congregational and Christian Churches. *Minutes, Third Regular Meeting*. New York: General Council, Congregational and Christian Churches, 1936. CLA.

———. *Digest Minutes of Meetings of the General Council, 1931–1965*. New York: Executive Committee, General Council, 1971. CLA.

Gerstle, Gary. *American Crucible: Race and Nation in the Twentieth Century*. Princeton, NJ: Princeton University Press, 2001.

Gleason, Philip. "American Identity and Americanization." In *Harvard Encyclopedia of American Ethnic Groups*, edited by Stephan Thernstrom. Cambridge, MA: Belknap Press, Harvard University Press, 1980.

Gordon, Linda. *The Great Arizona Orphan Abduction*. Cambridge, MA: Harvard University Press, 1999.

Gordon, Milton M. *Assimilation in American Life: The Role of Race, Religion, and National Origins*. New York: Oxford University Press, 1964.

Grant, Madison. *The Passing of the Great Race, or the Racial Basis of European History*. New York: Charles Scribner's Sons, 1916.

Green, Steven K. *Inventing a Christian America: The Myth of the Religious Founding*. New York: Oxford University Press, 2015.

Greene, Alison Collis. *No Depression in Heaven: The Great Depression, the New Deal, and the Transformation of Religion in the Delta*. New York: Oxford University Press, 2016.

Gribble, Richard. "The Immigration Restriction Debate, 1917–1929: Church and State in Conflict." *Journal of Church and State*. February 16, 2016. doi.org/10.1093/jcs/csw001.

Griffith, R. Marie. *Moral Combat: How Sex Divided American Christians and Fractured American Politics*. New York: Basic Books, 2017.

Griffith, Sarah Marie. *The Fight for Asian American Civil Rights: Liberal Protestant Activism, 1900–1950*. Champaign: University of Illinois Press, 2018.

Grijalva, Joshua. *A History of Mexican Baptists in Texas, 1881–1981*. Dallas, TX: Baptist General Convention of Texas, 1982.

———. "The Story of Hispanic Southern Baptists." *Baptist History and Heritage* 18, no. 3 (July 1983): 40–47.

Grodka, Sonia, and Gerhard Hennes. *Homeless No More: A Discussion on Integration Between Sponsor and Refugee*. New York: National Council of the Churches of Christ in the U.S.A., 1960.

Grose, Howard B. *Aliens or Americans?* Dayton, OH: Home Missionary Society of the United Brethren Church, 1906.

Guerin-Gonzales, Camille. *Mexican Workers and American Dreams: Immigration, Repatriation, and California Farm Labor, 1900–1939.* New Brunswick, NJ: Rutgers University Press, 1994.

Guglielmo, Thomas A. *White on Arrival: Italians, Race, Color, and Power in Chicago, 1890–1945.* New York: Oxford University Press, 2003.

Gulick, Sidney L. *Should Congress Enact Special Laws Affecting Japanese?* New York: National Committee on American Japanese Relations, 1922.

———. *Adventuring in Brotherhood among Orientals in America.* New York: American Missionary Association, 1925.

Hamburger, Philip. *Separation of Church and State.* Cambridge, MA: Harvard University Press, 2002.

Hankins, Barry. *Jesus and Gin: Evangelicalism, the Roaring Twenties and Today's Culture Wars.* New York: Palgrave Macmillan, 2010.

Hansen, Marcus L. *The Problem of the Third Generation Immigrant.* Rock Island, IL: Augustana Historical Society, 1938.

Hansen, Marcus Lee, and Arthur M. Schlesinger. *The Immigrant in American History.* Cambridge, MA: Harvard University Press, 1940.

Hargis, Billy James. *Facts about Communism and Our Churches.* Tulsa, OK: Christian Crusade, 1962.

Harkness, Georgia E. *The Church and the Immigrant.* New York: George H. Doran, 1921.

Harper, Keith. *The Quality of Mercy: Southern Baptists and Social Christianity, 1890–1920.* Tuscaloosa: University of Alabama Press, 1996.

Hedstrom, Matthew S. *The Rise of Liberal Religion: Book Culture and American Spirituality in the Twentieth Century.* New York: Oxford University Press, 2012.

Herberg, Will. *Protestant, Catholic, Jew: An Essay in American Religious Sociology.* 1955. Reprint, Chicago: University of Chicago Press, 1983.

Hernández, Kelly Lytle. *Migra!: A History of the U.S. Border Patrol.* Berkeley: University of California Press, 2010.

Higham, John. *Strangers in the Land: Patterns of American Nativism 1860–1925.* Corrected ed. Westport, CT: Greenwood Press, 1981.

———. "Ethnicity and American Protestants: Collective Identity in the Mainstream." In *New Directions in American Religious History,* edited by Harry S. Stout and D. G. Hart. New York: Oxford University Press, 1997.

———. *Hanging Together: Unity and Diversity in American Culture,* edited by Carl J. Guarneri. New Haven, CT: Yale University Press, 2001.

Hirobe, Izumi. *Japanese Pride, American Prejudice: Modifying the Exclusion Clause of the 1924 Immigration Act.* Stanford, CA: Stanford University Press, 2001.

Hirota, Hidetaka. *Expelling the Poor: Atlantic Seaboard States and the Nineteenth-Century Origins of American Immigration Policy.* New York: Oxford University Press, 2017.

Hoffman, Abraham. *Unwanted Mexican Americans in the Great Depression: Repatriation Pressures, 1929–1939.* Tucson: University of Arizona Press, 1974.

Holcomb, Carol Crawford. "The Kingdom at Hand: The Social Gospel and the Personal Service Department of Woman's Missionary Union, Auxiliary to the Southern Baptist Convention." *Baptist History and Heritage* 35 (Spring 2000): 49–66.

Hollinger David A. "Pluralism, Cosmopolitanism, and the Diversification of Diversity." In *Postethnic America: Beyond Multiculturalism*, 10th anniversary edition. New York: Basic Books, 2000.

———. *After Cloven Tongues of Fire: Protestant Liberalism in Modern American History.* Princeton, NJ: Princeton University Press, 2013.

———. *Protestants Abroad: How Missionaries Tried to Change the World but Changed America.* Princeton, NJ: Princeton University Press, 2017.

Holmes, David L. *A Brief History of the Episcopal Church.* Harrisburg, PA: Trinity Press International, 1993.

Home Missions Council. *Thirteenth Annual Meeting of the Home Missions Council.* New York: Home Missions Council, 1920.

Home Missions Council and Council of Women for Home Missions. *Fifteenth Annual Meeting of the Home Missions Council and Council of Women for Home Missions.* New York: Home Missions Council, Council of Women for Home Missions, 1922.

Hong, Jane H. *Opening the Gates to Asia: A Transpacific History of How America Repealed Asian Exclusion.* Chapel Hill: University of North Carolina Press, 2019.

Hopkins, Charles Howard. *The Rise of the Social Gospel in American Protestantism, 1865–1915.* New Haven, CT: Yale University Press, 1940.

Horsman, Reginald. *Race and Manifest Destiny: The Origins of American Racial Anglo-Saxonism.* Cambridge, MA: Harvard University Press, 1981.

Hudnut-Beumler, James, and Mark Silk, eds. *The Future of Mainline Protestantism in America.* New York: Columbia University Press, 2018.

Huntington, Samuel P. *Who Are We?: The Challenges to America's National Identity.* New York: Simon & Schuster, 2004.

Hutchison, William R. "The Americanness of the Social Gospel: An Inquiry in Comparative History." *Church History* 44, no. 3 (September 1975): 367–81.

———, ed. *Between the Times: The Travail of the Protestant Establishment in America, 1900–1960.* New York: Cambridge University Press, 1989.

———. *Religious Pluralism in America: The Contentious History of a Founding Ideal.* New Haven, CT: Yale University Press, 2003.

Jacobson, Matthew Frye. *Whiteness of a Different Color: European Immigrants and the Alchemy of Race.* Cambridge, MA: Harvard University Press, 1998.

———. *Barbarian Virtues: The United States Encounters Foreign Peoples at Home and Abroad, 1876–1917.* New York: Hill and Wang, 2001.

Jacobson, Robin Dale. *The New Nativism: Proposition 187 and the Debate over Immigration.* Minneapolis: University of Minnesota Press, 2008.

Jenkins, Philip. *The Next Christendom: The Coming of Global Christianity.* Rev. ed. New York: Oxford University Press, 2007.

Jones, Henry D. *The Evangelical Movement among Italians in New York City: A Study.* New York: Unit for City, Immigrant and Industrial Work Board of National Missions of the Presbyterian Church, 1935. In *Protestant Evangelism among Italians in America*, edited by Francesco Cordasco et al. New York: Arno Press, 1975.

Jones, Robert C., and Louis R. Wilson. *The Mexican in Chicago.* Chicago: Comity Commission of the Chicago Church Federation, 1931.

Jones, Robert P. *The End of White Christian America.* New York: Simon & Schuster, 2016.

Kallen, Horace M. *Cultural Pluralism and the American Idea: An Essay in Social Philosophy.* Philadelphia: University of Pennsylvania Press, 1956.

———. *Culture and Democracy in the United States.* 1924. Reprint, New Brunswick, NJ: Transaction Publishers, 1998.

Kang, S. Deborah. *The INS on the Line: Making Immigration Law on the US-Mexico Border, 1917–1954.* New York: Oxford University Press, 2017.

Kaufman, Matthew J. *Horace Kallen Confronts America: Jewish Identity, Science, and Secularism.* Syracuse, NY: Syracuse University Press, 2019.

Kennedy, John F. *A Nation of Immigrants.* 1964. Reprint, New York: Harper Perennial, 2018.

Kenny, Gale L. "The World Day of Prayer: Ecumenical Churchwomen and Christian Cosmopolitanism, 1920–1946." *Religion and American Culture* 27 (Summer 2017): 129–58.

Kinney, Mary Martin. *The World at My Door.* Philadelphia, PA: Judson Press, 1938.

Kinzer, Donald L. *An Episode in Anti-Catholicism: The American Protective Association.* Seattle: University of Washington Press, 1964.

Kittelstrom, Amy. "The International Social Turn: Unity and Brotherhood at the World's Parliament of Religions, Chicago, 1893." *Religion and American Culture: A Journal of Interpretation* 19, no. 2 (Summer 2009): 243–74.

———. *The Religion of Democracy: Seven Liberals and the American Moral Tradition.* New York: Penguin Press, 2015.

Kivisto, Peter, and Dag Blanck, eds. *American Immigrants and Their Generations: Studies and Commentaries on the Hansen Thesis after Fifty Years.* Urbana: University of Illinois Press, 1990.

Koed, Betty K. "The Politics of Reform: Policymakers and the Immigration Act of 1965." PhD diss., University of California, Santa Barbara, 1999.

Kraut, Alan M. "A Century of Scholarship in American Immigration and Ethnic History." In *A Century of American Historiography,* edited by James M. Banner, Jr. Boston: Bedford/St. Martin's, 2010.

Kruse, Kevin M. *One Nation Under God: How Corporate America Invented Christian America.* New York: Basic Books, 2015.

Kunzel, Regina G. *Fallen Women, Problem Girls: Unmarried Mothers and the Professionalization of Social Work, 1890–1945.* New Haven, CT: Yale University Press, 1993.

Landis, Benson Y. *Protestant Experience with United States Immigration, 1910–1960.* New York: Church World Service, 1961.

Lantzer, Jason S. *Mainline Christianity: The Past and Future of America's Majority Faith.* New York: New York University Press, 2012.

Lawrence, J. B. *History of the Home Mission Board.* Nashville, TN: Broadman Press, 1958.

Lawrence, Una Roberts. *Winning the Border: Baptist Missions among the Spanish-Speaking Peoples of the Border.* Atlanta, GA: Home Mission Board, SBC, 1935.

Leach, Henry Goddard. "The Next Forty Years." *Forum* 75 (March 1926): 414–19.

Lee, Elizabeth M., and John S. Kulisz. *The Methodist Program under the Refugee Relief Act of 1953.* New York: Methodist Committee for Overseas Relief, 1957. UMAHC.

Lee, Erika. *The Making of Asian America: A History.* New York: Simon & Schuster, 2015.

——. *America for Americans: A History of Xenophobia in the United States.* New York: Basic Books, 2019.

Leech, Patrick Charles. "The Forgotten Crisis: The Untold Story of Tracy S. Voorhees and the President's Committee for Hungarian Refugee Relief, 1956–1957." MA thesis, Texas A&M University, Central Texas, 2017.

Lew-Williams, Beth. *The Chinese Must Go: Violence, Exclusion, and the Making of the Alien in America.* Cambridge, MA: Harvard University Press, 2018.

Lippy, Charles H. *Pluralism Comes of Age: American Religious Culture in the Twentieth Century.* Armonk, NY: M.E. Sharpe, 2000.

Lissak, Rivka Shpak. *Pluralism and Progressives: Hull House and the New Immigrants, 1890–1919.* Chicago: University of Chicago Press, 1989.

Littell, Franklin H. *From State Church to Pluralism: A Protestant Interpretation of Religion in American History.* Garden City, NY: Anchor Books, 1962.

Lowe, Kevin M. *Baptized with the Soil: Christian Agrarians and the Crusade for Rural America.* New York: Oxford University Press, 2015.

Luker, Ralph E. *The Social Gospel in Black and White: American Racial Reform, 1885–1912.* Chapel Hill: University of North Carolina Press, 1991.

Machen, J. Gresham. *Christianity and Liberalism.* New York: Macmillan, 1923.

Marinari, Maddalena. "Divided and Conquered: Immigration Reform Advocates and the Passage of the 1952 Immigration and Nationality Act." *Journal of American Ethnic History* 35 (Spring 2016): 9–40.

——. *Unwanted: Italian and Jewish Mobilization against Restrictive Immigration Laws, 1882–1965.* Chapel Hill: University of North Carolina Press, 2020.

Marinari, Maddalena, Madeline Y. Hsu, and María Cristina García, eds. *A Nation of Immigrants Reconsidered: US Society in an Age of Restriction, 1924–1965.* Urbana: University of Illinois Press, 2019.

Marsden, George. *The Twilight of the American Enlightenment: The 1950s and the Crisis of Liberal Belief.* New York: Basic Books, 2014.

Martin, Susan F. *A Nation of Immigrants.* New York: Cambridge University Press, 2011.

Maryland Baptist Union Association. *Minutes of the One Hundred and Seventh Annual Session of the Maryland Baptist Union Association,* 1942.

Maston, T. B. *"Of One": A Study of Christian Principles and Race Relations.* Atlanta, GA: Home Mission Board, Southern Baptist Convention, 1946.

Maxwell, Melody. "'We Are Happy to Co-Operate': The Institutionalization and Control of Birmingham's Baptist Good Will Center, 1909–1928." *Perspectives in Religious Studies* 38, no. 3 (Fall 2011): 249–65.

May, Henry F. *Protestant Churches and Industrial America*. 1949. Reprint, New York: Harper Torchbooks, 1967.

Mazzenga, Maria, ed. *American Religious Responses to Kristallnacht*. New York: Palgrave Macmillan, 2009.

McBeth, Leon. *The Baptist Heritage*. Nashville, TN: Broadman Press, 1987.

———. *Texas Baptists: A Sesquicentennial History*. Dallas, TX: Baptistway Press, 1998.

McClatchy, V. S. *Japanese Immigration and Colonization*. Washington, DC: Government Printing Office, 1921.

McGreevy, John T. *Catholicism and American Freedom: A History*. New York: W. W. Norton, 2003.

McLean, Robert N. *That Mexican!: As He Really Is, North and South of the Rio Grande*. New York: Fleming H. Revell, 1928.

———. "The Mexican Return," 1932. In *The Great American Mosaic: An Exploration of Diversity in Primary Documents*, Vol. 4, edited by Gary Y. Okihiro and Guadalupe Compeán. Santa Barbara, CA: Greenwood, ABC-CLIO, 2014.

McLean, Robert, and Grace Petrie Williams. *Old Spain in New America*. New York: Association Press, 1916.

Melkonian-Hoover, Ruth M., and Lyman A. Kellstedt. *Evangelicals and Immigration: Fault Lines Among the Faithful*. Cham, Switzerland: Palgrave Macmillan, 2019.

Methodist Church. *Composite Annual Report, Section of Home Missions, Division of Home Missions and Church Extension*, November 22–29, 1940. Philadelphia, PA: Board of Missions and Church Extension, Methodist Church, 1940. UMAHC.

———. *Journal of the 1948 General Conference of the Methodist Church*, April 28–May 8, 1948.

———. *Mid-Century Report, Division of Home Missions and Church Extension of the Board of Missions and Church Extension of the Methodist Church*, December 10–13, 1950. UMAHC.

Methodist Episcopal Church. *Journal of the Thirty-First Delegated General Conference of the Methodist Episcopal Church*, edited by John M. Arters. New York: Methodist Book Concern, 1932.

———. *Journal of the Thirty-Second Delegated General Conference of the Methodist Episcopal Church*, edited by John M. Arters. New York: Methodist Book Concern, 1936.

———. *Reports Presented at the 1936 Annual Meeting of the Board of Home Missions and Church Extension of the Methodist Episcopal Church for the year ending October 31, 1936*. UMAHC.

Methodist Episcopal Church, South. *Seventy-Eighth Annual Report, Board of Missions*, compiled and edited by A. J. Weeks. Nashville, TN: Publishing House of MECS, 1924.

———. *Seventy-Ninth Annual Report, Board of Missions*, compiled and edited by A. J. Weeks. Nashville, TN: Publishing House of MECS, 1925.

———. *Missionary Yearbook of the Methodist Episcopal Church, South, 1930*, edited by Elmer T. Clark. Nashville, TN: Board of Missions, MECS, 1930.

Miglio, Sarah. "The Near Eastern Front of the Great War and the Self-Secularization of Christian Humanitarian Work." In *Remembering Armageddon: Religion and the First World War*, edited by Philip Jenkins. Waco, TX: ISR Books, 2015.

Miller, Robert Moats. *American Protestantism and Social Issues, 1919–1939*. Chapel Hill: University of North Carolina Press, 1958.

———. *Harry Emerson Fosdick: Preacher, Pastor, Prophet*. New York: Oxford University Press, 1985.

———. *Bishop G. Bromley Oxnam: Paladin of Liberal Protestantism*. Nashville, TN: Abingdon Press, 1990.

Mislin, David. *Saving Faith: Making Religious Pluralism an American Value at the Dawn of the Secular Age*. Ithaca, NY: Cornell University Press, 2015.

Montejano, David. *Anglos and Mexicans in the Making of Texas, 1836–1986*. Austin: University of Texas Press, 1987.

Morris, Samuel L. *The Task That Challenges: Home Mission Text Book*. Richmond, VA: Presbyterian Committee of Publication, 1917.

Morse, Hermann N., ed. *Home Missions Today and Tomorrow: A Review and Forecast*. New York: Home Missions Council, 1934.

———. *Toward a Christian America: The Contribution of Home Missions*. New York: Council of Women for Home Missions and Missionary Education Movement, 1935.

National Council of the Churches of Christ in the U.S.A. *Witness for Immigration: Report of the Consultation on Immigration Policy in the United States, Washington, D.C., April 13 and 14, 1961.*

National Council of the Congregational Churches of the United States. *The Congregational Year-Book*, Vol. 47. New York: National Council of Congregational Churches, 1924.

———. *Twenty-Second Regular Meeting*. New York: National Council, 1927. CLA.

———. *Minutes, Twenty-Third Regular Meeting*. New York: National Council, 1929. CLA.

Newman, Mark. *Getting Right with God: Southern Baptists and Desegregation, 1945–1995*. Tuscaloosa: University of Alabama Press, 2001.

Ngai, Mae M. *Impossible Subjects: Illegal Aliens and the Making of Modern America*. Princeton, NJ: Princeton University Press, 2004.

Nixon, Justin Wroe. *Protestantism's Hour of Decision*. Philadelphia, PA: Judson Press, 1940.

North American Home Missions Congress. *Reports of Commissions, Addresses and Findings, Washington, D.C., December 1–5, 1930.*

Nurser, John S. *For All Peoples and All Nations: The Ecumenical Church and Human Rights*. Washington, DC: Georgetown University Press, 2005.

Okrent, Daniel. *The Guarded Gate: Bigotry, Eugenics, and the Law That Kept Two Generations of Jews, Italians, and Other European Immigrants Out of America*. New York: Scribner, 2020.

Orsi, Robert A. *The Madonna of 115th Street: Faith and Community in Italian Harlem, 1880–1950.* 3rd ed. New Haven, CT: Yale University Press, 2010.

Oxx, Katie. *The Nativist Movement in America: Religious Conflict in the Nineteenth Century.* New York: Routledge, 2013.

Petit, Jeanne D. *The Men and Women We Want: Gender, Race, and the Progressive Era Literacy Test Debate.* Rochester, NY: University of Rochester Press, 2010.

Phalen, William J. *American Evangelical Protestantism and European Immigrants, 1800–1924.* Jefferson, NC: McFarland, 2011.

Plainfield, J. F. *The Stranger within Our Gates.* Atlanta, GA: Home Mission Board, Southern Baptist Convention, n.d.

Presbyterian Church in the United States of America. *One Hundred Sixteenth Annual Report, Board of Home Missions of the Presbyterian Church in the United States of America.* New York: Presbyterian Building, 1918.

———. *Minutes of the General Assembly of the Presbyterian Church in the U.S.A.* Vol. 1, Part 1. Philadelphia: Office of the General Assembly, 1922.

President's Commission on Immigration and Naturalization. *Whom We Shall Welcome: Report of the President's Commission on Immigration and Naturalization.* Washington, DC: US Government Printing Office, 1953.

Preston, Andrew. *Sword of the Spirit, Shield of Faith: Religion in American War and Diplomacy.* New York: Alfred A. Knopf, 2012.

Prichard, Robert W. *A History of the Episcopal Church*, 3rd rev. ed. New York: Morehouse, 2014.

Protestant Episcopal Church. *The Annual Report of the National Council, The Domestic and Foreign Missionary Society of the Protestant Episcopal Church in the United States of America*, 1924, 1930, 1933. AEC.

———. *Domestic and Foreign Missionary Society of the Protestant Episcopal Church in the United States of America, Original Minutes, Meeting of the National Council*, 1930, 1938, 1939, 1944, 1945, 1959, 1960. AEC.

———. *Episcopal Church Annual, 1960.* New York: Morehouse-Barlow, 1960.

———. *Episcopal Church Annual, 1963.* New York: Morehouse-Barlow Co., 1963.

———. *Journal of the General Convention of the Protestant Episcopal Church, 1928.* New York: Abbott Press & Mortimer-Walling, 1929.

———. *Journal of the General Convention of the Protestant Episcopal Church in the United States of America, 1931.* Saint Louis, MO: Frederick Printing and Stationary Co., 1932.

———. *Living Church Annual, Churchman's Year Book, and American Church Almanac, 1924.* Milwaukee, WI: Morehouse Publishing, 1923.

———. *Living Church Annual, Churchman's Year Book, and American Church Almanac, 1931.* Milwaukee, WI: Morehouse, 1931.

———. *Living Church Annual, Year Book of the Episcopal Church, 1935.* Milwaukee, WI: Morehouse, 1934.

———. *Living Church Annual, Year Book of the Episcopal Church, 1941.* New York: Morehouse-Gorham, 1940.

———. *Living Church Annual, Year Book of the Episcopal Church, 1943.* New York: Morehouse-Gorham, 1942.

———. *Living Church Annual, Year Book of the Episcopal Church, 1945.* New York: Morehouse-Gorham, 1944.

Pruitt, Nicholas T. "American Sojourners: Congregationalists and Immigration at the Turn of the Twentieth Century." *Bulletin of the Congregational Library and Archives* 14, no. 1 (2019): 6–13.

Ratner, Sidney. "Horace M. Kallen and Cultural Pluralism." *Modern Judaism* 4 (May 1984): 185–200.

Rees, Elfan. *We Strangers and Afraid: The Refugee Story Today.* New York: Carnegie Endowment for International Peace, 1959.

Reeves, Richard. *Infamy: The Shocking Story of the Japanese-American Internment in World War II.* New York: Henry Holt, 2015.

Reeves-Ellington, Barbara, Kathryn Kish Sklar, and Connie A. Shemo, eds. *Competing Kingdoms: Women, Mission, Nation, and the American Protestant Empire, 1812–1960.* Durham, NC: Duke University Press, 2010.

Reimers, David M. "An Unintended Reform: The 1965 Immigration Act and Third World Immigration to the United States." *Journal of American Ethnic History* 3 (Fall 1983): 9–28.

Robinson, Greg. *By Order of the President: FDR and the Internment of Japanese Americans.* Cambridge, MA: Harvard University Press, 2001.

Rodríguez, Moisés. "The Cultural Context of Southern Baptist Work Among Mexican Americans in Texas." PhD diss., Baylor University, 1997.

Roediger, David R. *The Wages of Whiteness: Race and the Making of the American Working Class.* Rev. ed. 1991. Reprint, New York: Verso, 2003.

———. *Working Toward Whiteness: How America's Immigrants Became White: The Strange Journey from Ellis Island to the Suburbs.* Second edition paperback. New York: Basic Books, 2018.

Rosenfield, Harry N. "The Prospects for Immigration Amendments." *Law and Contemporary Problems* 21, no. 2 (Spring 1956): 401–26.

Ross, Robert W. *So It Was True: The American Protestant Press and the Nazi Persecution of the Jews.* Eugene, OR: Wipf and Stock, 1980.

Ross, William G. *Forging New Freedoms: Nativism, Education, and the Constitution, 1917–1927.* Lincoln: University of Nebraska Press, 1994.

Roy, Ralph Lord. *Communism and the Churches.* New York: Harcourt, Brace, and Co., 1960.

Saenger, Gerhart. *Today's Refugees, Tomorrow's Citizens: A Story of Americanization.* New York: Harper & Brothers, 1941.

Sánchez, George J. *Becoming Mexican American: Ethnicity, Culture, and Identity in Chicano Los Angeles, 1900–1945.* New York: Oxford University Press, 1993.

Schultz, Kevin M. *Tri-Faith America: How Catholics and Jews Held Postwar America to Its Protestant Promise.* New York: Oxford University Press, 2013.

———. "The Blessings of American Pluralism, and Those Who Rail Against It." In *Faith in the New Millennium: The Future of Religion and American Politics*, edited by Matthew Avery Sutton and Darren Dochuk. New York: Oxford University Press, 2016.

Seaver, Charles H. *As We Do unto Others*. New York: Department of International Justice and Goodwill, National Council of the Churches of Christ in the U.S.A. [1954].

Shaffer, Robert. "Opposition to Internment: Defending Japanese American Rights during World War II." *The Historian* 61 (Spring 1999): 597–619.

Shattuck, Gardiner H. *Episcopalians and Race: Civil War to Civil Rights*. Lexington: University Press of Kentucky, 2000.

Shea, William M. *The Lion and the Lamb: Evangelicals and Catholics in America*. New York: Oxford University Press, 2004.

Shenton, James P., and Kevin Kenny. "Ethnicity and Immigration." In *The New American History*. Rev. ed., edited by Eric Foner. Philadelphia: Temple University Press, 1997.

Southern Baptist Convention. *Annual of the Southern Baptist Convention*. 1925, 1927, 1935, 1941, 1942, 1946–1949, 1956, 1963, 1965. Southern Baptist Historical Library and Archives. www.sbhla.org.

———. "News Copy, For Release: 3:40 P.M., Friday, May 26, 1961." Southern Baptist Historical Library and Archives. www.sbhla.org.

Spear, Sheldon. "The United States and the Persecution of Jews in Germany, 1933–1939." *Jewish Social Studies* 30, no. 4 (October 1968): 215–42.

Spiro, Jonathan. *Defending the Master Race: Conservation, Eugenics, and the Legacy of Madison Grant*. Lebanon, NH: University of Vermont Press, University Press of New England, 2009.

Steiner, Edward A. *From Alien to Citizen: The Story of My Life in America*. New York: Fleming H. Revell, 1914.

———. *The Making of a Great Race: Racial and Religious Cross-Currents in the United States*. New York: Fleming H. Revell, 1929.

Stockhausen, Ulrike. "'The Strangers in Our Midst': Evangelicals and Immigration, 1960–2014." PhD diss., Westphalian Wilhelms University of Münster, 2017.

Stowe, Walter Herbert. *Immigration and the Growth of the Episcopal Church*. Richmond, VA: Joint Commission of General Convention on Strategy and Policy, 1942.

Strong, Josiah. *The Challenge of the City*. New York: Missionary Education Movement of the United States and Canada, 1911.

Sylvest, Edwin E., Jr. "Hispanic American Protestantism in the United States." In *On the Move: A History of the Hispanic Church in the United States*, by Moises Sandoval. Maryknoll, NY: Orbis Books, 1990.

Taylor, Jack E. *God's Messengers to Mexico's Masses: A Study of the Religious Significance of the Braceros*. Eugene, OR: Institute of Church Growth, 1962.

Taylor, Sandra C. *Advocate of Understanding: Sidney Gulick and the Search for Peace with Japan*. Kent, OH: Kent State University Press, 1984.

Thompson, Michael G. *For God and Globe: Christian Internationalism in the United States between the Great War and the Cold War*. Ithaca, NY: Cornell University Press, 2015.

Thomson, Charles A. *Enter the Mexican*. New York: Presbyterian Church in the U.S.A., Federal Council of Churches of Christ in America, 1929. SBHLA.

Tichenor, Daniel J. *Dividing Lines: The Politics of Immigration Control in America*. Princeton, NJ: Princeton University Press, 2002.

Tillich, Paul J. "Christianity and Emigration," *Presbyterian Tribune*, October 29, 1936.

———. "Mind and Migration." *Social Research* 4 (September 1937): 295–305.

Truett, George W. "Baptists and Religious Liberty." In *Proclaiming the Baptist Vision: Religious Liberty*, edited by Walter B. Shurden. Macon, GA: Smyth and Helwys, 1997.

Turek, Lauren Frances. *To Bring the Good News to All Nations: Evangelical Influence on Human Rights and U.S. Foreign Relations*. Ithaca, NY: Cornell University Press, 2020.

Turpin, Andrea L. *A New Moral Vision: Gender, Religion, and the Changing Purposes of American Higher Education, 1837–1917*. Ithaca, NY: Cornell University Press, 2016.

United States Department of Commerce. Bureau of the Census. *Historical Statistics of the United States, 1789–1945*. Washington, DC: Government Printing Office, 1949.

———. *Religious Bodies: 1926, Vol. I, Summary and Detailed Tables*. Washington, DC: Government Printing Office, 1930.

———. *Religious Bodies: 1936, Vol. I, Summary and Detailed Tables*. Washington, DC: Government Printing Office, 1941.

US House of Representatives. 79th Congress. First Session. *To Grant a Quota to Eastern Hemisphere Indians and to Make Them Racially Eligible for Naturalization; Hearings before the Committee on Immigration and Naturalization*. Washington, DC: US Government Printing Office, 1945.

US Senate. 87th Congress. Second Session. *Hearings before the Subcommittee to Investigate Problems Connected with Refugees and Escapees*, Part 2. Washington, DC: US Government Printing Office, 1963.

———. 89th Congress. First Session. *Hearings before the Subcommittee on Immigration and Naturalization of the Committee on the Judiciary*, Parts 1 and 2. Washington, DC: US Government Printing Office, 1965.

Wagner, Stephen Thomas. "The Lingering Death of the National Origins Quota System: A Political History of United States Immigration Policy, 1952–1965." PhD diss., Harvard University, 1986.

Watson, E. O., ed. *Year Book of the Churches, 1921–22*. Washington, DC: Hayworth Publishing House, 1922.

Wattles, Jeffrey. *The Golden Rule*. New York: Oxford University Press, 1996.

Wepman, Dennis. "di Donato, Pietro." *American National Biography Online*. www.anb. org (accessed January 6, 2017).

Wheeler, Lauren E. "Southern Baptists and Their Missions to Jews: 1930–1960." Unpublished paper. Baylor University, 2012.

White, Ronald C., Jr. *Liberty and Justice for All: Racial Reform and the Social Gospel (1877–1925)*. Louisville, KY: Westminster John Knox Press, 2002.

White, Ronald C., Jr., and C. Howard Hopkins. *The Social Gospel: Religion and Reform in Changing America*. Philadelphia, PA: Temple University Press, 1976.

Wild, Mark. *Renewal: Liberal Protestants and the American City after World War II.* Chicago: University of Chicago Press, 2019.

Willis, Alan Scot. *All According to God's Plan: Southern Baptist Missions and Race, 1945–1970.* Lexington: University Press of Kentucky, 2005.

Witte, John, Jr. *Religion and the American Constitutional Experiment.* 2nd ed. Boulder, CO: Westview Press, 2005.

Woman's Division of Christian Service, Methodist Church. *First Annual Report of the Woman's Division of Christian Service,* 1940–1941. New York: Woman's Division of Christian Service, Methodist Church, n.d. UMAHC.

———. *Patterns for Peace; Thirteenth Annual Report of the Woman's Division of Christian Service of the Board of Missions of the Methodist Church,* 1951–1952. UMAHC.

———. *Twenty-First Annual Report of the Woman's Division of Christian Service, Board of Missions, The Methodist Church,* 1959–1960. UMAHC.

Woman's Home Missionary Society of the Methodist Episcopal Church. *Fifty-Fifth Annual Report, For the Year 1935–1936.* Cincinnati, OH: Woman's Home Missionary Society, Methodist Episcopal Church, n.d. UMAHC.

Wuthnow, Robert. *The Restructuring of American Religion.* Princeton, NJ: Princeton University Press, 1988.

Wuthnow, Robert, and John H. Evans, eds. *The Quiet Hand of God: Faith-Based Activism and the Public Role of Mainline Protestantism.* Berkeley: University of California Press, 2002.

Yang, Jia Lynn. *One Mighty and Irresistible Tide: The Epic Struggle Over American Immigration, 1924–1965.* New York: W. W. Norton, 2020.

Yohn, Susan M. *A Contest of Faiths: Missionary Women and Pluralism in the American Southwest.* Ithaca, NY: Cornell University Press, 1995.

Yoo, David K. *Contentious Spirits: Religion in Korean American History, 1903–1945.* Stanford, CA: Stanford University Press, 2010.

Zeidel, Robert F. *Immigrants, Progressives, and Exclusion Politics: The Dillingham Commission, 1900–1927.* DeKalb: Northern Illinois University Press, 2004.

Ziegler, Benjamin Munn, ed. *Immigration: An American Dilemma.* Boston: D. C. Heath and Co., 1953.

Zolberg, Aristide R. *A Nation by Design: Immigration Policy in the Fashioning of America.* New York: Russell Sage Foundation; Cambridge, MA: Harvard University Press, 2008.

Zubovich, Gene. "For Human Rights Abroad, against Jim Crow at Home: The Political Mobilization of American Ecumenical Protestants in the World War II Era." *Journal of American History* 105 (September 2018): 267–90.

Zunz, Olivier. *Why the American Century?* Chicago: University of Chicago Press, 1998.

INDEX

Abel, Theodore, 81–83

Adams, Henry C., 35

Addams, Jane, 17, 35–36, 40, 70, 176–177

African Americans, 8–9, 15–16, 85, 94, 104, 130, 153, 157; and the civil rights movement, 16, 37–38, 130, 168; home missions to, 10, 15, 37, 45–46, 73, 125, 126, 127, 129–130, 169

African Methodist Episcopal Church, 8–9

Aid Refugee Chinese Intellectuals, Inc., 226n4

"America the Beautiful," 36

American Baptists/American Baptist Convention (ABC), 126–127, 140, 141, 143, 160, 162, 173, 176, 189. *See also* Northern Baptists/Northern Baptist Convention

American Baptist Home Mission Society, 42, 43, 82

American Christian Committee for German Refugees, 88

American Christian Committee for Refugees, 88, 100, 113, 136, 230n69

American Committee for Protection of Foreign Born, 166

American Federation of Labor, 110

American Friends, 103, 158, 175

American identity, 1, 7, 24, 39, 42–45, 57, 67, 91–92, 96, 115–116, 121, 130, 132, 142, 146–149, 162–163, 166, 177–178, 183–184, 185, 186, 209n1. *See also* Americanization; American Way of Life; Christian national-ism; Judeo-Christian; immigrant heritage

American Immigration and Citizenship Conference, 152, 241n97

American Jewish Committee, 41, 153

American Legion, 110

American Missionary Association (AMA), 32, 33, 35, 37, 51–52, 73, 78

American Veterans Committee, 153

American Way of Life, 19, 91–92, 93–94, 98, 117, 132, 149, 150, 176, 178, 184, 187

Americanization, 12, 23, 26, 31, 40, 42–46, 55, 56, 63, 65, 75–76, 79–80, 81–83, 93–94, 97, 134, 187, 206n68, 206n70; Americanism, 37, 78; and gender norms, 17, 76–77; resistance to, 19, 46–48, 77–78, 82, 83, 127–128, 130

Anderson, Frank L., 83

Angel Island, 27, 28, 59, 68, 125

anti-Catholicism, 14, 38, 39, 45, 53, 55, 68, 79, 80–83, 95, 103, 105, 132–134, 137, 146, 165, 166, 177–178, 181, 189, 215n103, 218n6, 219n23

anti-communist, 4, 19, 20, 90, 109, 118–119, 134, 144, 149, 154, 155, 156, 161, 163, 165, 166–167, 189

Anti-Defamation League of B'nai B'rith, 152, 156, 173

anti-Semitism, 47, 53, 99, 105, 137, 163, 165, 193, 218n6

Armenian Apostolic Church, 30, 70

Armenian immigrants, 30, 69–70, 87–88, 127

ABOUT THE AUTHOR

NICHOLAS T. PRUITT is Assistant Professor of History at Eastern Nazarene College, where he has been teaching since 2016. He completed his undergraduate studies at Wayland Baptist University and his graduate work at Baylor University. His research focuses on the intersection of religion, culture, and politics in US history.